£8.50

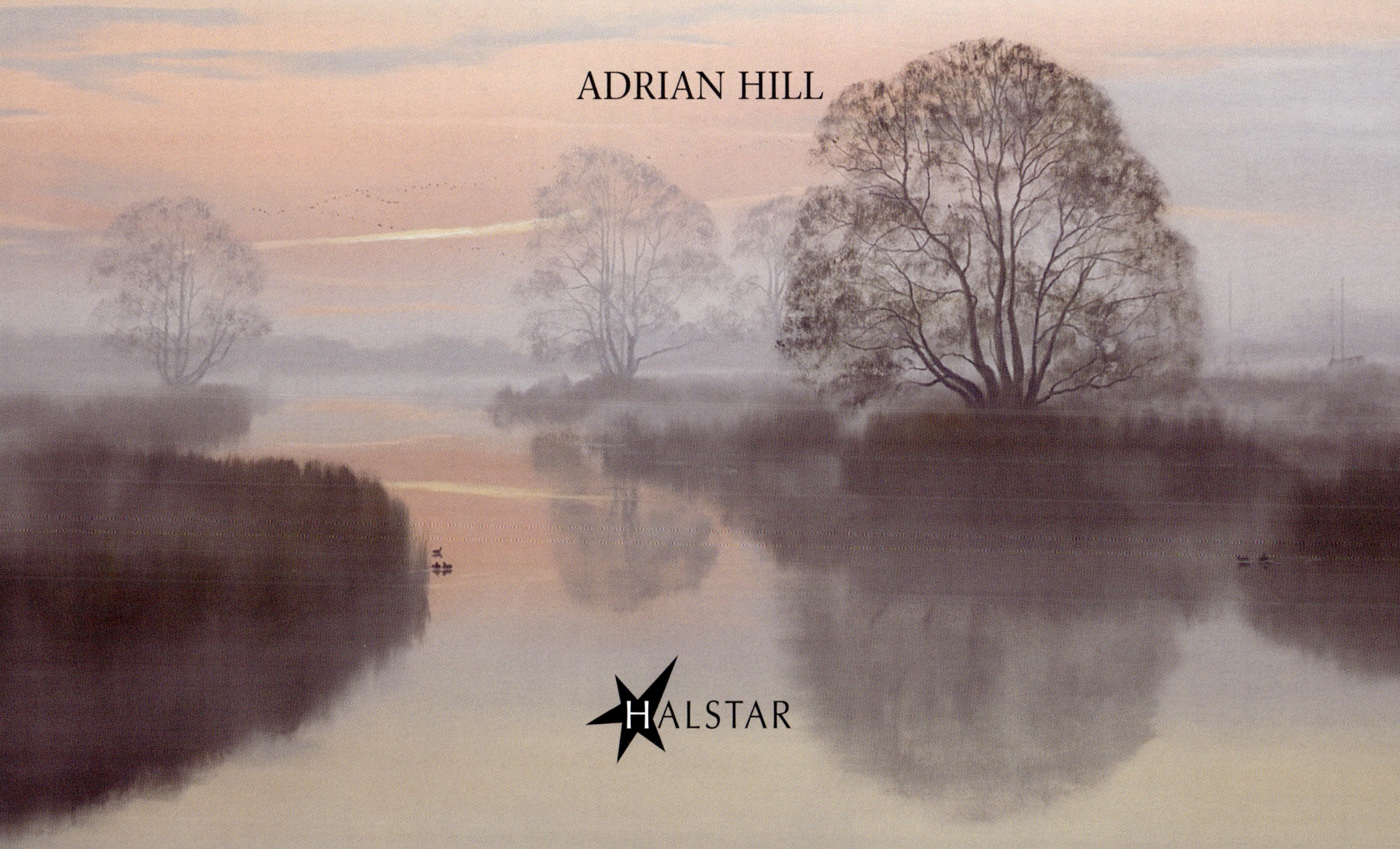

Tony *Garner's* ENCHANTED LIGHT

PASTELS OF NORFOLK & THE BROADS

ADRIAN HILL

HALSTAR

First published in Great Britain in 2010

British Library Cataloguing-in-Publication Data
A CIP record for this title is available from the British Library

ISBN 978 1 906690 26 7

HALSTAR
Halsgrove House,
Ryelands Industrial Estate,
Bagley Road, Wellington, Somerset TA21 9PZ
Tel: 01823 653777   Fax: 01823 216796
email: sales@halsgrove.com

An imprint of Halstar Ltd, part of the Halsgrove group of companies
Information on all Halsgrove titles is available at: www.halsgrove.com

Printed and bound in Italy by Grafiche Flaminia

CONTENTS

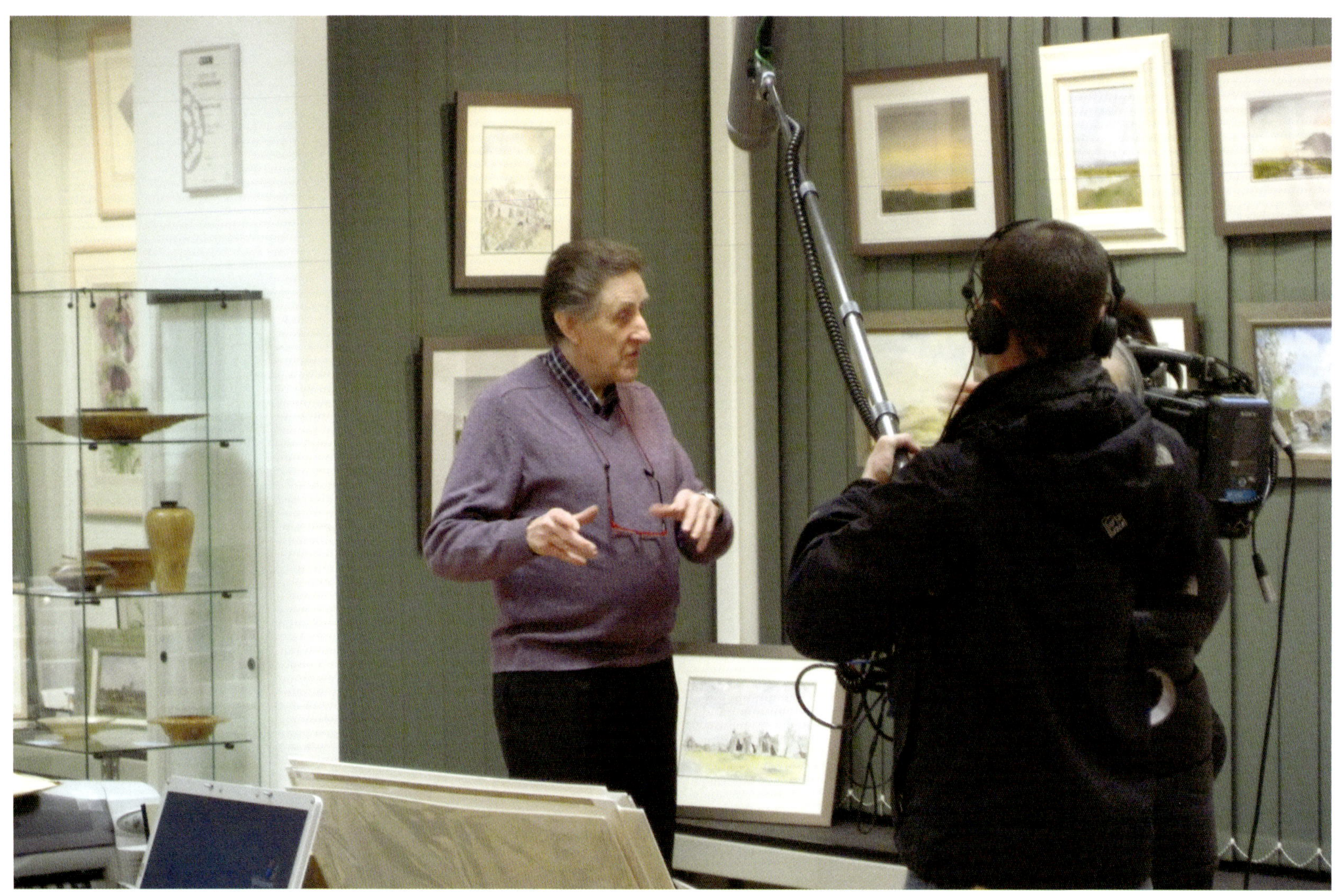

Tony Garner working with a Japanese TV crew at Picturecraft Gallery.

attend Wensum Lodge in Norwich for art classes. He recalls, "I felt that I had been kicked in the stomach, came home and put my paints and brushes away and did not touch them for six months. I am not sure why I picked up my brushes again, I've often wondered what prompted me to start painting once more."

Following his break from painting, Tony actually decided to attend painting and drawing classes at Wensum Lodge. He recalls, "I stuck it out for five weeks and accept that a few ground rules had proven useful, but I hated it so much that I didn't bother to go any more." He found it difficult to overcome the insensitivity of the gallery owner's words too: "Of all the things that could have stopped me from painting this was the one thing that could have tipped the balance, but somehow it didn't. Despite the unquestionable knock to my confidence, I hung on to the fact that it wasn't all about the finished product... it was the pleasure that I experienced from painting." He confesses, "There was a little bit inside me that questioned why I should be beaten by one person's opinions, after all who the hell was he anyway?"

Charged for a new challenge, Tony set about finding somewhere else to exhibit his paintings. A flea market in Hoveton Village Hall was his first venue, and to his surprise a few unframed paintings were sold helping to decrease his "pile of stock"! A second chance to showcase his work was at the annual Broadland Rotary Club Art Exhibition. Ten watercolour paintings were exhibited and he was successful in selling three works.

Late in 1987, on a cold winter's afternoon, Tony and his wife Gaynor were to make the acquaintance of my grandfather, the late John Hill, at the Old Reading Room Gallery in Kelling on the north Norfolk coast. This gallery was purchased to run in conjunction with Picturecraft of Holt and had a fine reputation for a warm friendly welcome. Using Tony Garner's own words he recalls with great affection, "I was to meet John Hill whilst on a jaunt around the coast. I chanced upon this small gallery, and found myself entertained in front of a roaring log fire. This kindly old man talked and talked... and then talked again, about art and everything that was Norfolk! That afternoon I was to learn about a gallery in Holt which was being run by his son Michael. He enthused that the Holt gallery was a wonderful place where a unique display system enabled space to be hired in order to exhibit one's own paintings. Pondering over this fascinating conversation I decided to pay the gallery a visit. A day or two later, I assembled a collection of my work and presented myself to Michael Hill at the Picturecraft Gallery in Holt. Within a couple of months I had exhibited and sold most of my framed work. The relationship built with the gallery remains firmly in place to this day."

Ironically it would be the Picturecraft Gallery in Holt where Tony would sell his first pastel painting. He recalls, "Whilst sailing with some friends, the evening wind died and we became becalmed. I had my camera with me and took a picture of the setting sun. The fabulous golden rays of sunshine burst from below the cloud line and reflected on the surface of the water. As soon as I got home I tried to replicate this in watercolour, but just could not portray the intensity of the light".

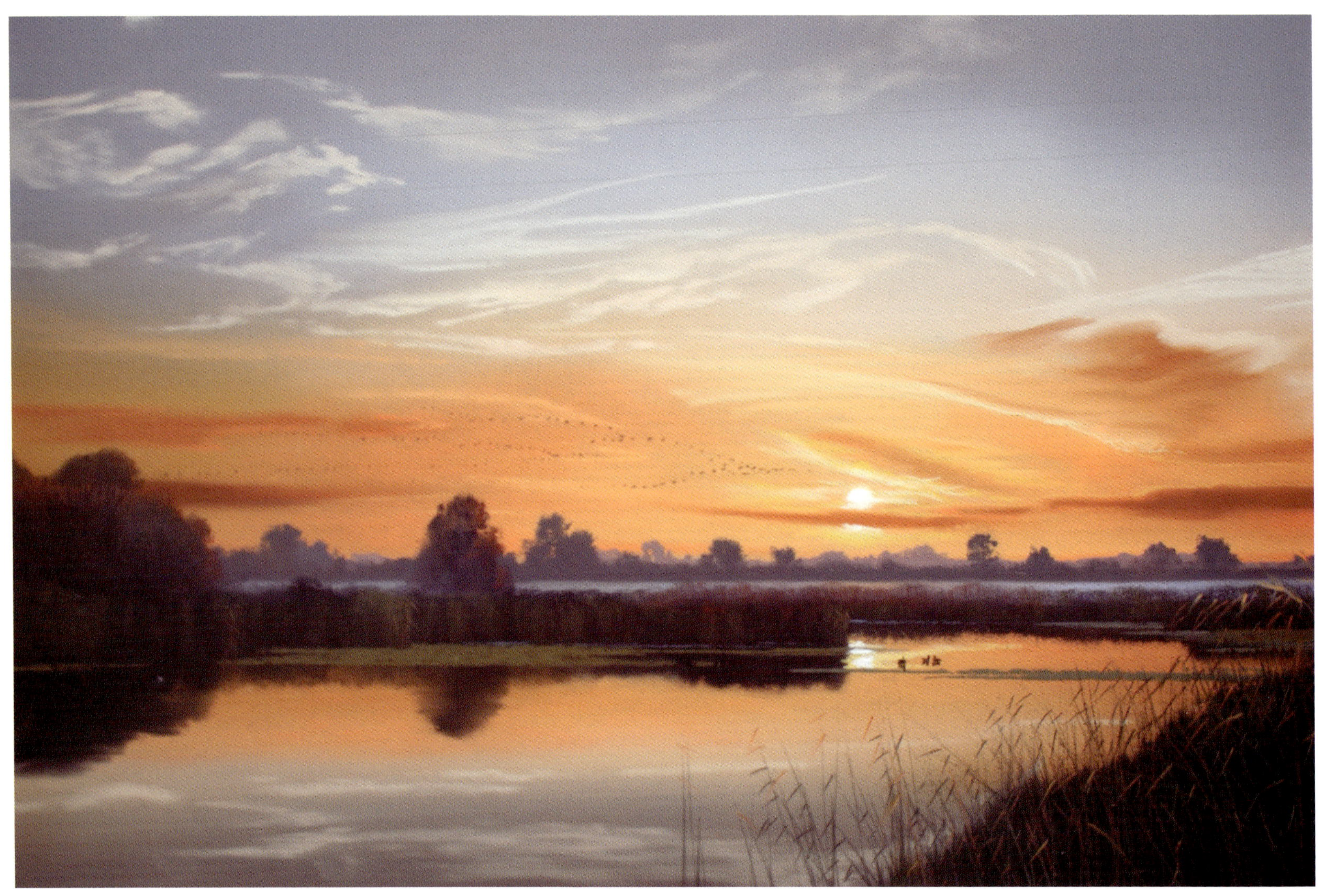

'The luminosity of pastel'. Late Evening - an early work.

Despite this failure in watercolour, Tony remained undaunted and decided to try to capture the same scene in pastel. "The luminosity of the pastel pigment ideally suited my first sunset painting. I was so delighted with the effect, I immediately started work on another and the resulting two pictures, when framed, were taken to the Picturecraft Gallery. They were hung and sold in a matter of hours, before I had even managed to get back home!"

More pastels were to follow and watercolours became few and far between, "My journey of painting light in the landscape had begun."

Outside the art world, Tony Garner had been fortunate in 1989 to be offered a position in sales for Assett, a local conservatory company. During the following four years he was able to scale down his selling activities in order to build towards a dream of becoming a professional artist. Throughout this period he exhibited extensively at Picturecraft in both their Holt and Kelling art galleries. He also exhibited annually at the Wymondham Rotary Club Art Exhibition, successfully selling all his paintings at every exhibition. Following one of the Rotary events, he was approached by Mary Gundry to exhibit at her Garden Gallery, based in Southwold, Suffolk. Soon the expense of travelling around to exhibit at amateur shows became a burden and the search for more permanent exhibition space was needed.

An approach had been made by Richard Weller inviting Tony to exhibit at the Le Strange Old Barns, a gallery based at Old Hunstanton in west Norfolk. Another popular gallery was A Room With A View, based in the city of Norwich. Two places to exhibit were recommended by Tony Garner's picture framer, namely Thelma's Gallery at Horning, and Ramblers Gallery at Thurne, which were being run by a Mrs Parsons. However, one of the best exhibition venues for Tony Garner proved to be a local public house, The Fur and Feather, which agreed to sell on a 'commission-free' basis. His paintings sold in good numbers and contributed so effectively in decorating the pub!

Teaching art was now to feature significantly in Tony Garner's life. The first opportunity arose in 1991 to promote the use of watercolour through classes organised by Norfolk's Adult Education network based at Cromer, but before long he was teaching students at North Walsham, Hoveton, Thorpe and Hellesdon. One ironic situation for Tony was to find himself returning to Wensum Lodge, but this time as a teacher as opposed to a student. He continued to provide art instruction at Wensum Lodge until 2005 and actually gained a teaching qualification there in 1998.

One particular Adult Education class in South Walsham became quite special, for when it came to an end, he adopted this class and continued teaching the students privately until 2009. Throughout this time, he also chose to demonstrate to Art Societies across the region and was responsible for showcasing materials from many major artists' materials companies, including Rexel Derwent, St Petersburgh Artists, Sennelier and Unison pastels.

In 1992, Tony Garner was approached by the BBC to produce a painting of a new hide on the Ted Ellis Trust at Wheatfen. This was in conjunction with 'Children in Need' and the

BBC's 'Challenge Anneka' programme. The painting was countersigned by naturalist David Bellamy, and when auctioned, together with print sales, raised £2000.

Another promotional avenue developed in early 1993 when Tony opened his own working artists' studio in The Bygone Village at Fleggburgh, a major tourist attraction at that time. The concept of The Bygone Village was to enable the public to watch artists and craftspeople working at their various trades, and this proved highly motivational. It was possible to paint and build up a stock of paintings to meet all the needs of his newly arranged portfolio of galleries throughout the area.

The complexities of working in front of the public presented a number of intriguing situations and Tony especially recalls one particular incident: "I had only been open for a few months and one afternoon I was aware that a lady was watching me most intently, quietly observing my every move. I applied some underpainting to a pastel board and, using a much deeper tone, introduced some strong dark shadows to the painting. I was tremendously startled when she suddenly proclaimed quite loudly 'You have ruined it!' Given the severity of the interruption and break of my concentration, I longed that she would disappear. I remained quiet and just stood still, leaving my painting well alone until she finally moved off".

Tony was surprised at the number of people who would queue in fascination to watch him work. One of the most common interjections would be for someone to boldly claim, "I know someone who paints!" These familiar quips soon earned themselves a witty response from Tony, "There must be at least seventeen artists per street in Norfolk!"… which caused much amusement to the other visitors.

Performing in front of the public was a continual strain, comically described by Tony as experiencing, "homicidal tendencies".   He began to find the running costs of this business venture rising higher and out of proportion. A decision was made to move, best explained as "keeping costs down and sanity intact".

He felt that it would be much more cost effective to only pay commission when a painting was sold and not be burdened with renting a studio outlet. In 1996 he moved to a small village on the outskirts of Acle in Norfolk where he set up his own studio enabling him to work in isolation, "away from prying eyes and inane comments".

The Norfolk Broads was a continual source of new subject material, but also a wonderful place to take a break from painting in order to spend time on his sailing boat. One fine day, Tony stumbled across an unusual business opportunity. He vividly recalls, "After a weekend racing the boat at Barton Regatta we returned down the river to moor near Ludham Bridge. Immediately opposite there was a mock-up of an old, flat bottomed, Edwardian working boat for sale called *Pragmatist*. It had apparently been built by an 'eccentric old boy', who lived in Dydler's Mill, and its main purpose was specifically to enable him to fetch his morning papers from the Horning Village Shop. He had chosen to gift it to the Nancy

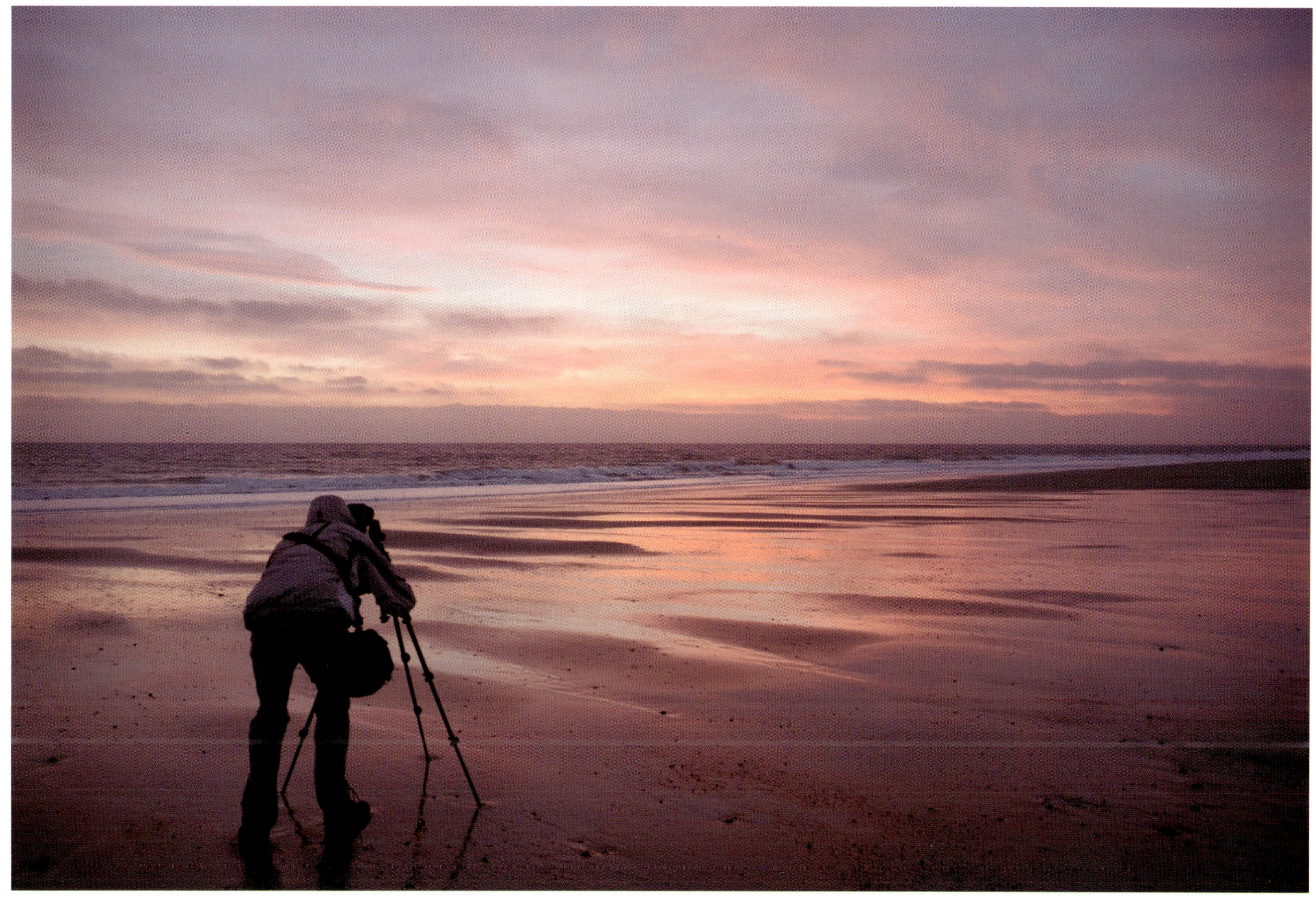

'Capturing the moment'.

Oldfield Trust to help raise them funds but they were unable to use it themselves and had put it up for sale."

Without any hesitation, Tony purchased the boat, had it thoroughly checked and made structurally sound at a local boat yard. Once it had been fully restored and painted it was renamed *Easel Weasel.* On contacting the *Eastern Daily Press*, they were incredibly interested and published a significant editorial feature on this new 'floating studio'. This generated further publicity when BBC Television arrived with a camera crew to compile a report which was featured on their 'Look East' programme, where roving reporter Mike Liggins was shown receiving a painting lesson from Tony. The novelty of the idea and light-hearted manner of the broadcast not only captured the imagination of a very wide audience, but the programme managed to portray some wonderful photographic effects of the Norfolk Broads.

The quest to explore additional exhibition opportunities prompted a visit to Snape Maltings where a rather 'unhelpful' woman in the gallery rejected Tony Garner's work without seeing it. Feeling rather deflated, on the way home he called in to see Simon Simpson, a Norwich-based furniture manufacturer. On seeing his paintings, Simon offered him wall space for a one-man show, his first solo exhibition. This exhibition proved incredibly successful and an invitation was extended to return the following year. Three exhibitions were staged in total.

The inevitable strain of maintaining and regularly changing artwork in numerous galleries made it almost impossible to undertake large solo shows. Tony was then made aware of comments that his "Work was excellent but far too cheap". Being unable to keep up with demand prompted him to seek professional help from a business advisor. The advice appeared basic and simple "Double the price, sell half as many plus one, and then you'll always be in front". This advice was heeded and certain alterations to presentation were made. The results were a doubling of sales!

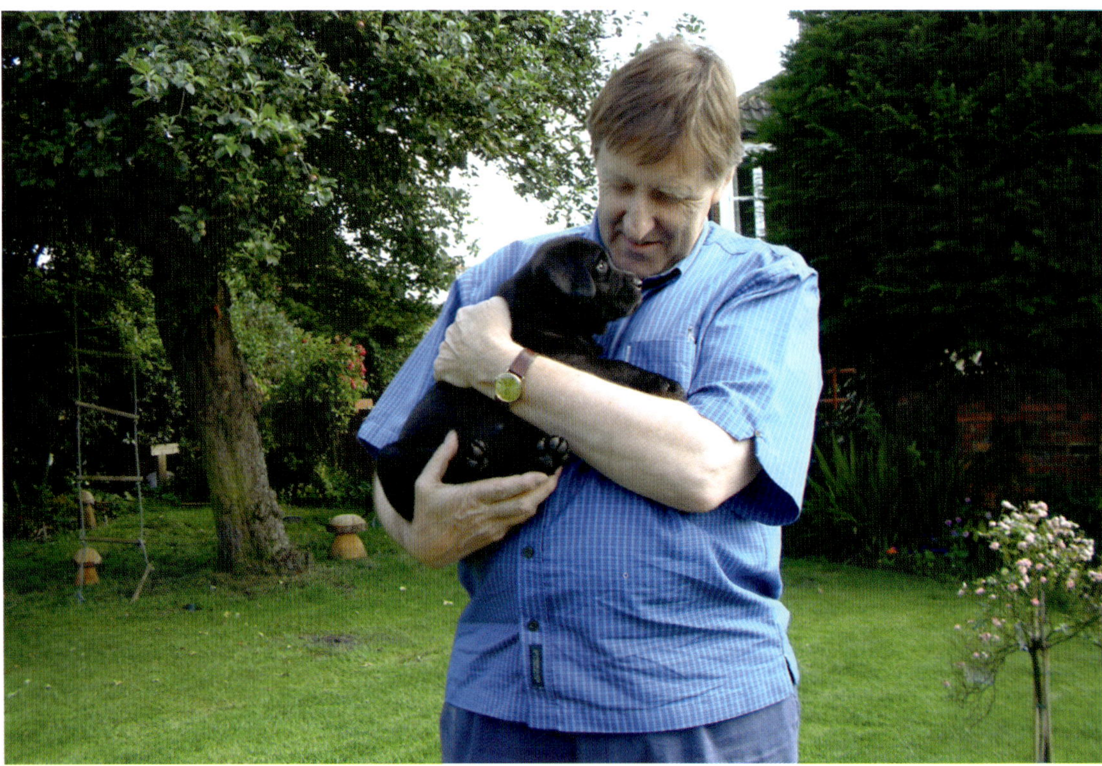

The new 'Member of Staff '.

For Tony to progress and cope a 'Member of Staff' was employed! He explains, "In July 2002 I decided to employ an apprentice. After scouring the country to find a suitable applicant I eventually decided on a young lady with rather large paws and a wet nose - a black Labrador puppy named Ronsard Millennium Flame, alias Bonnie. She has now reached the grand old age of 8 years and has been my constant painting, and refrigerator-door-opening companion. Bonnie has been known to walk all over my work from time to time. I'm not convinced that this is any way a critical comment, more the fact that it happens to be the most direct path to her food bowl!"

It was around this time that my path was to cross with Tony's again. My five-year career in retail management had developed and I had become a manager of Boots the Chemist based in Norwich. My busy working life was to suddenly came to a halt when I made the decision to offer assistance to my parents during my father's battle with cancer which had forced him to stop work. Recognising the unbearable pressures on my mother at that time, I made an approach to Boots who very kindly gave me the option to take a sabbatical year. My introduction to the family business was to take over the management of the Picturecraft Art Gallery in Holt which was midway through a total refurbishment programme.

Having overseen the finishing of a completely modernised gallery, it was my immediate priority to offer exhibition display space for artists to rent for the year ahead. My parents had prepared a list of contacts and I began the task of methodically telephoning each artist to introduce myself, and in some cases reacquaint myself, with all the names on the list. Of course, it came as no surprise to note Tony Garner's name and telephone number on the list.

My telephone conversation with Tony provoked an interesting response for he claimed he was unable to exhibit at that time because he had, "worn through the ends of his fingers". I confess to being totally mystified at this highly unusual explanation at the time, but have every reason to fully understand the situation today!

The next time I met Tony Garner was in early 2003 in my managerial capacity at the gallery. It seemed such a long time since I had been chatting with Tony and his wife at Jarrold's store in Norwich. He had arrived to purchase some artists' materials and was engaged in extremely playful conversation with my father. Unaware that we had already met, and extremely keen that we should be formally introduced, my father proudly brought Tony into the gallery and declared, "I would like you to meet the man who paints with his fingers".

I vividly recall this first 'official' meeting with Tony Garner and it was immediately evident that a strong friendship existed between him and my father. Here was a man with a fine sense of humour and with whom you immediately felt at ease, a breath of fresh air indeed! Although on that particular day I was unable to tempt him into our gallery policy of renting exhibition space, without question he certainly made a great impression on me at this very early stage of my art career.

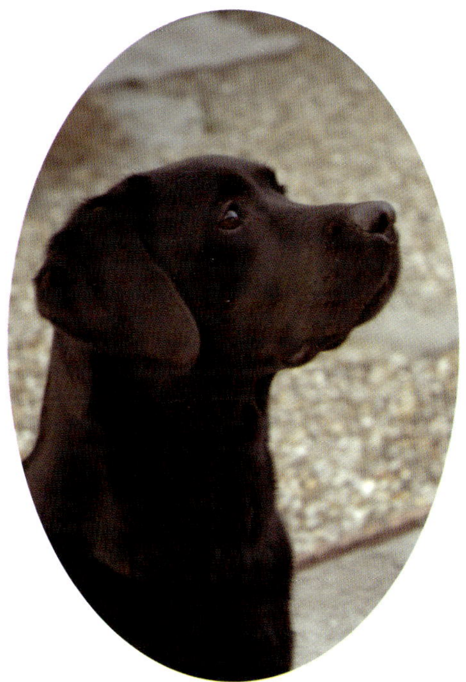

Bonnie.

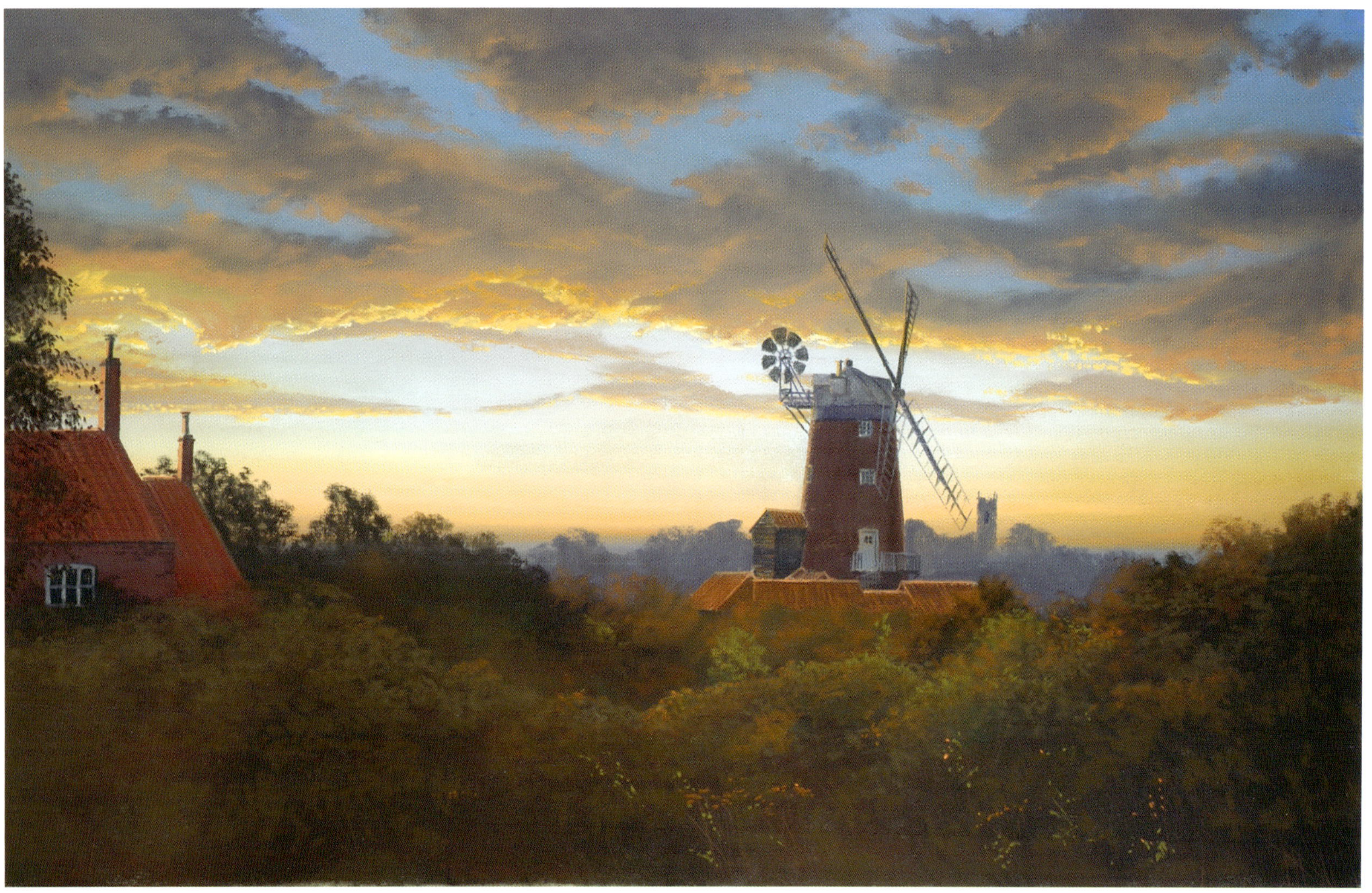

Cley Mill - early work.

Three months passed and Tony specifically returned to enquire if there was any display space available to rent in my gallery in order to exhibit some of his paintings. Keen to oblige, a small display panel was fortunately still available in the next exhibition session and I eagerly awaited the opportunity to finally see some of his original work. The date for delivering the paintings arrived whereupon Tony arrived with far too many pictures to fit into such a small panel. He was obviously delighted when I told him that he could have a much larger space at no additional cost in order to display his superb paintings.

My first introduction to Tony Garner's work was via a mixture of paintings, mostly pastels but there were also two large watercolours. Despite thirty-one other artists being represent-ed in the gallery at that time, and the quantity of exhibits being of a considerable scale, I can still clearly remember Tony's paintings to this day. The pastel paintings in particular were tremendously vibrant in colour, giving an appearance of silk on paper. I was to quickly learn that this technique of pastel painting was called 'blending'. The two landscape watercolours depicted 'a woodland path' and 'a resting boat', the latter being the first painting that I was to sell for him.

The first exhibition session was very successful with positive feedback and a number of sales. Greatly encouraged by this promising start Tony enthused with confidence and committed to becoming an annual exhibitor in the gallery. This privilege is usually only afforded to a small number of artists who have generated sufficient impact with a proven track record of achieving consistent sales. This early commitment of renting permanent space at Picturecraft Gallery certainly laid the foundations for his incredible success with me in the future.

A significant role that my gallery undertakes is to intersperse regular display sessions with special major 'solo' exhibitions. Within a very short time I could see the impact that Tony Garner's paintings were making in the gallery and in September 2003 I chose to enlighten him of the complex processes involved in staging a solo show. Following a relatively brief discussion, and with very little hesitation, Tony seized the opportunity to secure the date of September 2004 for his first one-man exhibition at Picturecraft.

The first consideration by Tony was his greatest desire to be connected with the public. He expressed a longing to work inside the gallery to enable visitors to witness for themselves the 'wonder of pastel painting'. I readily agreed and throughout the winter and spring months Tony regularly visited the gallery and the interest generated enabled me to build a substantial mailing list of customers who were completely fascinated to listen, learn and share in his knowledge and techniques. We were all to discover that pastel painting is a very messy process!

In essence (and my apologies for conveying the very basics of Tony Garner's painting technique), artists' soft pastel is applied to 'fine sandpaper' - a 400 grade bespoke high-quality glasspaper made specifically for artists. Using his fingers and the palm of his hands, Tony blends the colours of pastels together as they adhere to the 'gritty' surface of the paper. The result, as can be seen from the paintings illustrated in this book, is a seamless blend of tones achieving a most striking effect.

Watching a pastel painting 'coming together' is a mesmerizing experience and viewers found themselves entranced as a painting unfolded before them. The demonstrations also helped to cement the bond that Tony wished to create with the public, and their interest was stimulated sufficiently for them to become clients, collectors and good friends in the future.

It was essential to determine the number of paintings that would be needed for a major exhibition and I appreciate now that it would have been so much more helpful had I been

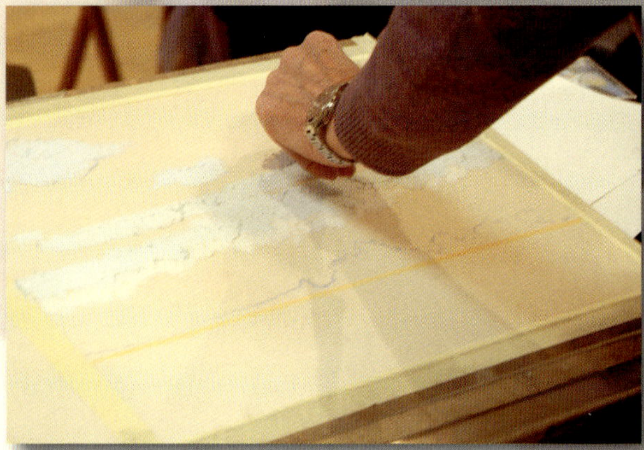

Stage 1. Roughing out the composition.

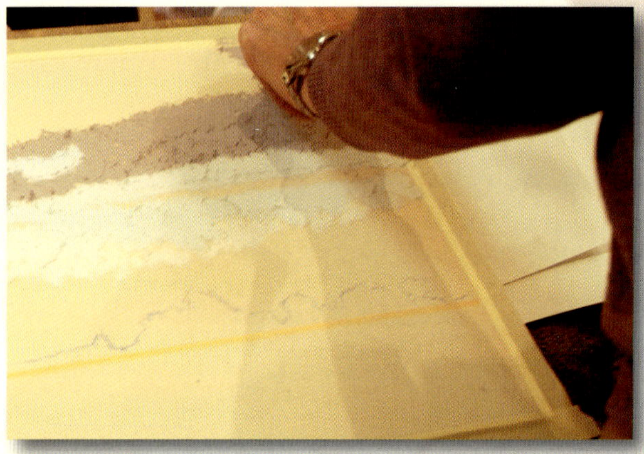

Stage 2. Establishing clouds.

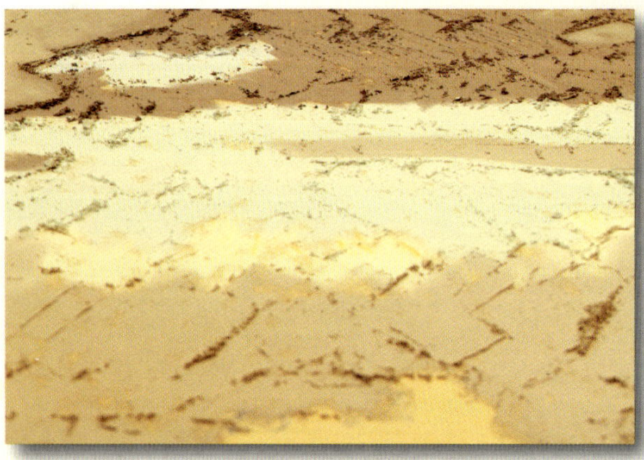

Stage 3. Close up of the initial 'chaos!'

Stage 4. Initial blending.

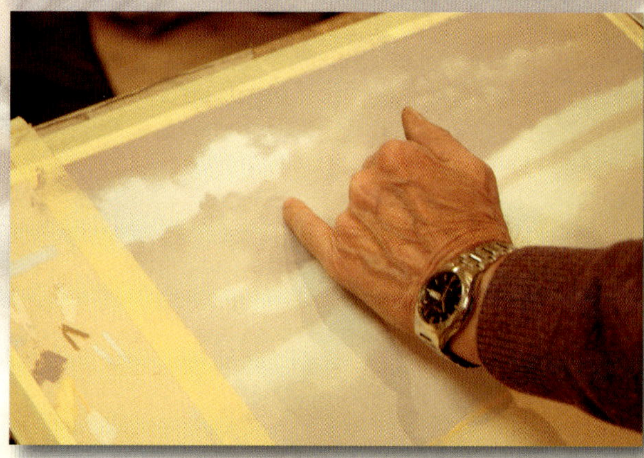

Stage 5. Putting the highlights in the clouds.

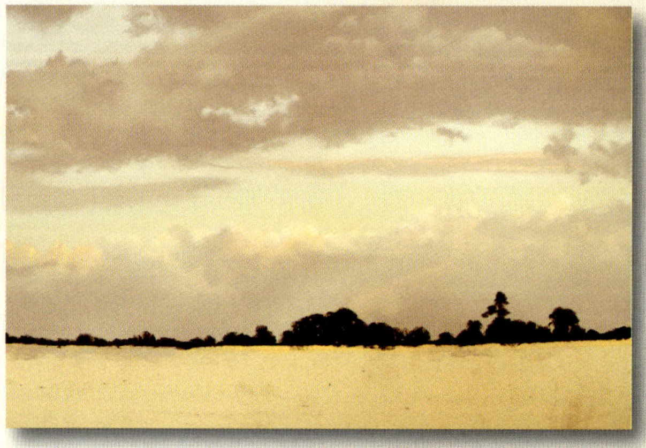

Stage 6. Background completed.

clearer in our deliberations. I casually suggested that ninety paintings would make a wonderful show… "30 small, 30 medium and 30 large." It was only in the weeks leading up to the exhibition that I realised Tony Garner had taken my advice quite literally. My very limited storage space at the gallery soon overflowed, for clearly my interpretation of 'large' was on an entirely different scale of measurements from that of his. Thirty enormous pastel paintings were the first pictures to arrive! Tony's past career in sales, where self-motivation and achieving targets was the order of the day, was just beginning to show.

The day arrived when the paintings were brought out of the stockroom into the gallery, and this proved to be one of the most memorable moments in Picturecraft's exhibition history. We spent most of the day preparing the paintings with titles, display labels and hanging fixings. My normal closing time of 5pm gave us the first opportunity to spread the paintings around the gallery in order to determine a suitable layout. Past experience in managing large-scale exhibitions is that this procedure should take relatively little time. It was usual to position larger paintings into key spaces first and then intersperse smaller paintings around them, depending on their size, subject and colour. It soon became apparent that Tony had produced over 100 paintings, the majority excessive in their size.

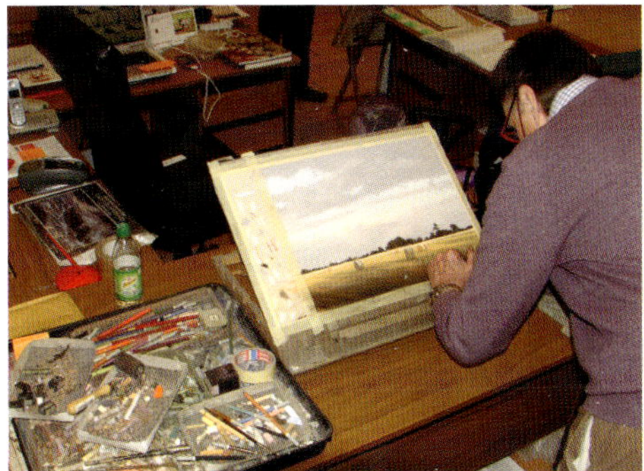

Applying the finishing touches.

The finished piece.

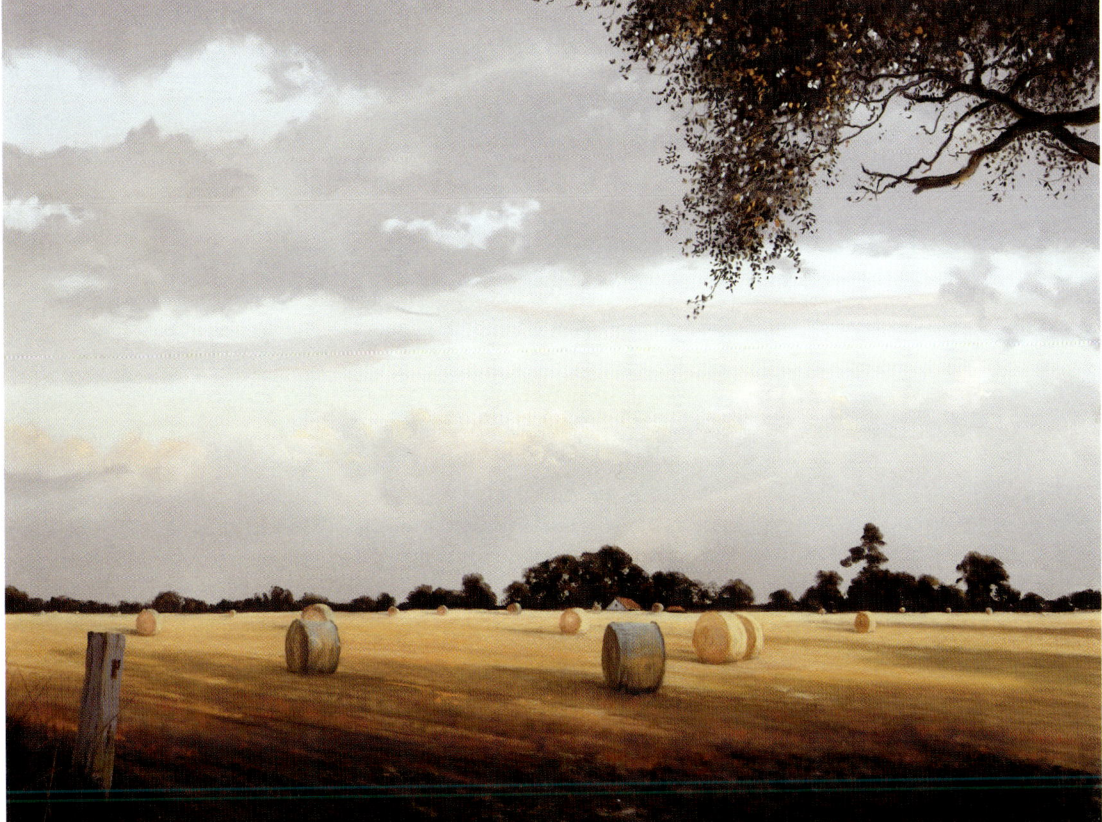

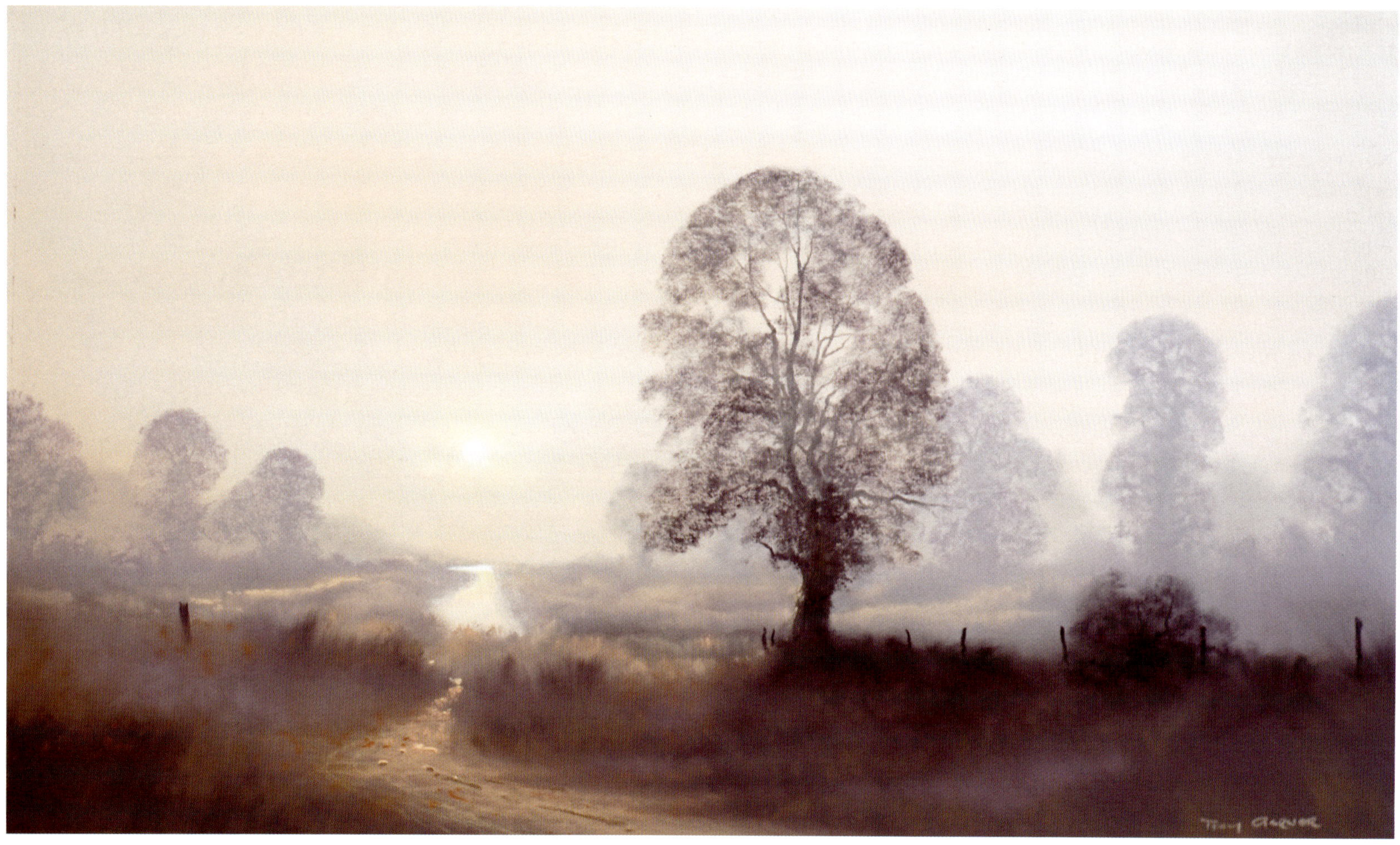

Hazy Light - early work.

My obvious concern was that the quantities and dimensions of the paintings far exceeded the availability of gallery wall space.

I managed to conceal my state of panic as the gallery door opened. My spirits were uplifted to discover it was my father arriving to see if we needed a hand. His many years of exhibition planning might prove invaluable to resolve my dilemma. His eyes scanned the gallery and the enormous volume of paintings immediately became apparent. Perhaps I should have expected his initial remark of sarcasm, "There are not enough paintings here to fill this place, what have you been doing all year!" Tony Garner leapt to his feet to declare, "It's OK, don't panic, I've got some more in the car!" It took us many, many hours, but we finally managed to arrange a most successful exhibition layout.

Tony's debut exhibition was entitled 'A Moment in Time', and it was only when all the paintings were finally hung in their place that the impact of the show could be fully appreciated. The gallery looked absolutely stunning and it was plain to see that Tony had reached a standard of pastel painting beyond compare. The room appeared lit by his paintings. His subjects were far ranging, but many conveyed the wonderful effects of light on the landscape for which Norfolk is renowned.

Nerves were on edge and anticipation high as the gallery opened at 3pm on Friday 24 September 2004. It was true to say that nobody could have been aware of what was to follow. All the determination and hard work to connect with the public certainly paid off. A long queue had formed outside the gallery door and their desire to see the exhibition was simply overwhelming. The preview attendance ran into hundreds, the atmosphere was electric with excitement and the sale of paintings phenomenal. The most-asked question throughout the preview was "Is there a date fixed for the next show?" Greatly encouraged by this unbelievable wave of enthusiasm, Tony booked his next show for September 2005.

With just a year to prepare, work commenced on his first painting for his next major show. This time he experimented with a new profile of picture-frame moulding and a change to the mounting presentation which involved the use of 'black core' mount card to further enhance and accentuate the drama of his paintings. His quest to complete 100 new paintings within a twelve-month time-frame placed pressures on his ability to show paintings in other galleries throughout East Anglia.

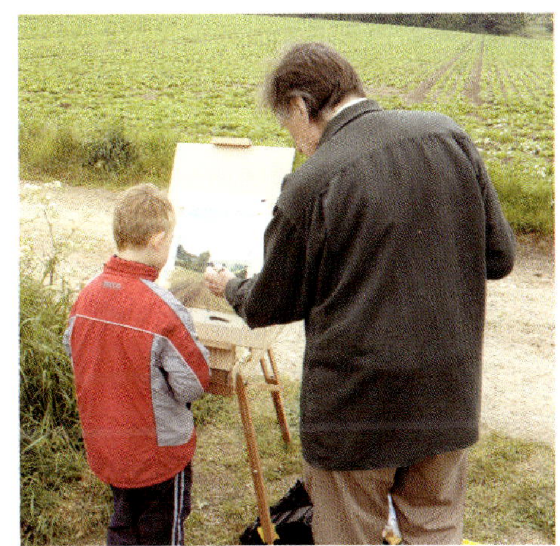

Kieron and Tony.

The desire to paint, as opposed to travelling around delivering paintings, involved serious rationalisation of many established outlets as Tony decided to confine his representation to just Norfolk and Suffolk. This newly concentrated area of distribution seemed to act as a catalyst and his technique evolved another step forward. Not only was he able to sustain a high level of quality within his work but concentration was particularly given to capturing and recording spectacular sunrises and sunsets.

Tony's second one-man exhibition was entitled 'Fleeting Moments', and this was to prove another highly successful show. However, this particular show was to reveal a condition which he had been totally unaware of throughout his life. He recalls the circumstances: "I was aware that my Mother had developed glaucoma later in her life and I thought that it would be wise to visit the optician. The routine eye test revealed that something was awry and I was subsequently referred to a consultant at the Norfolk and Norwich University Hospital. The examination commenced with a standard test where numbers needed to be found concealed within patterns made of various colours. I experienced tremendous difficulty with this test and was unable to discern hardly any of the numbers. I was staggered to discover, and it came as quite a shock, that I was colour blind".

While this was a startling revelation, Tony Garner appeared totally unaffected by his newly diagnosed condition. It was fascinating that his interpretation of some colours, notably the actual tones of colours, did not convey a detrimental effect to his work... indeed, quite the opposite. Perhaps this possibly gives an insight into his fearless method of using colour to most dramatic effect!

The *Eastern Daily Press* was quick to respond to news of Tony's eye condition and an extensive full-colour feature appeared just a day before his major exhibition opened. Needless to say, the public's response was immediate and attendance reached another new level. The publicity attracted tremendous interest and we were inundated with a completely new audience who wished to see the work of this 'colour blind' artist. The second major show surpassed all expectations, not just improving on the volume of paintings sold but also on the variety and strength of subject matter. The format of a major one-man exhibition for Tony at Picturecraft Gallery has now followed on an annual basis each September since 2004.

Today, the mutual and harmonious working practices between Tony Garner, Picturecraft and the Hill family continue and remain forever strong. Indeed my gallery now exclusively represents the original paintings of Tony and examples of his work can be viewed throughout the year. Publicity also steadily continues in promoting exhibitions, including television features, magazine articles and radio interviews, and Tony continues to attract a great deal of interest when he can be found regularly painting at the gallery.

And not content with sharing his skills with an adult audience, Tony Garner has also been instrumental in motivating Kieron Williamson, the seven-year-old child artist. Different pastel techniques are explored and an open invitation has been extended to Kieron to attend Tony Garner's pastel workshops. More recently, they have both experienced 'plein air' opportunities to share in another love of working in oil paints to capture the essence of the Norfolk landscape.

Sadly, a problem caused by degenerating hands has hampered Tony, and meeting deadlines has become more problematic. "I don't know how long I can keep 'up to speed' or indeed, if I can continue exhibiting on an annual basis. However, I have a close association with Kieron Williamson, the young man who promises to take up the baton. He is a seven-year-old 'superstar' who has already risen to international recognition. His progress has been meteoric. I do feel that the future of Norfolk landscape painting is potentially in very safe hands and so any assistance I can give to him, however small, will make all of the last 27 years of learning worthwhile."

So what of the future? The following pages of this book reveal not just the results of twelve months' hard work, but many years of dedicated experience in painting.

Tony Garner is a true master of the art of pastel painting.

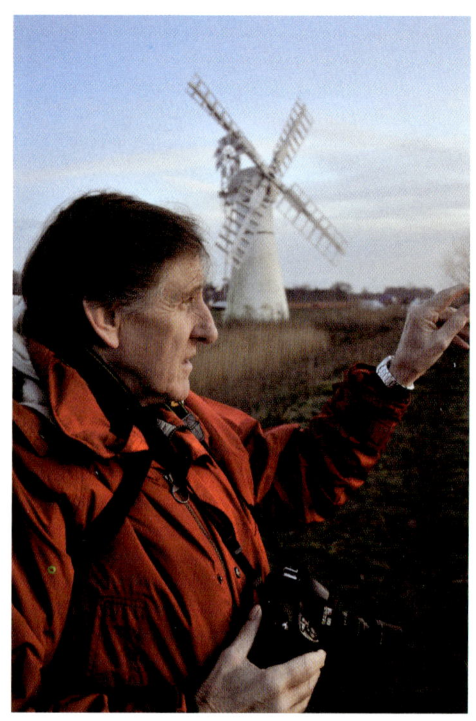

Seeking inspiration, Thurne Mill, December 2009.

EARLIER WORKS

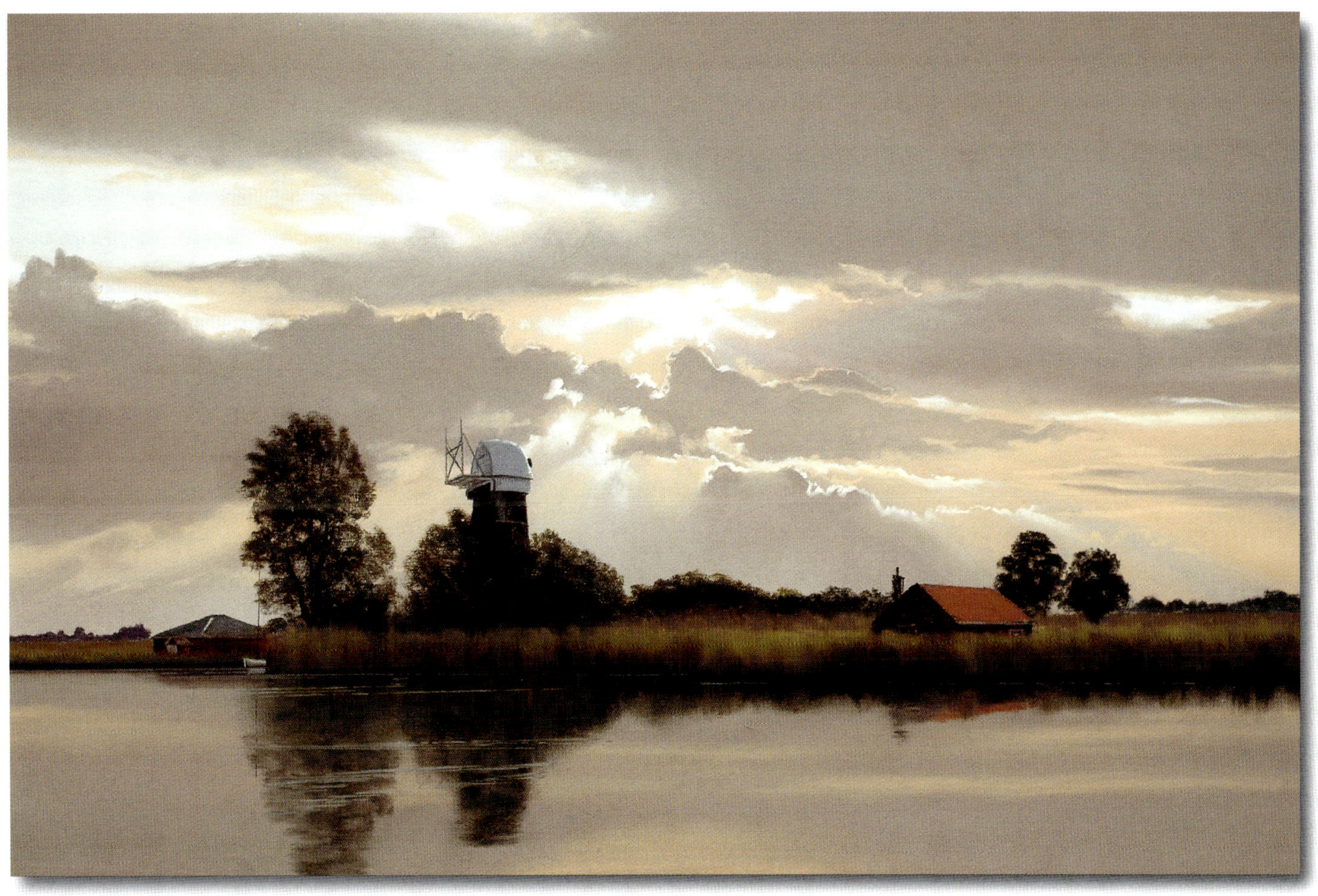

The Black Mill on the Bure.

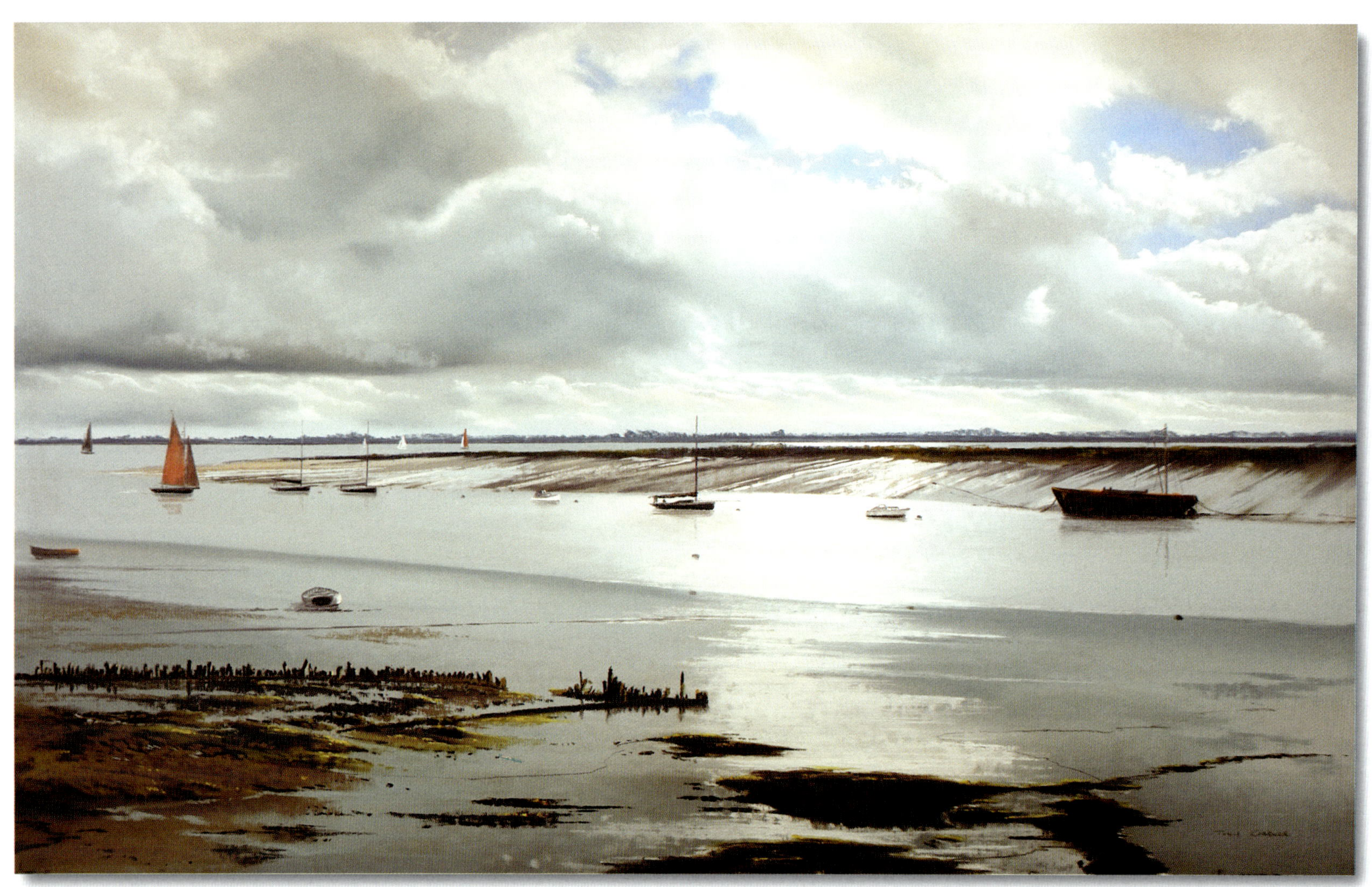

Coming Home.

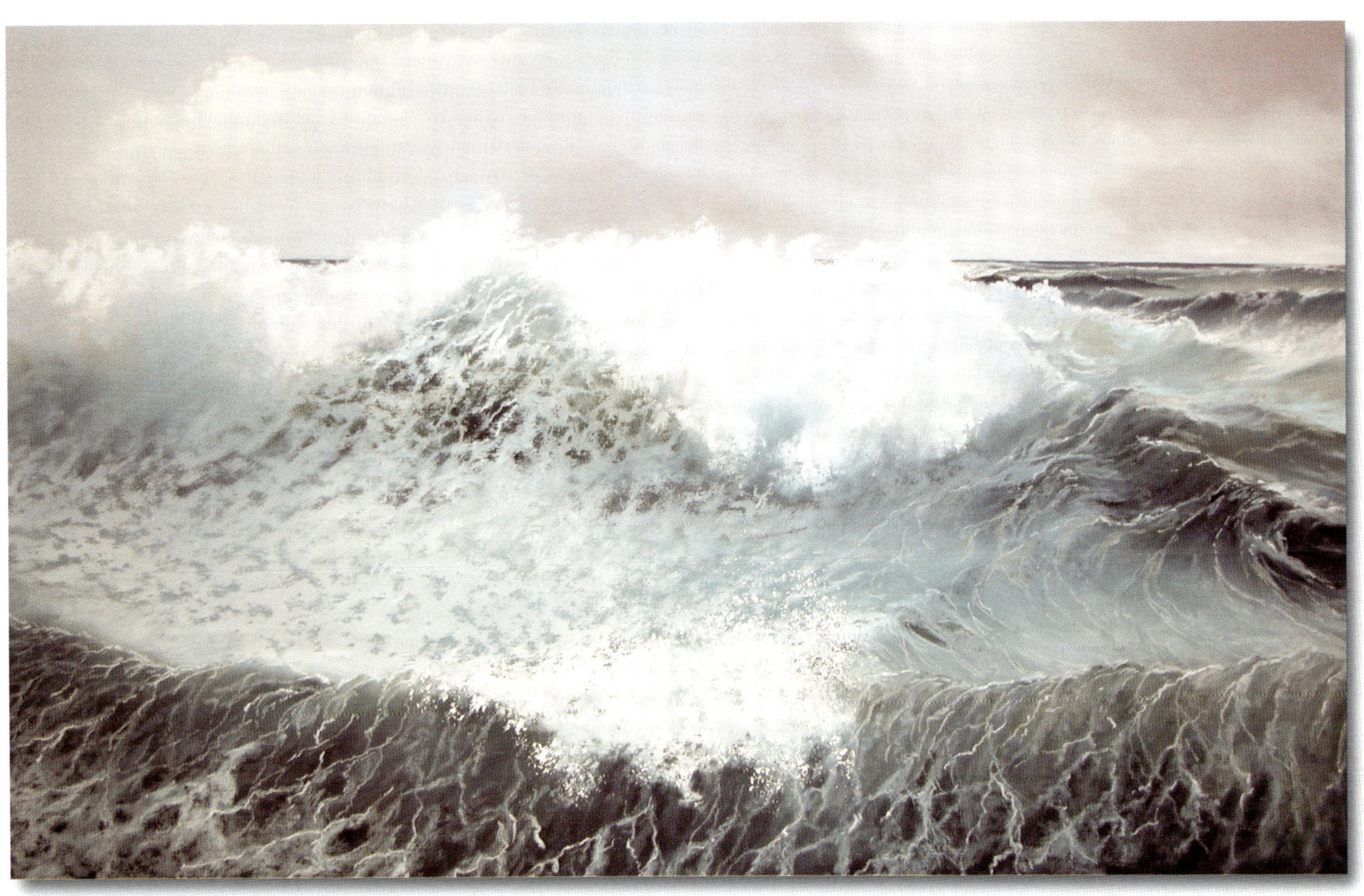

No Paddling.

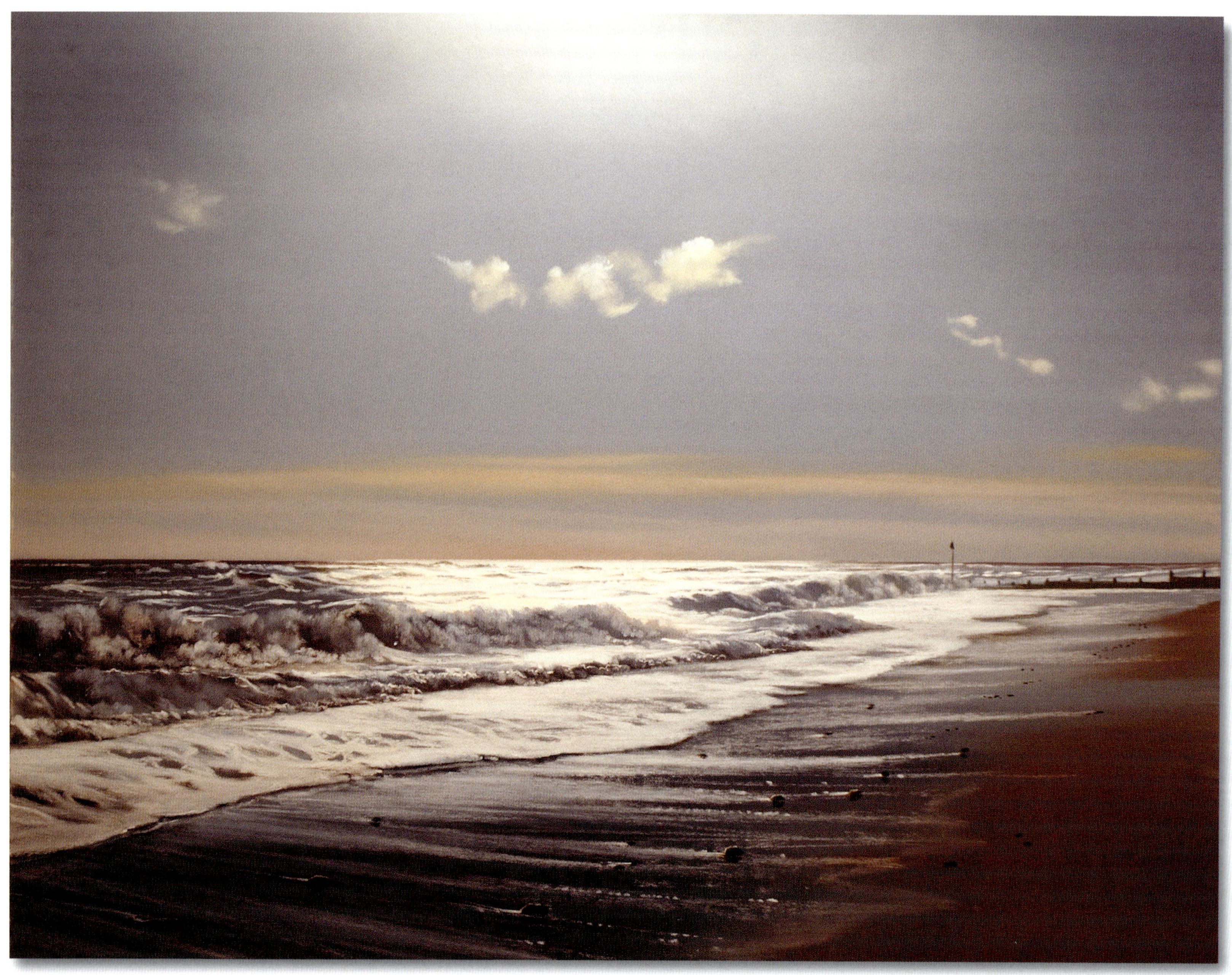

Light on the Surf.

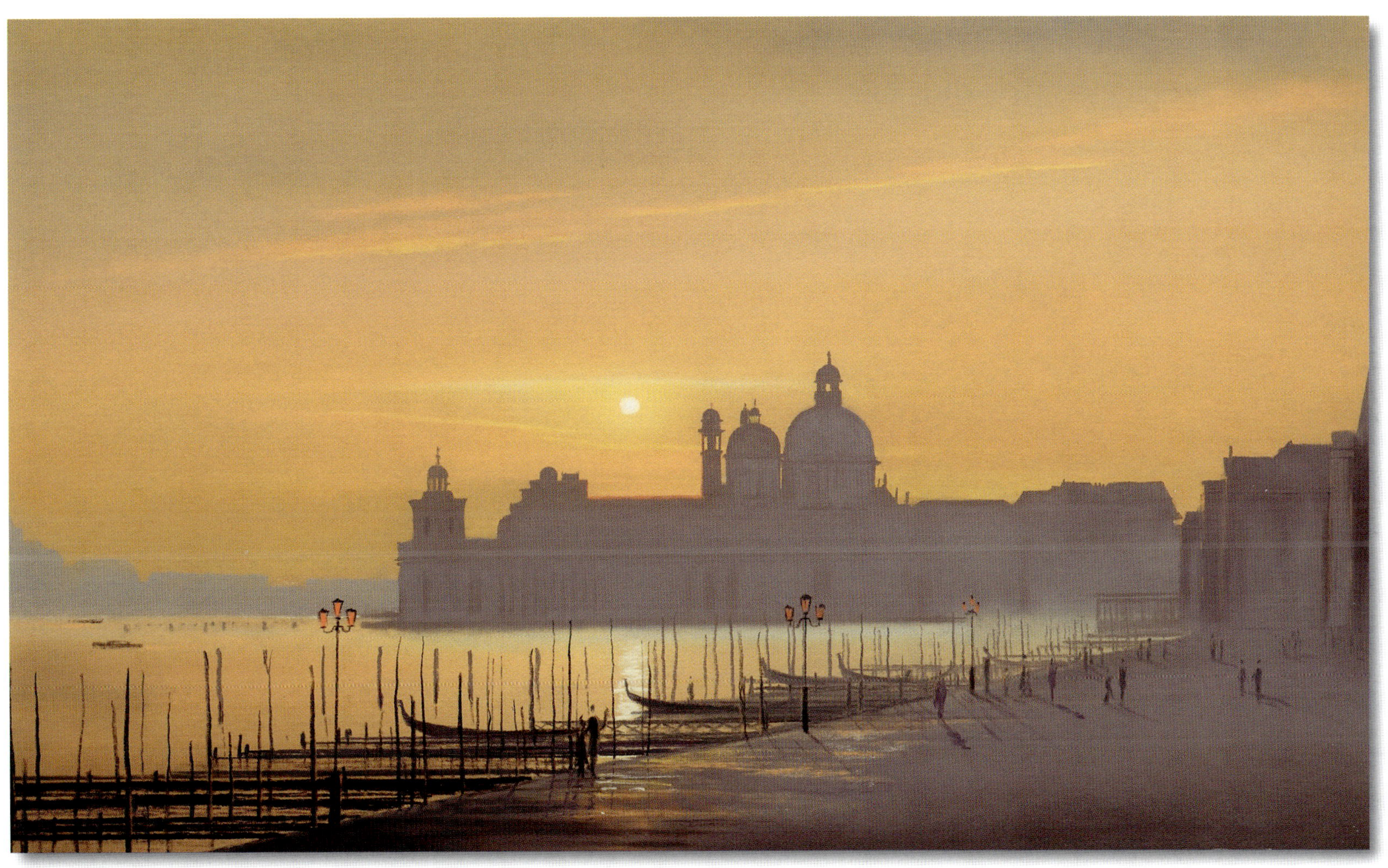

A Tourist in Venice.

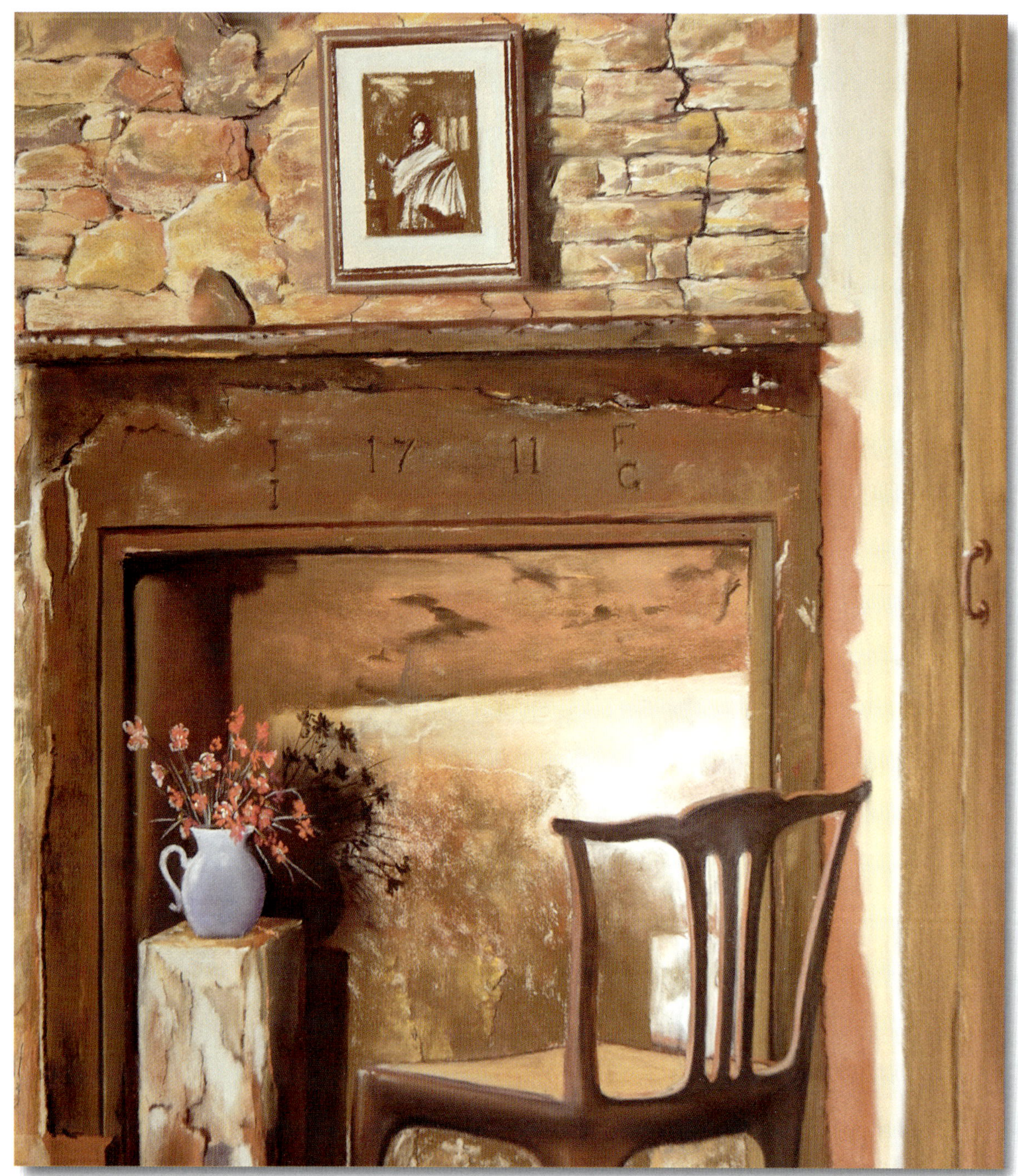

A Seat by the Fireside.

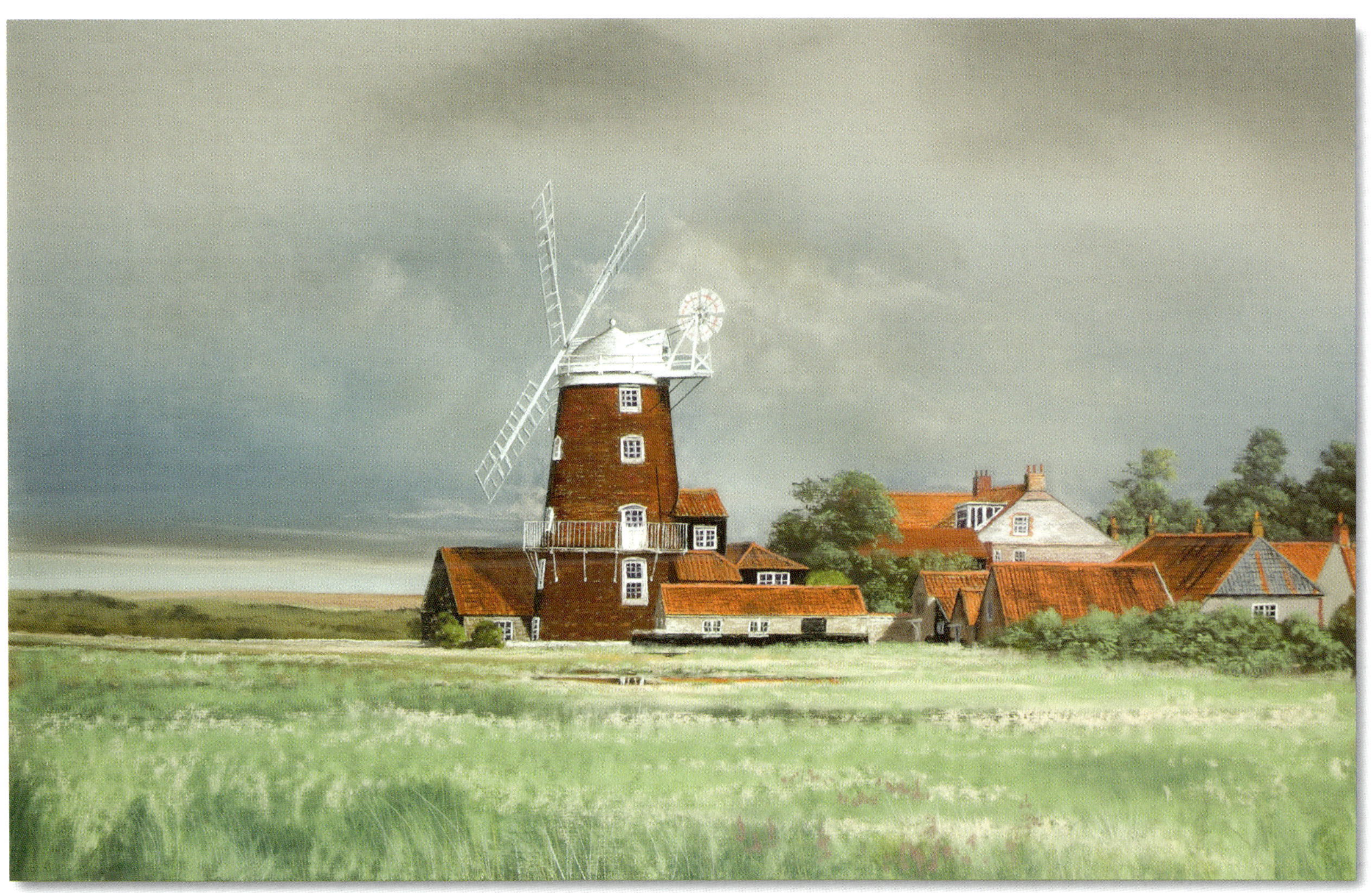

Stormclouds Over Cley.

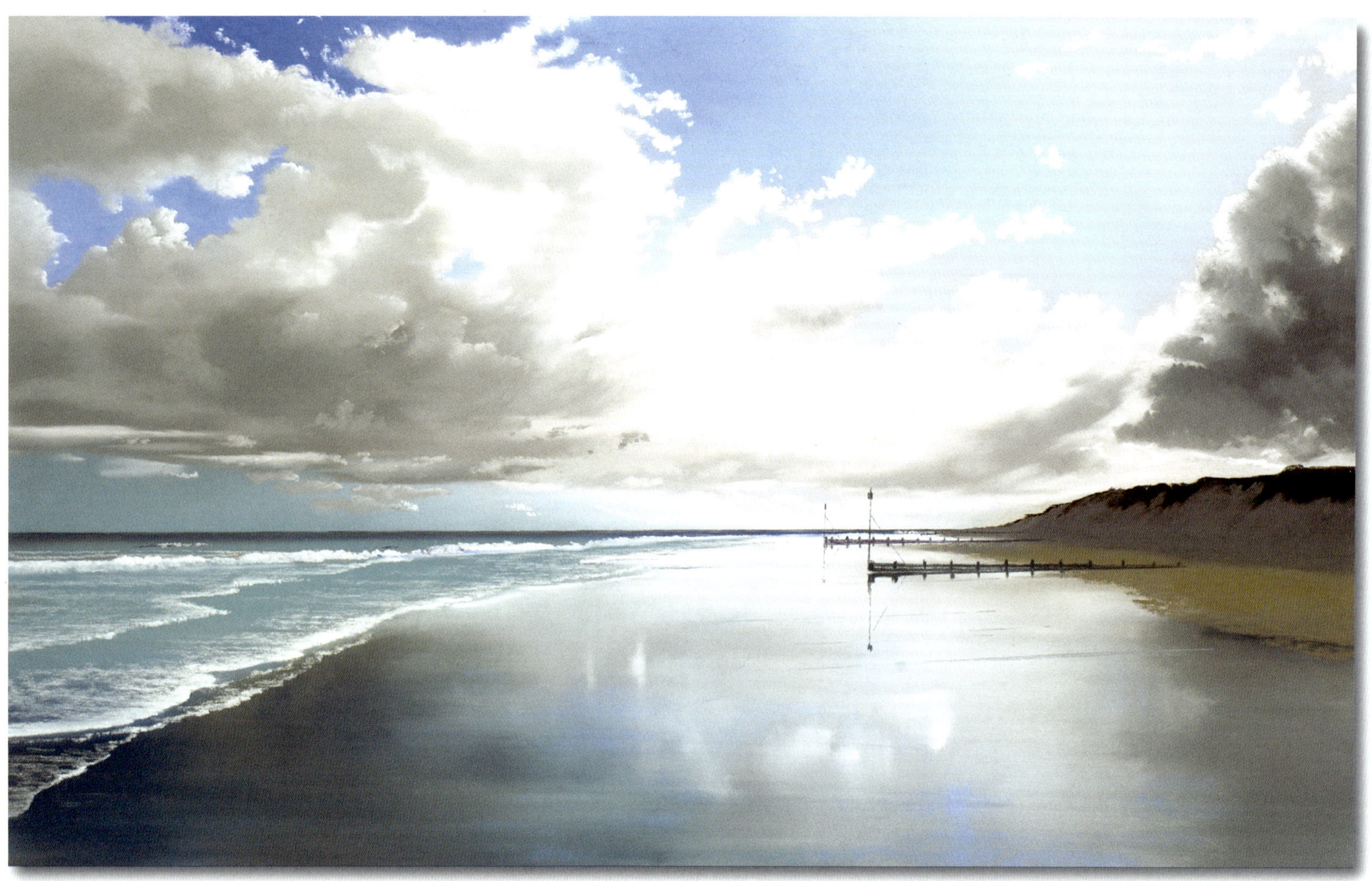

Reflective Sand.

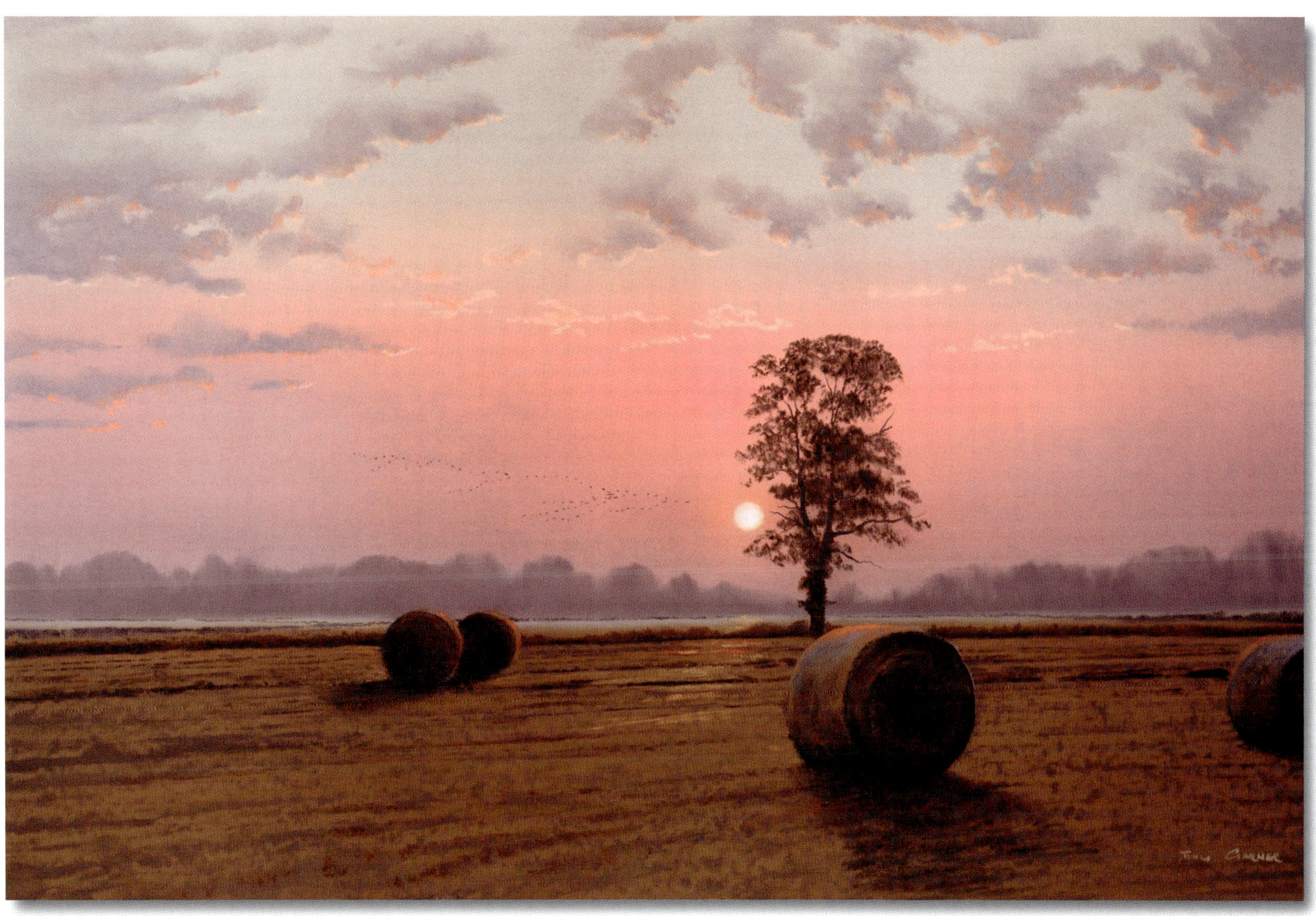

Harvest Skies.

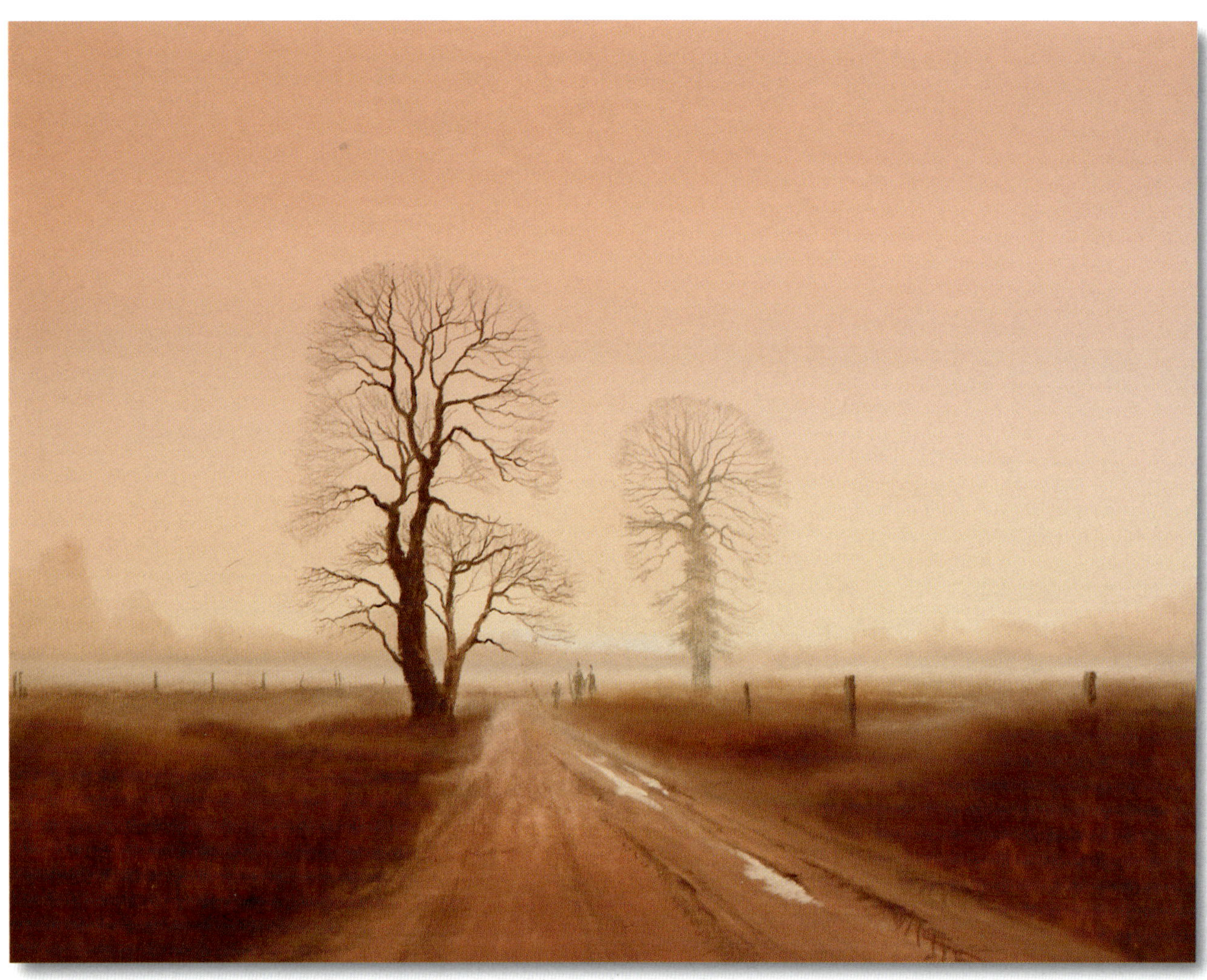

Family Walk.

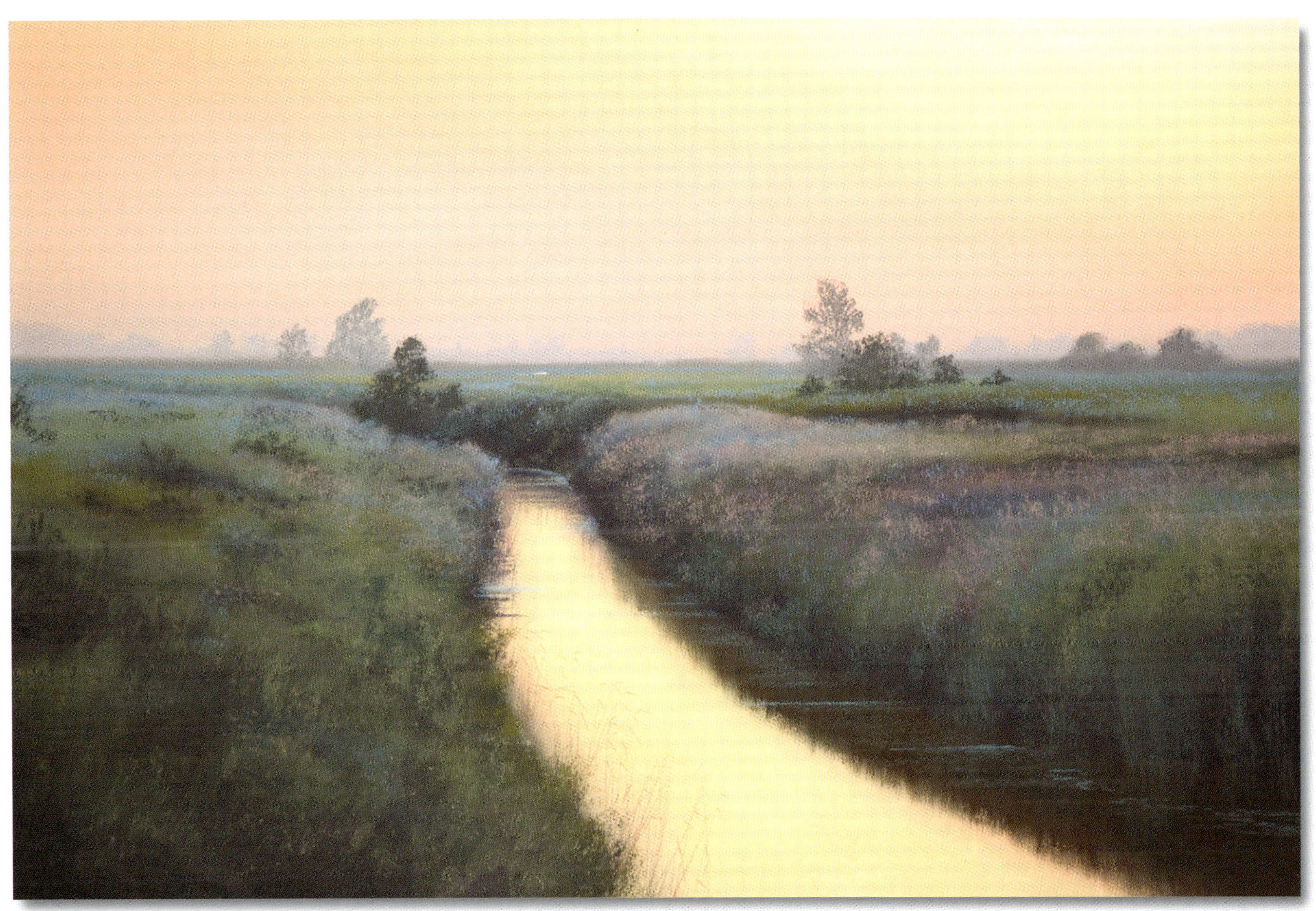

Sunset Dyke.

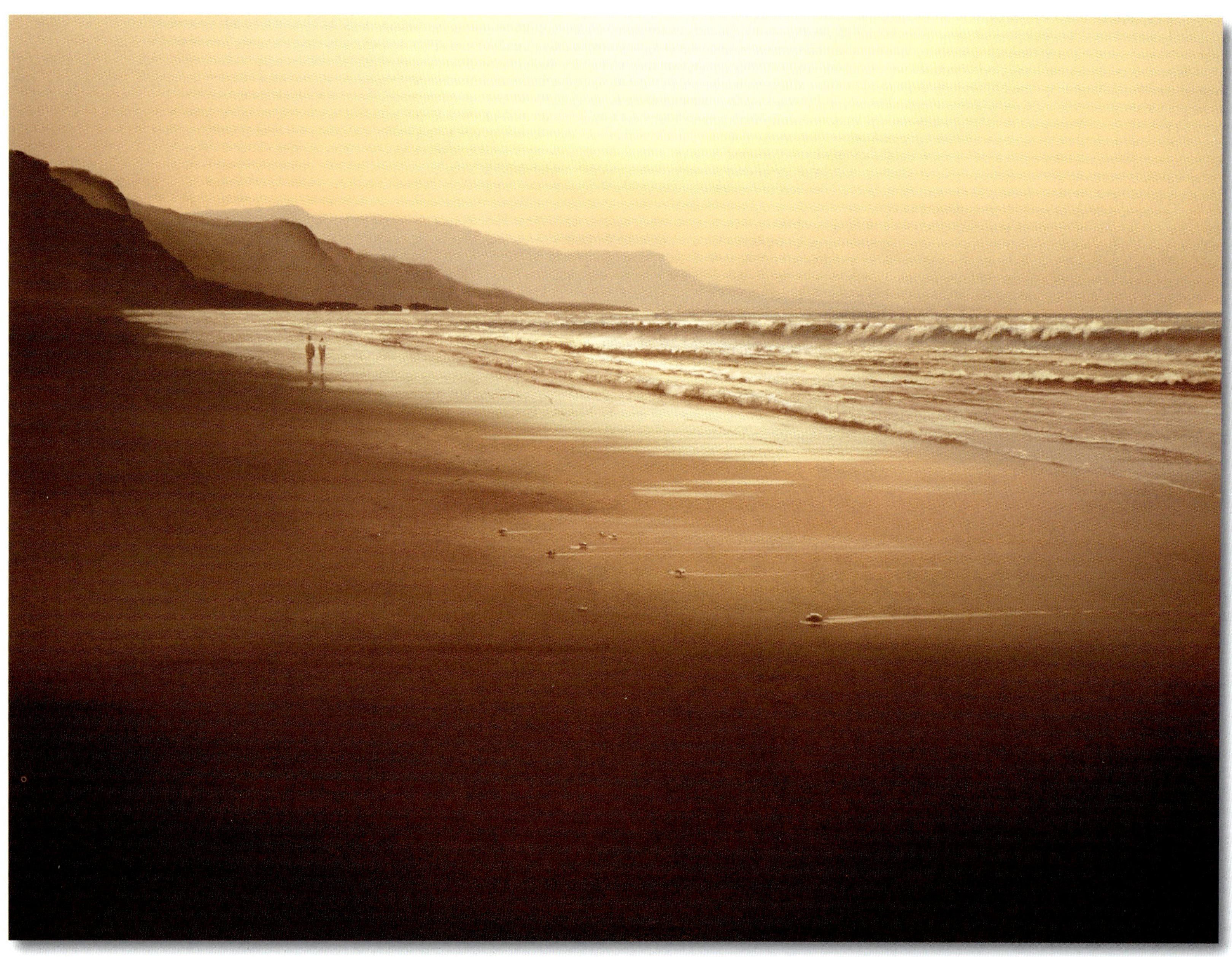

Walking the Tideline.

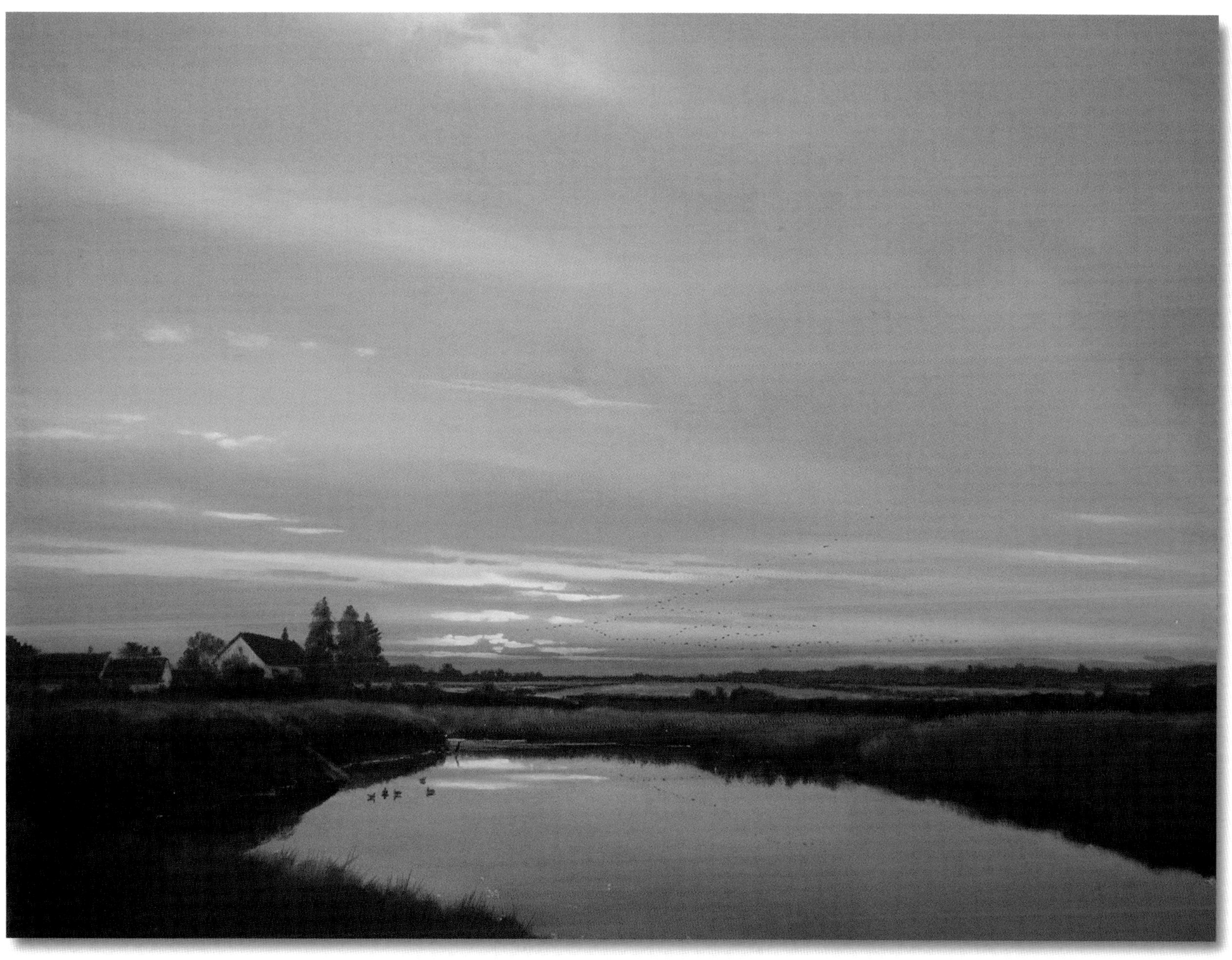

Red Sky at Morston.

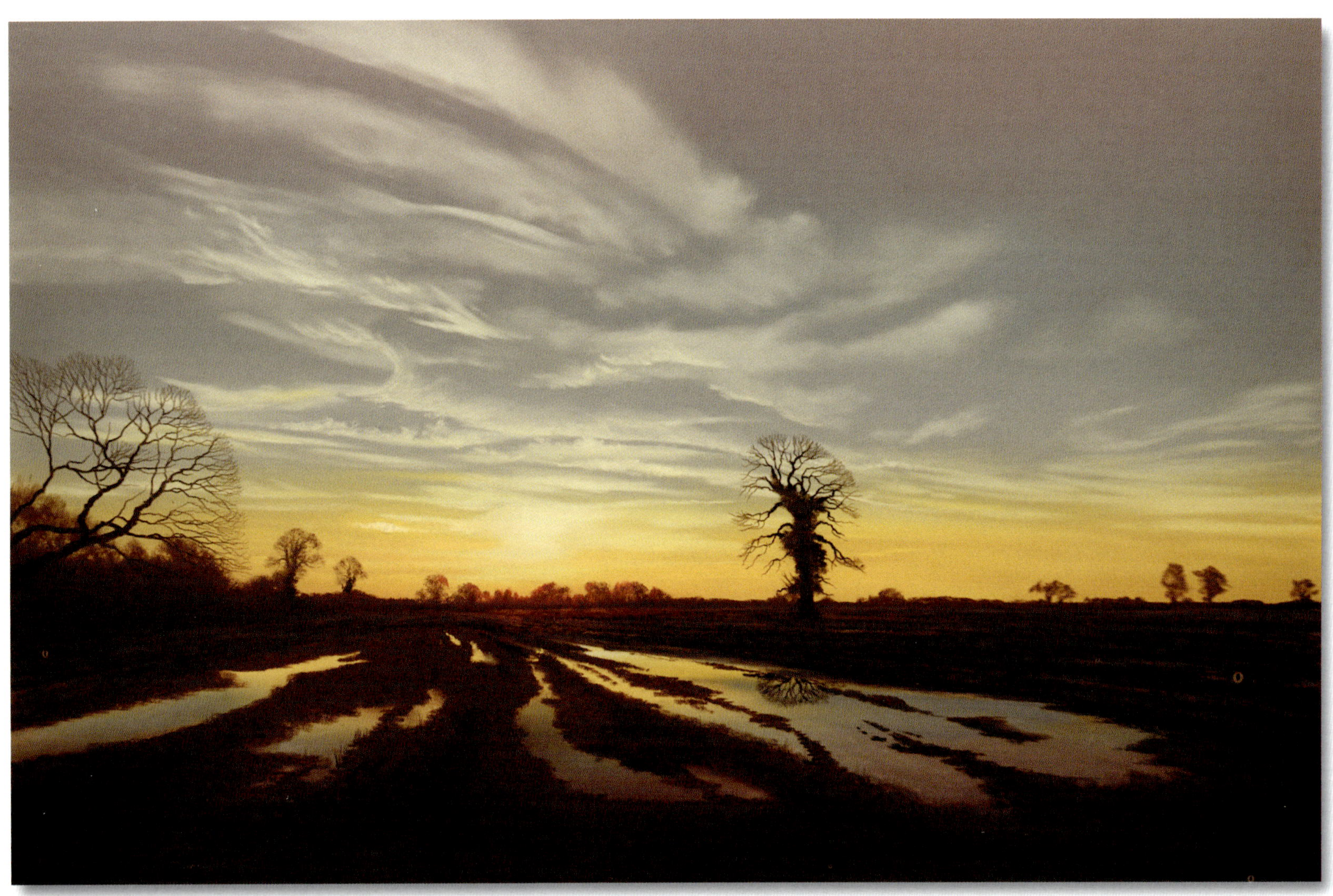

Morning After the Rain.

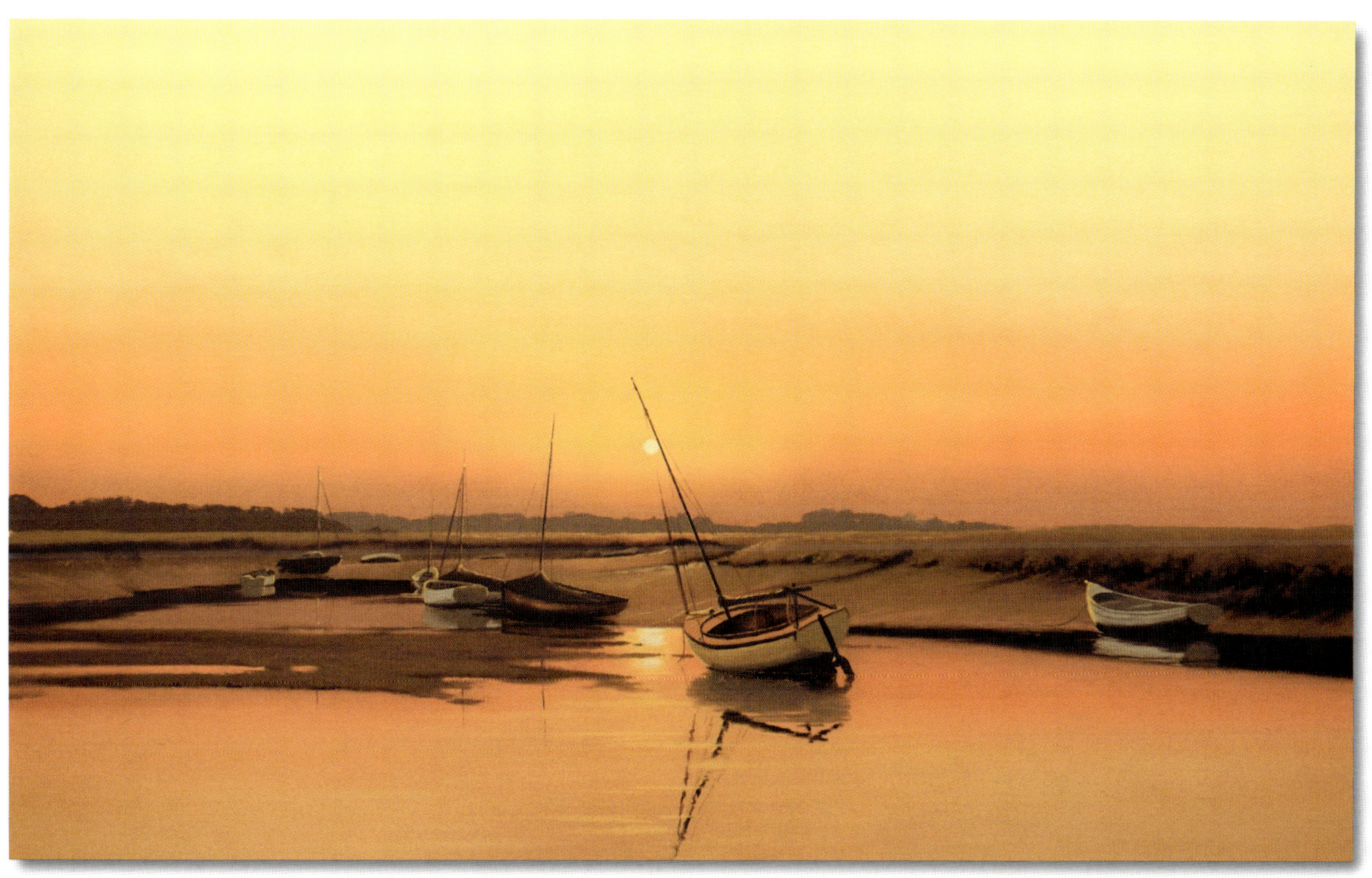

Golden Glow, Burnham.

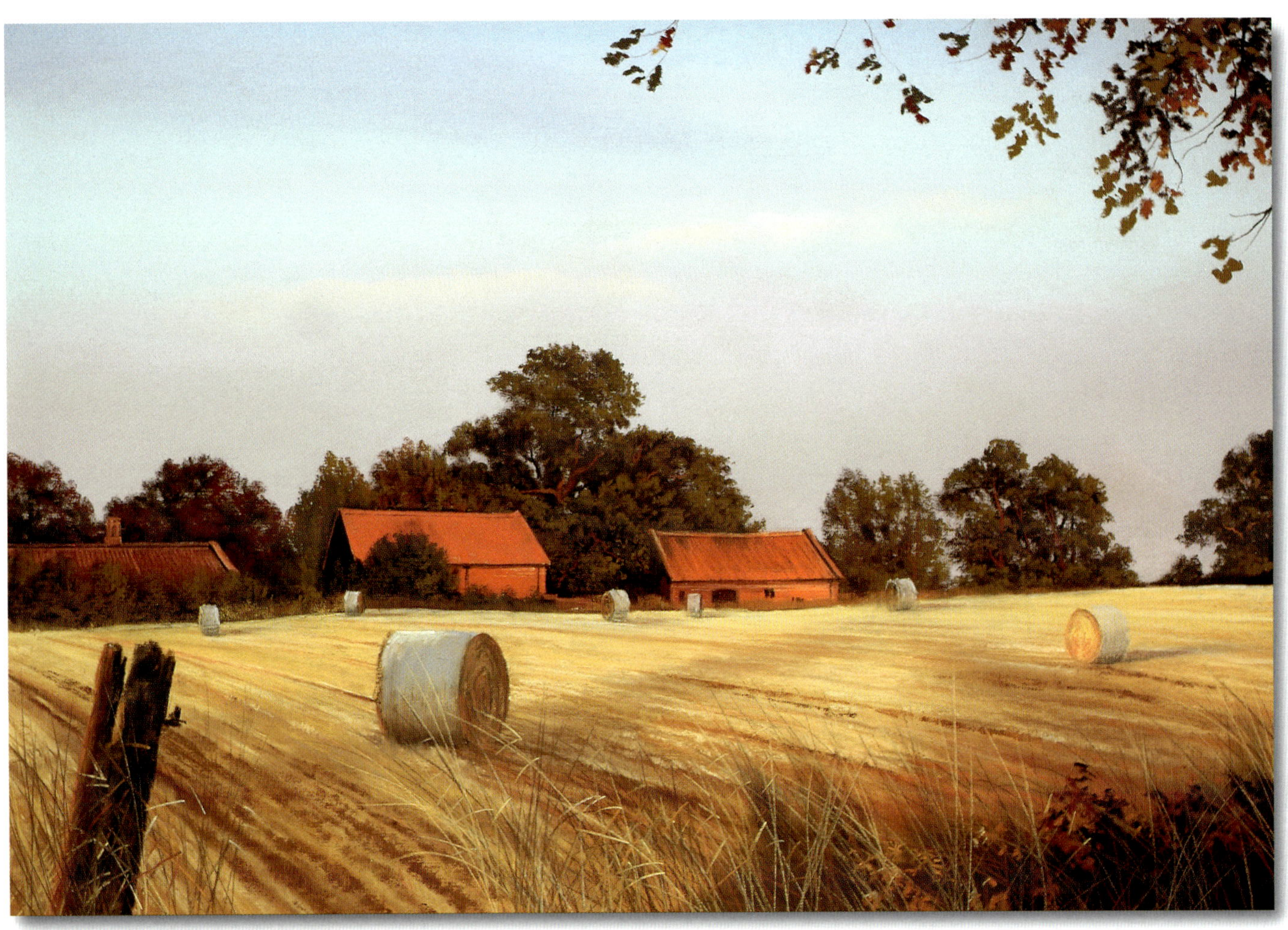

Happiness is…

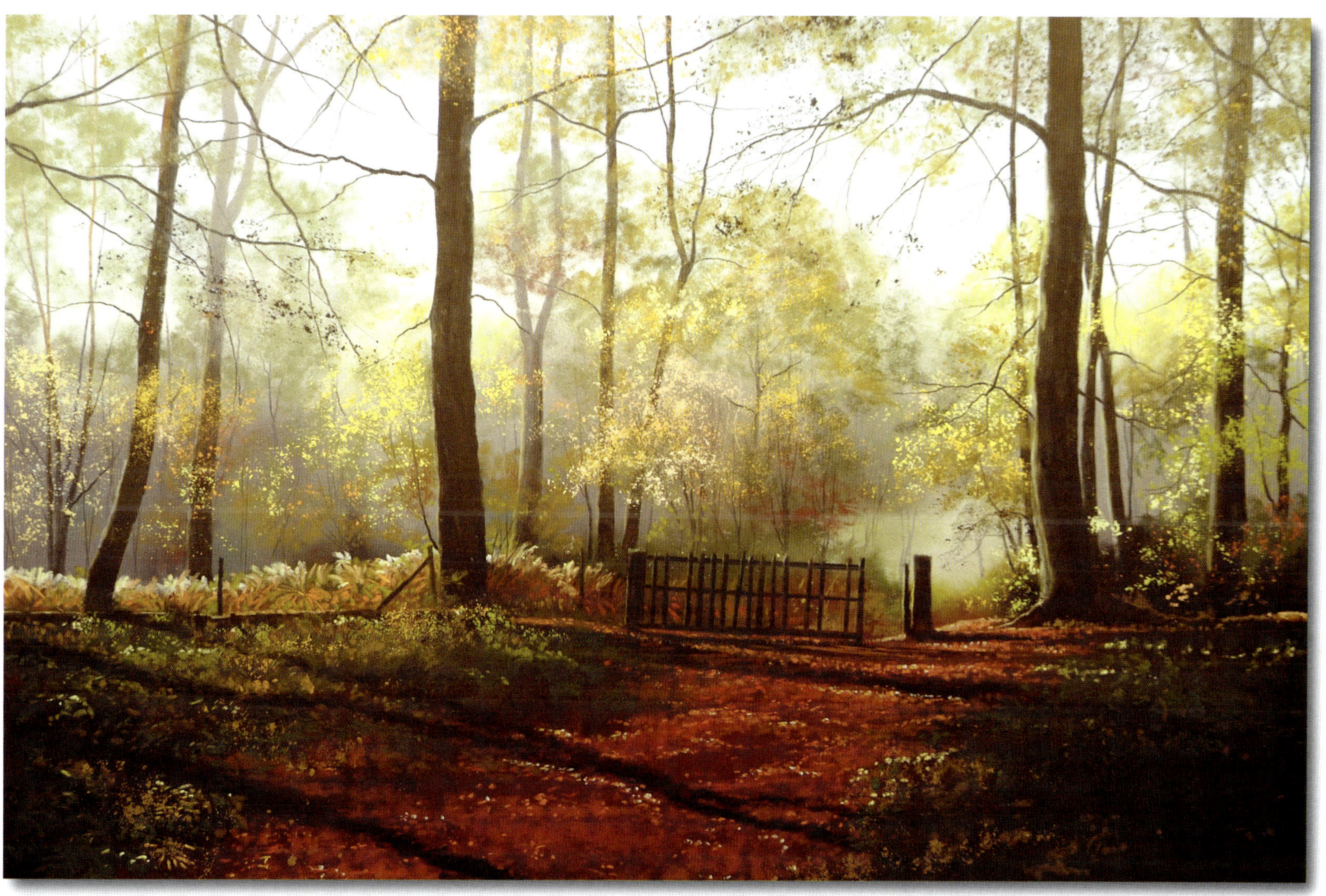

Autumn Light.

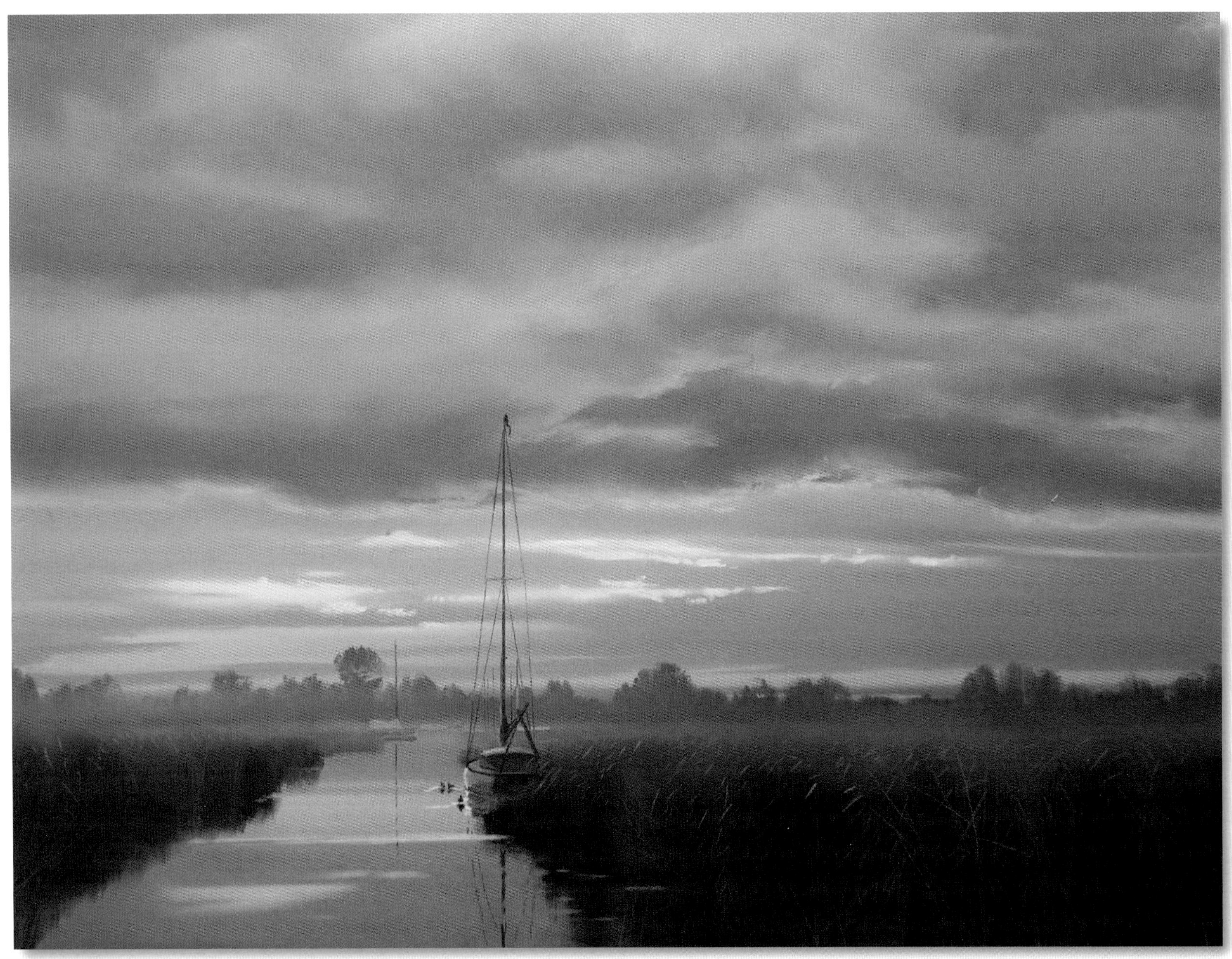

A Quiet Mooring.

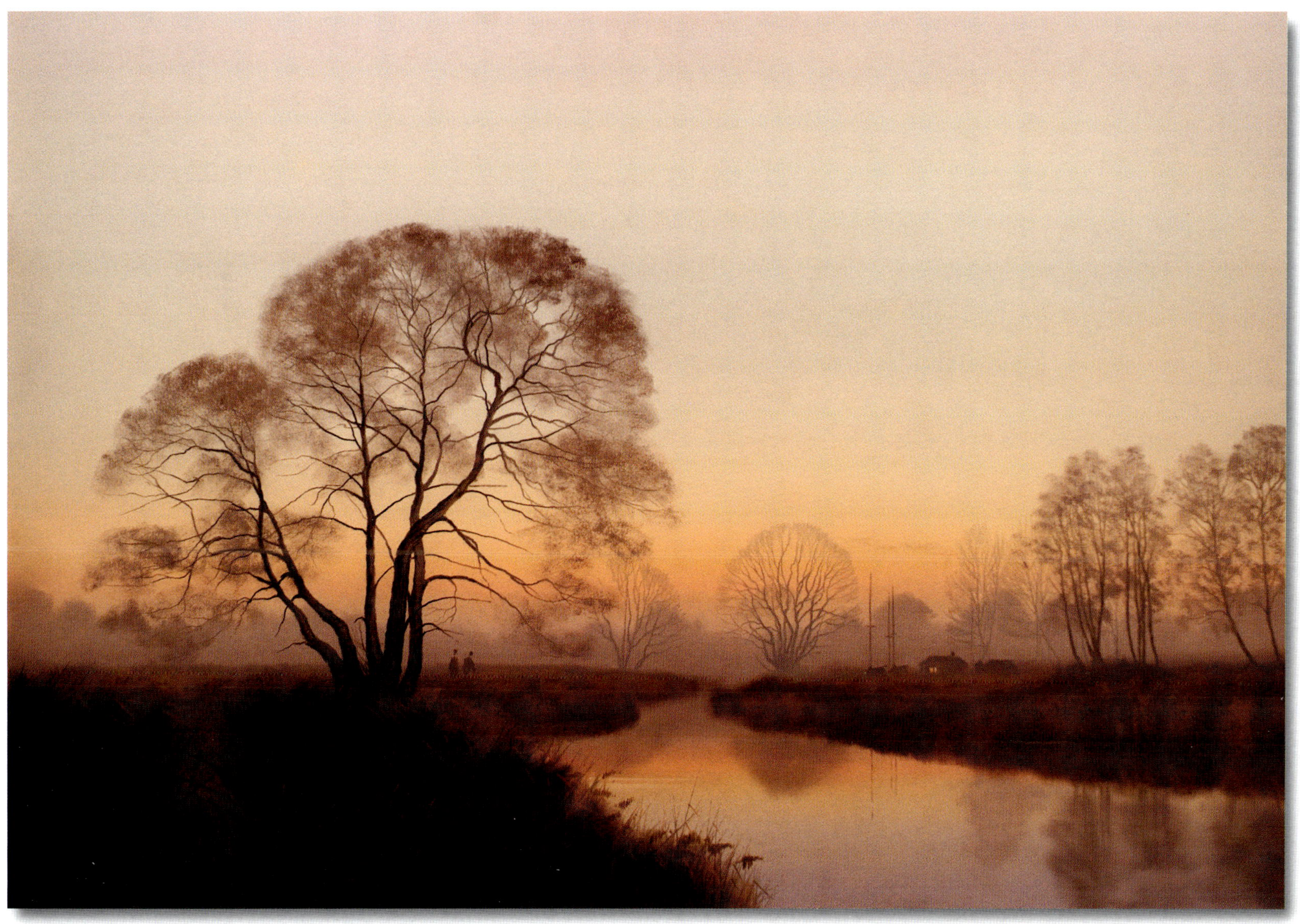

Daybreak.

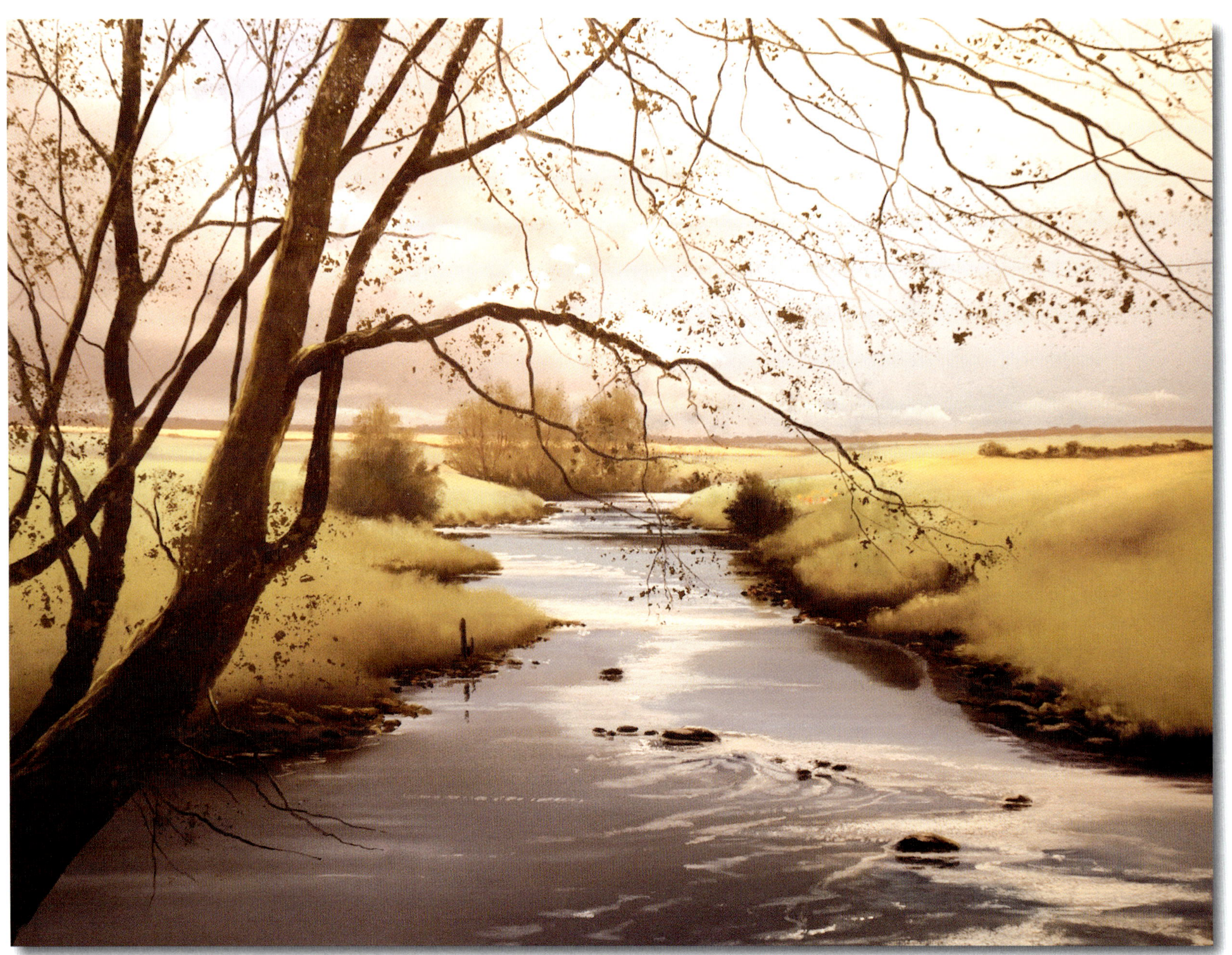

Sparkling Waters.

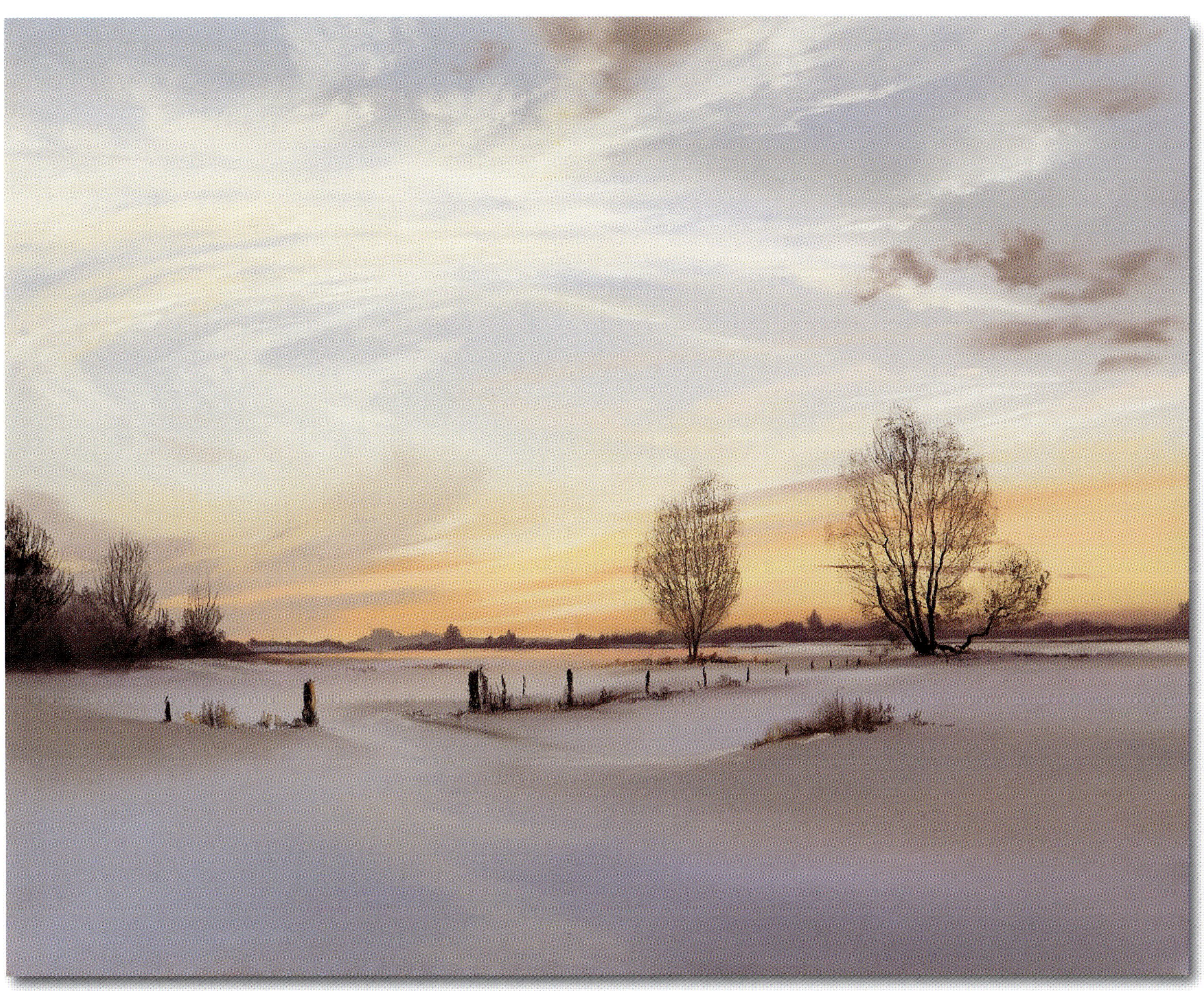

Winter Sun.

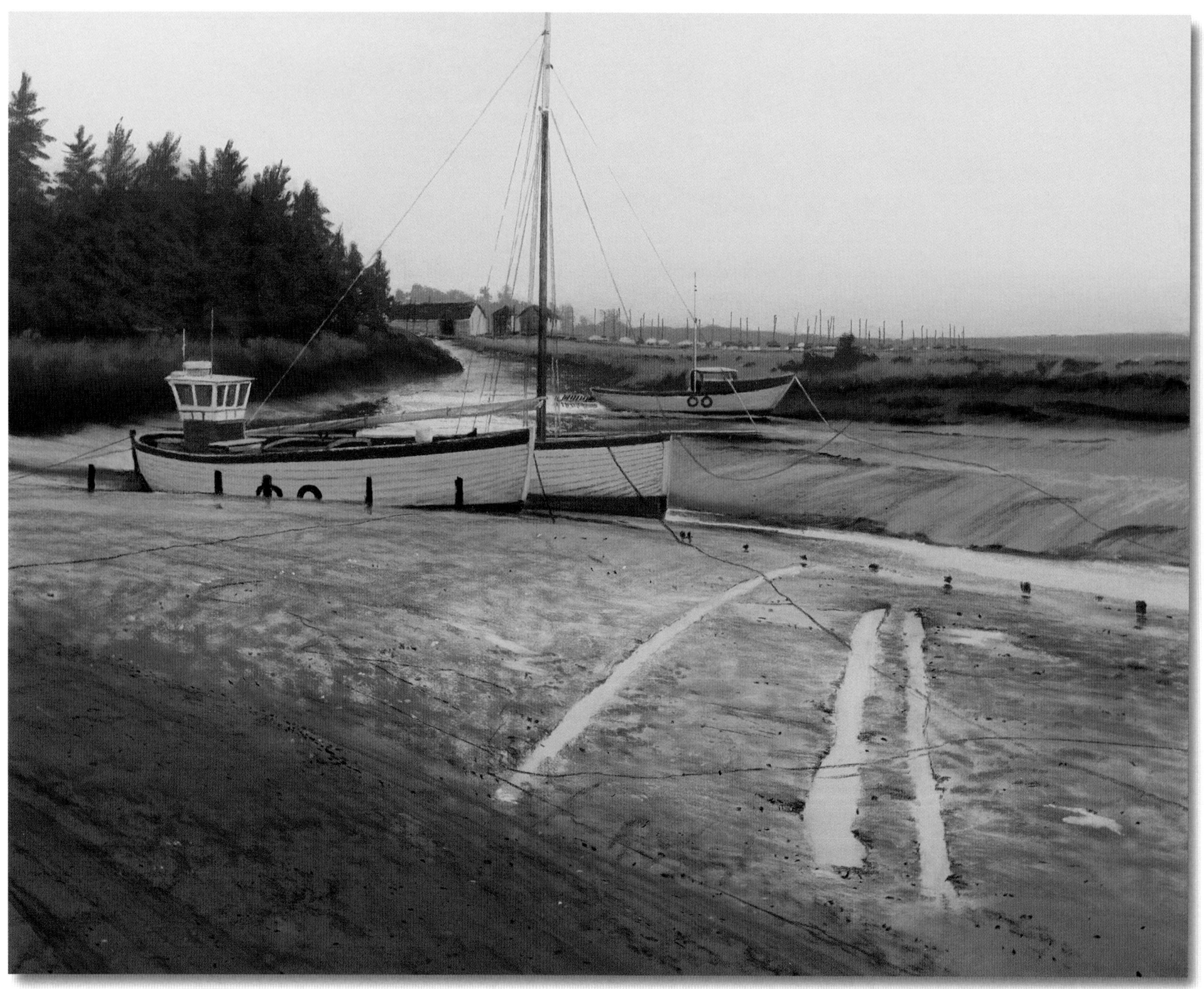

Sundown, Brancaster.

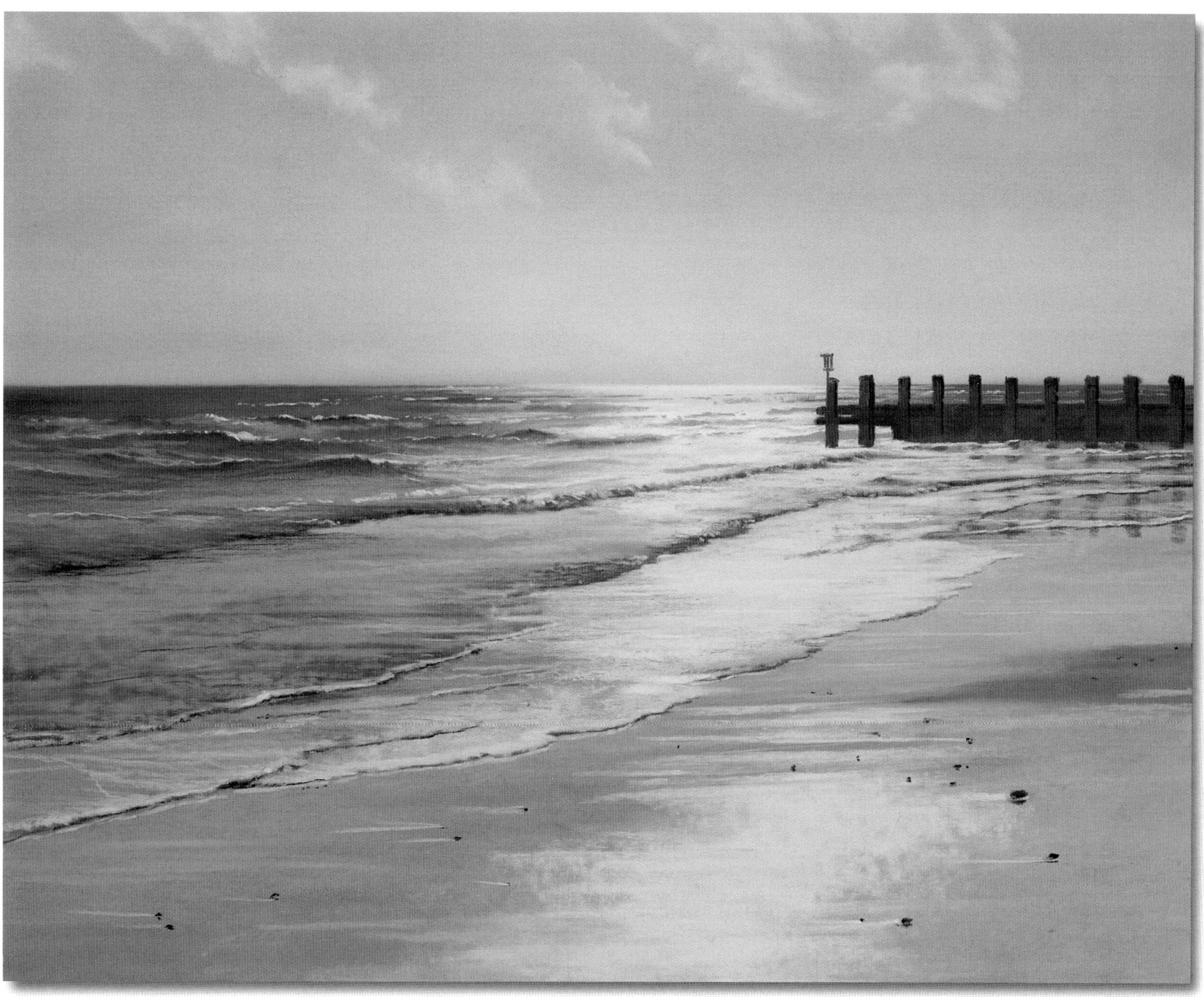

Lowestoft Sun.

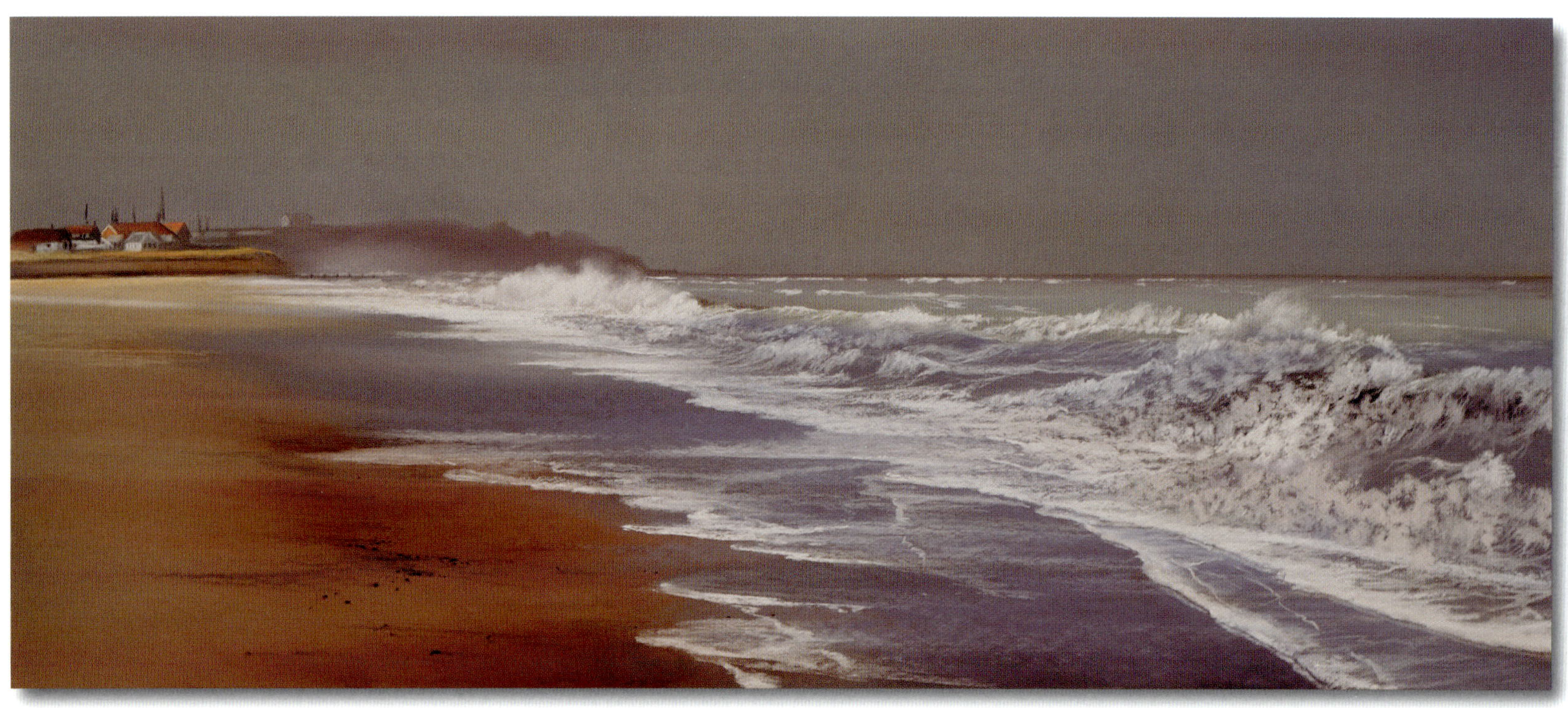

Memories of a Windy Day.

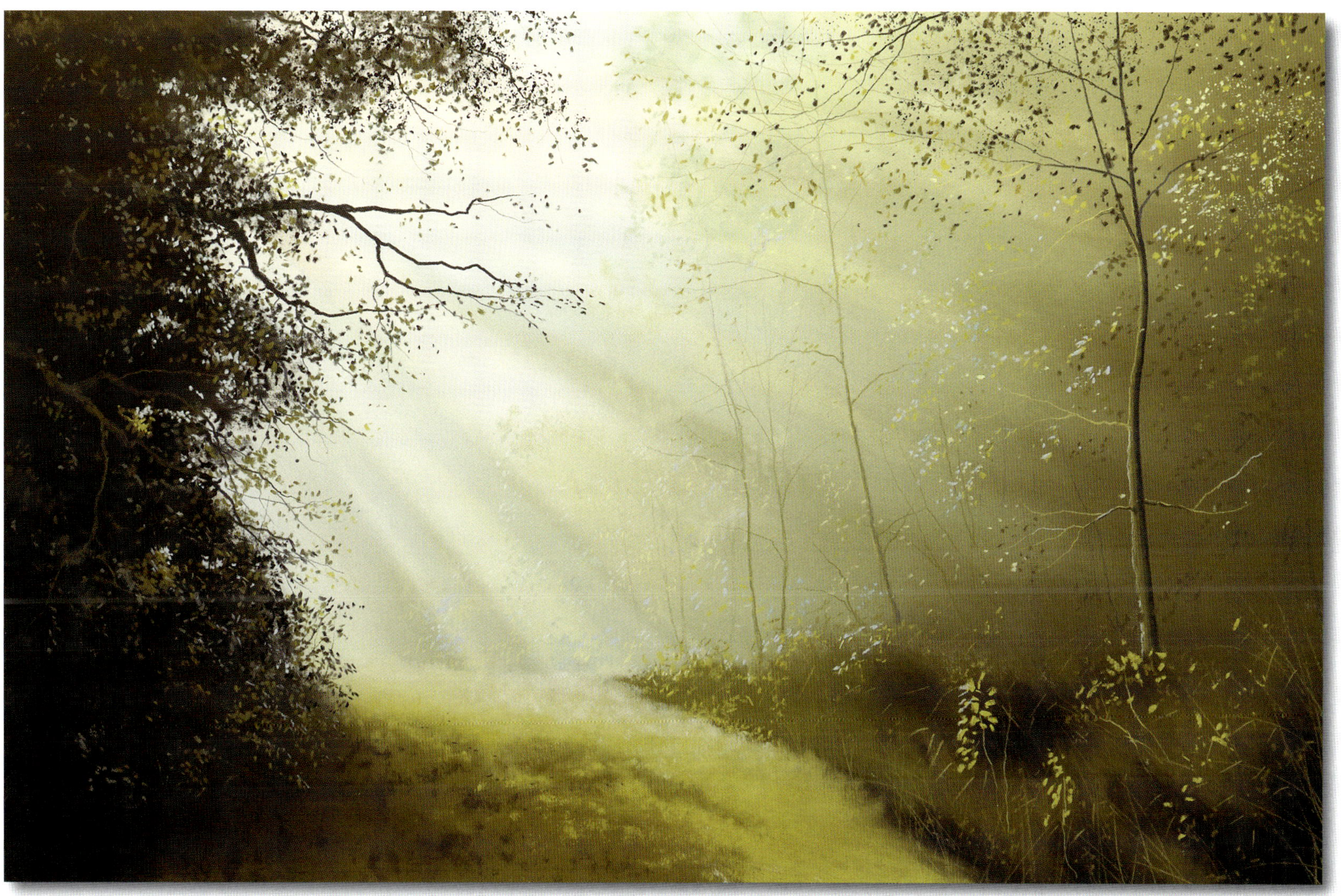

Shafts of Light.

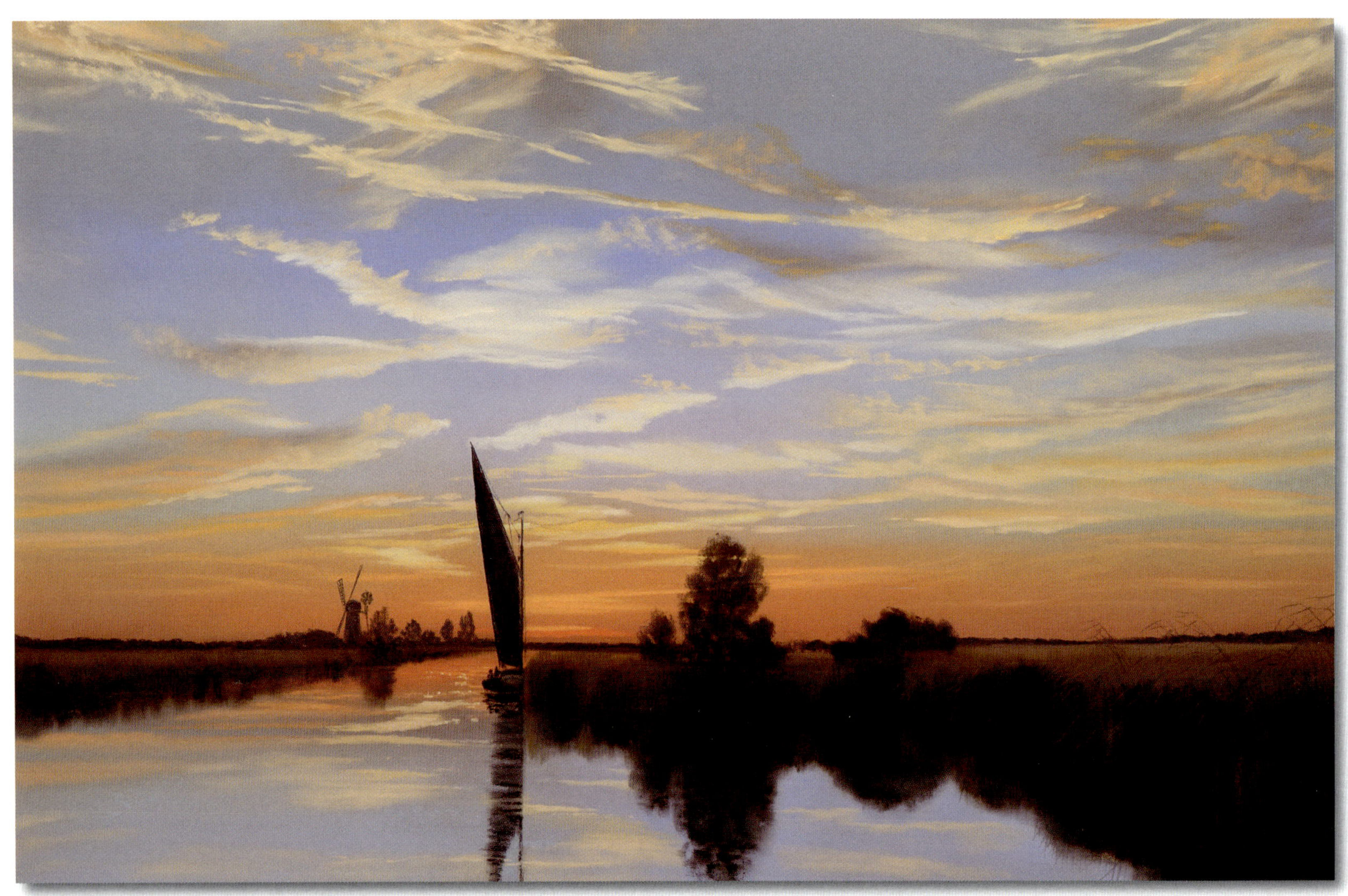

Going Home.

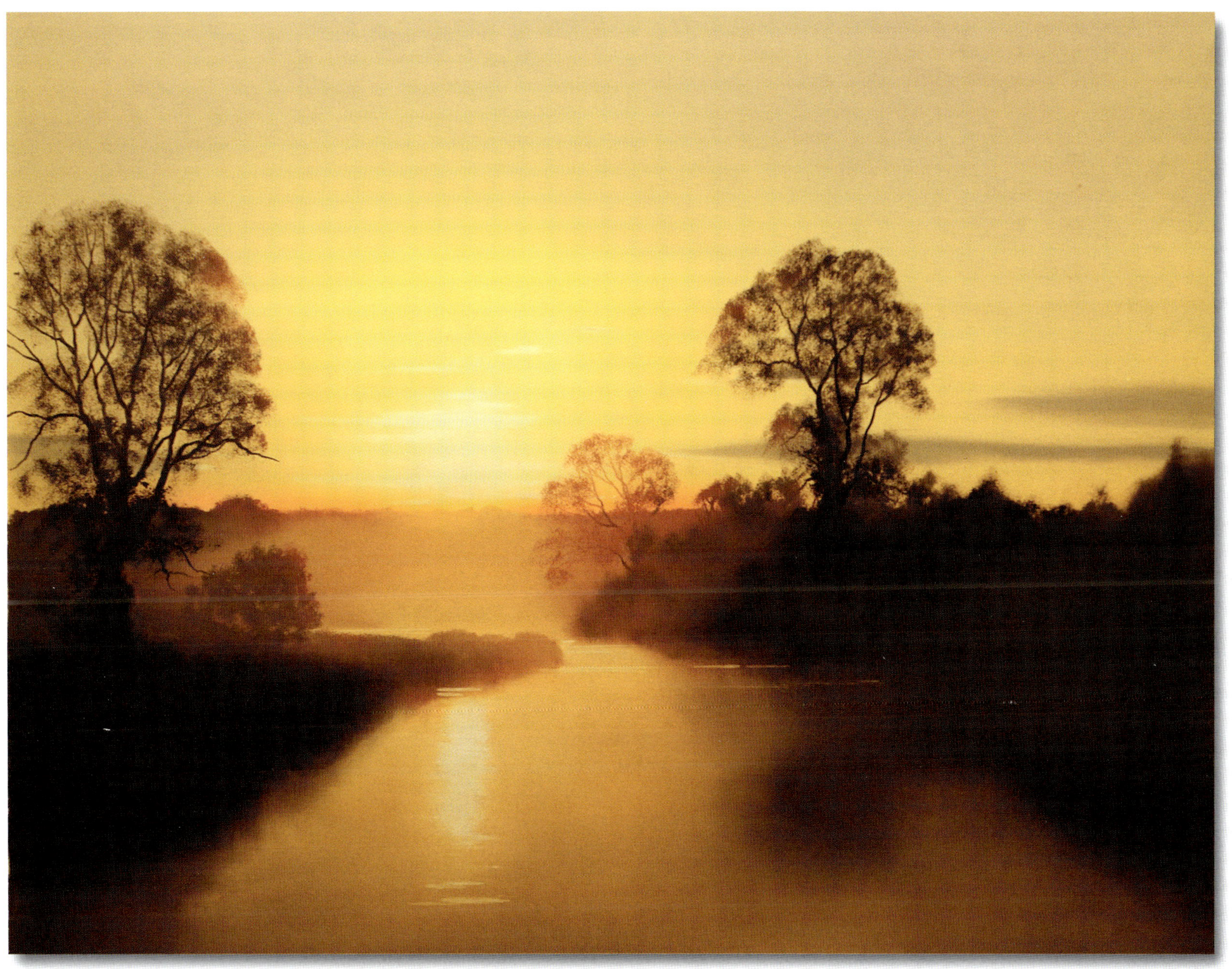

Golden Dawn.

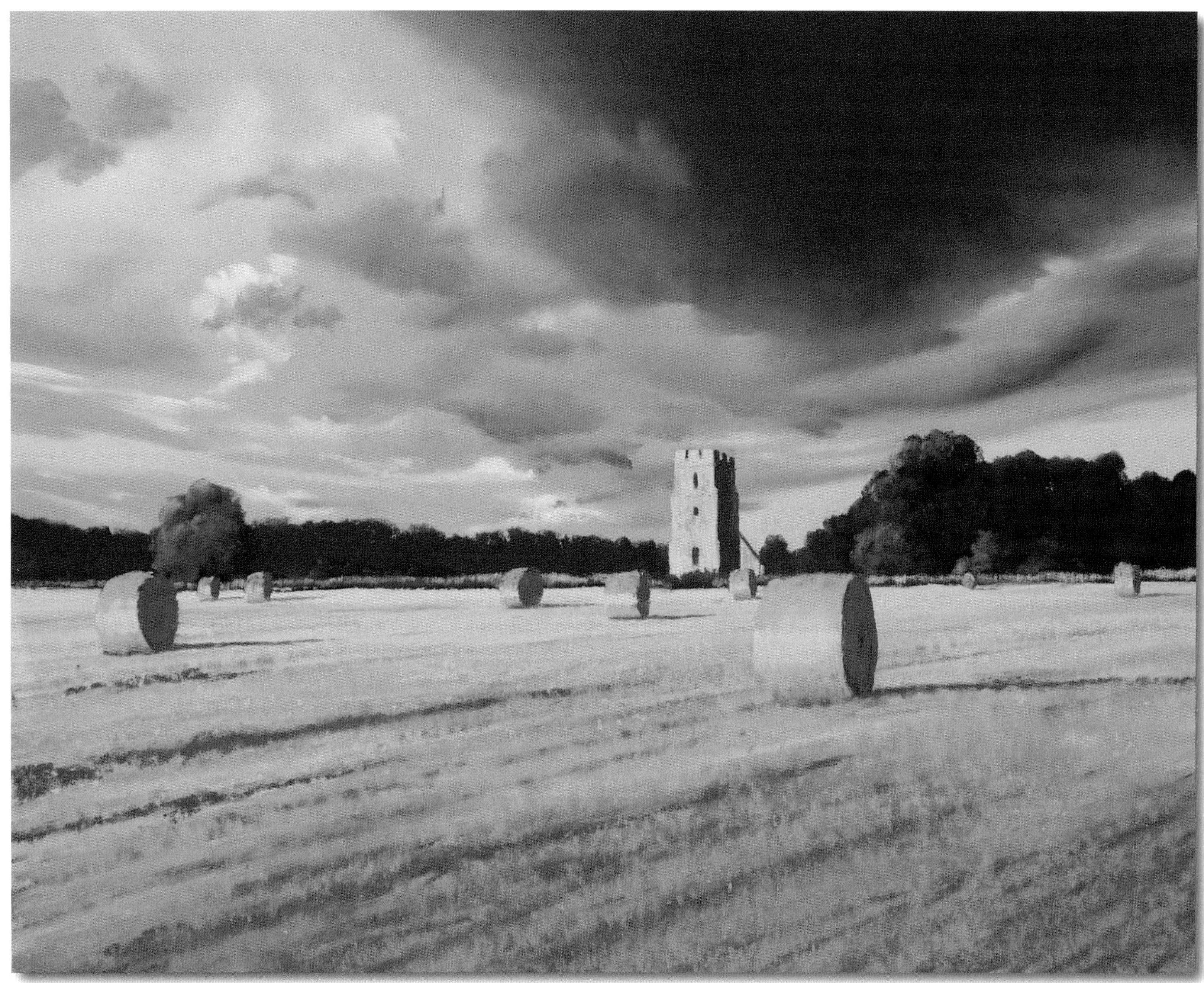

Harvest Stormclouds.

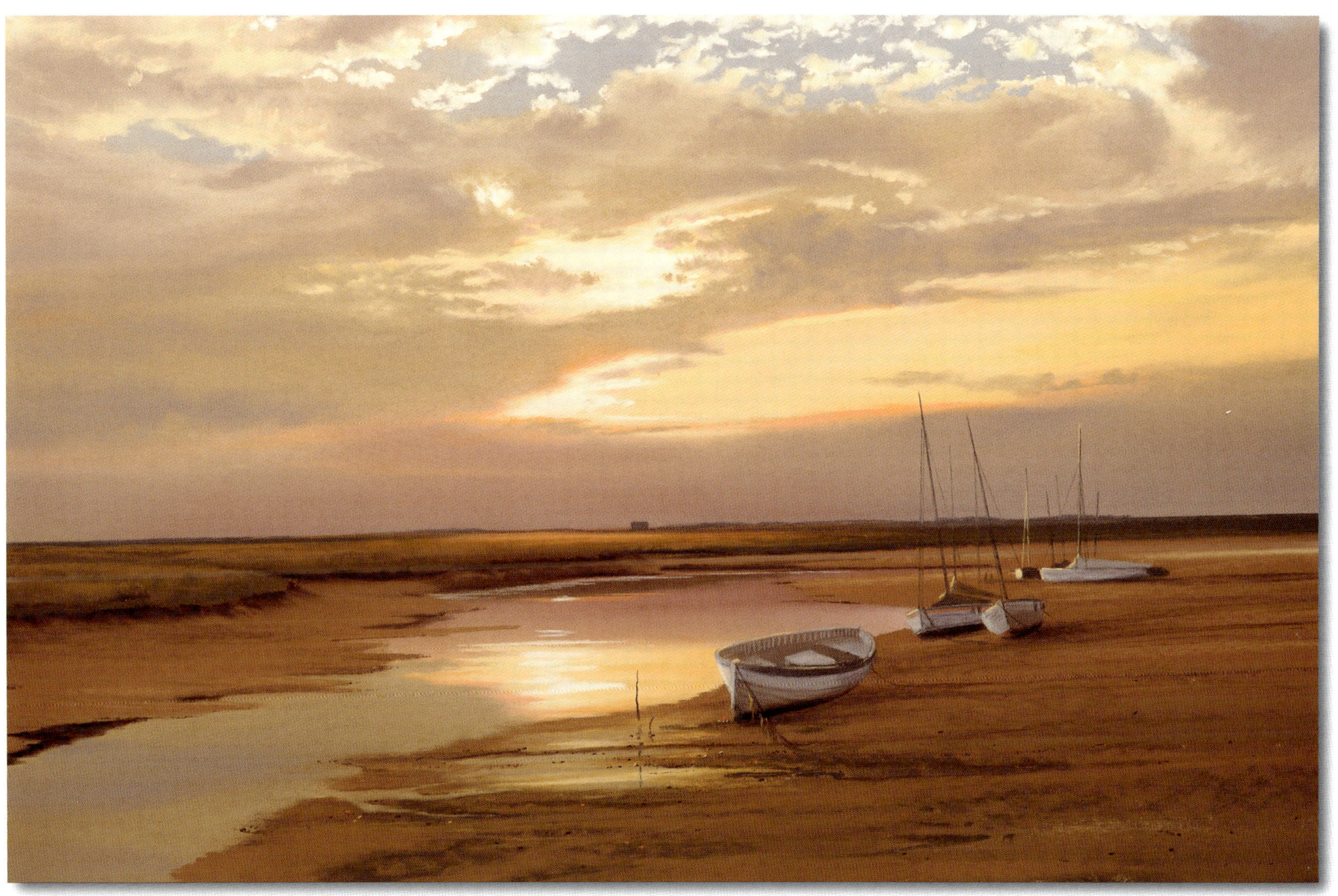

Blakeney Creek.

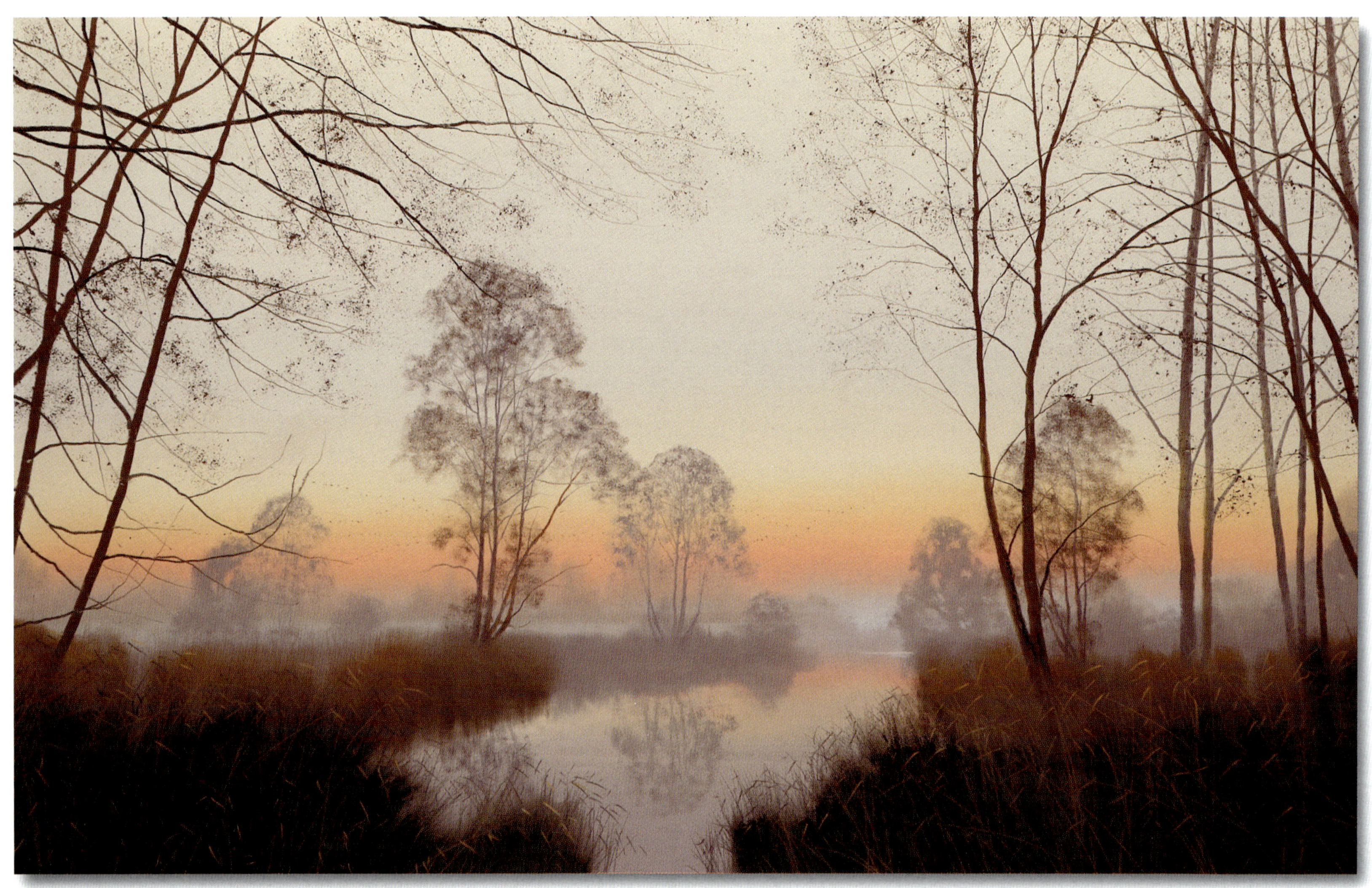

First Light.

RECENT WORK

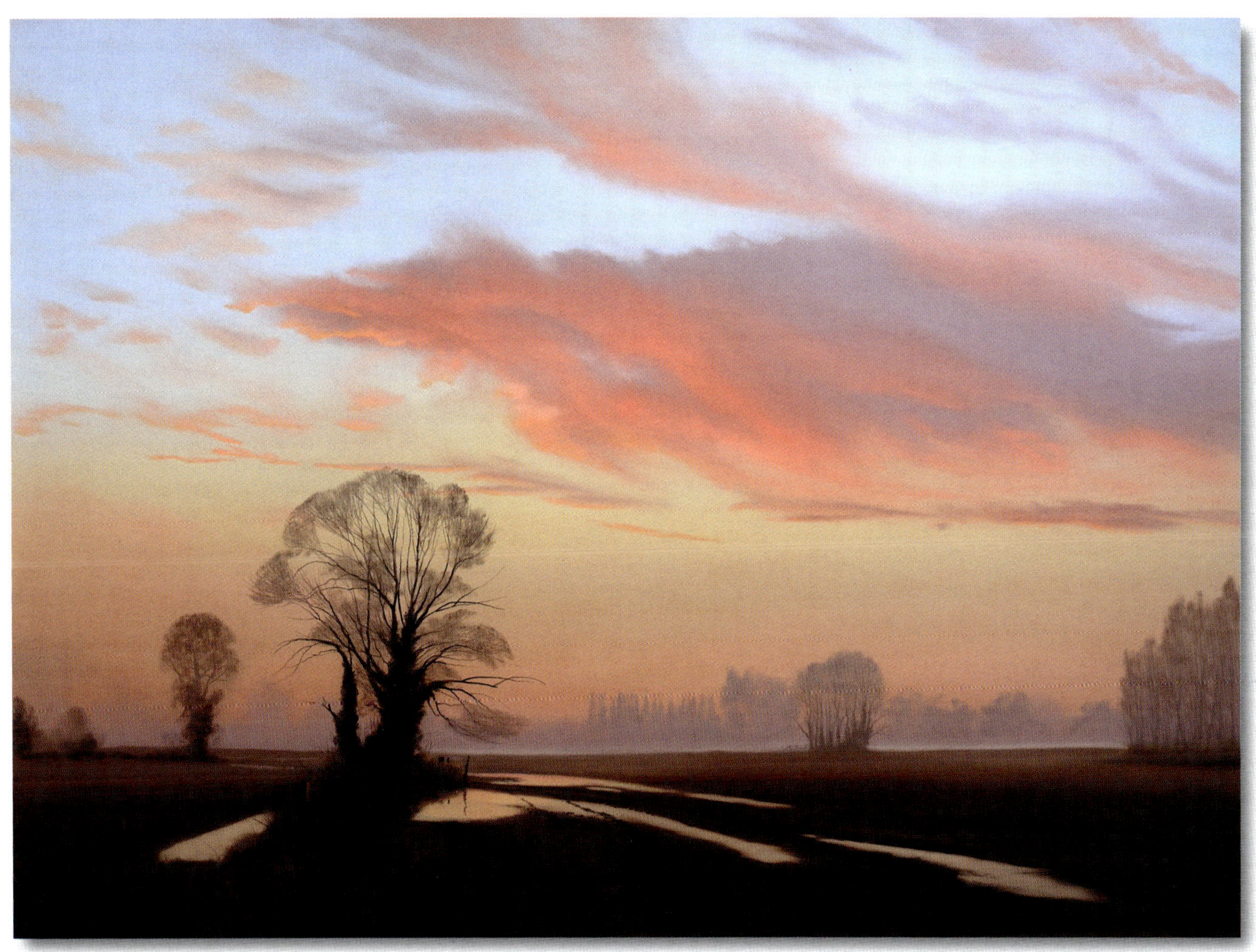

Winter Sun, Buxton.

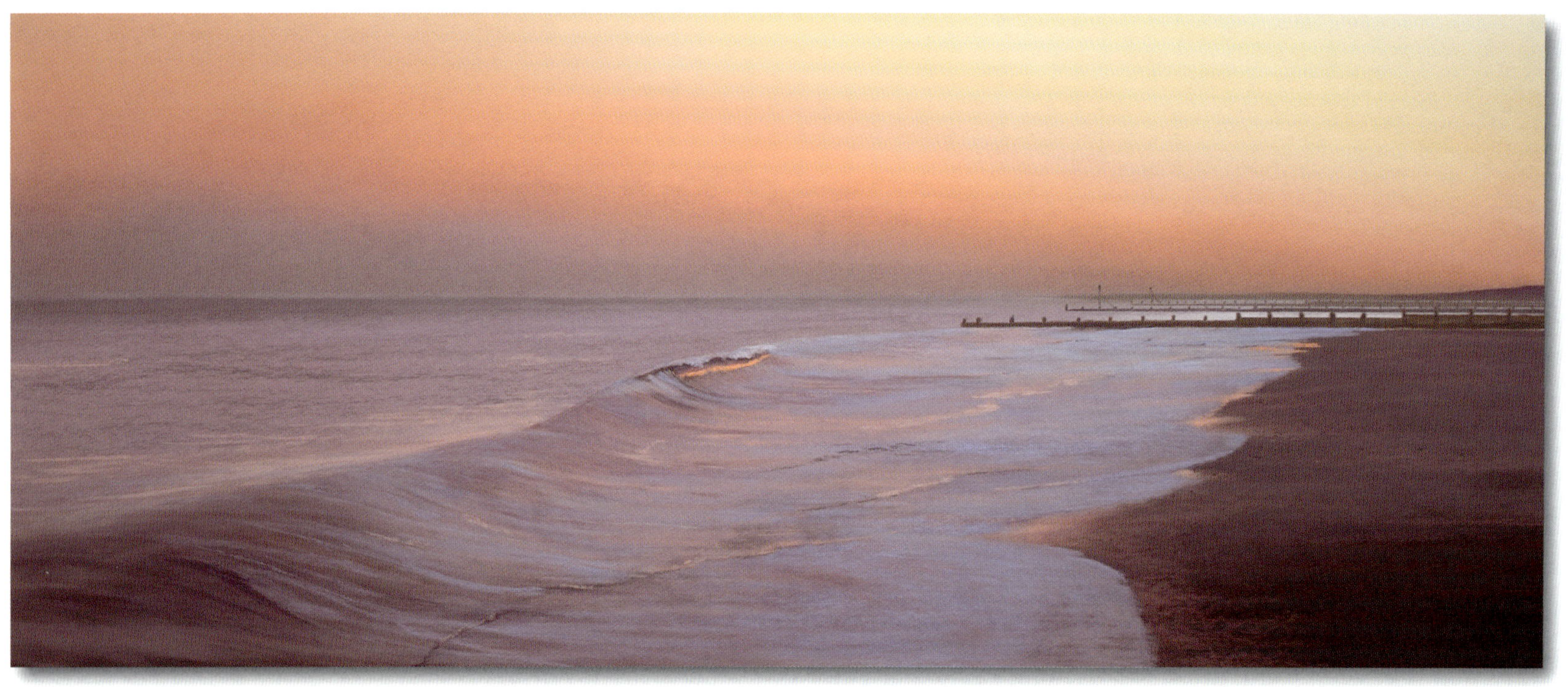

A Glorious Start.

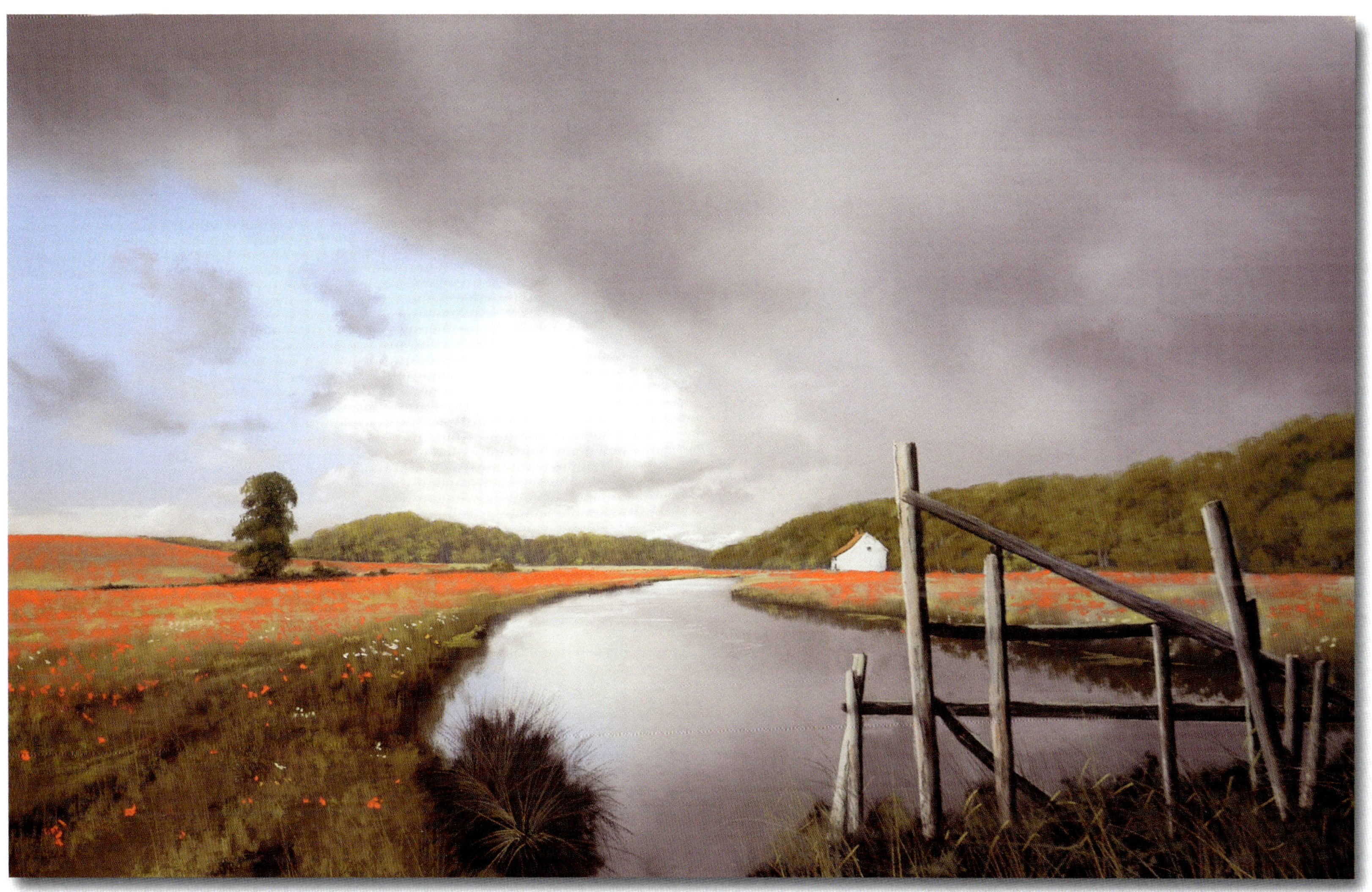

Poppies and Stormclouds.

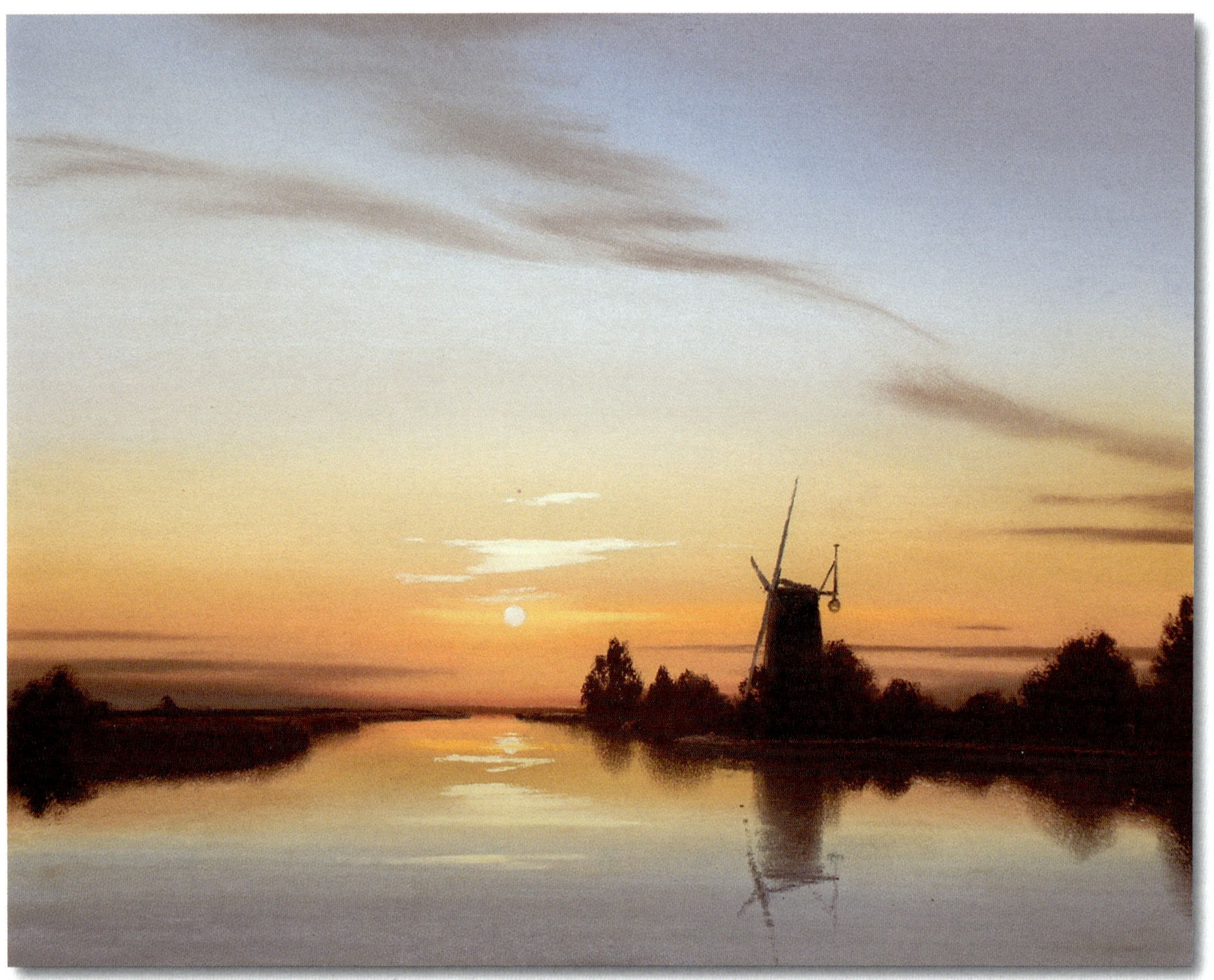

Broadland Memories.

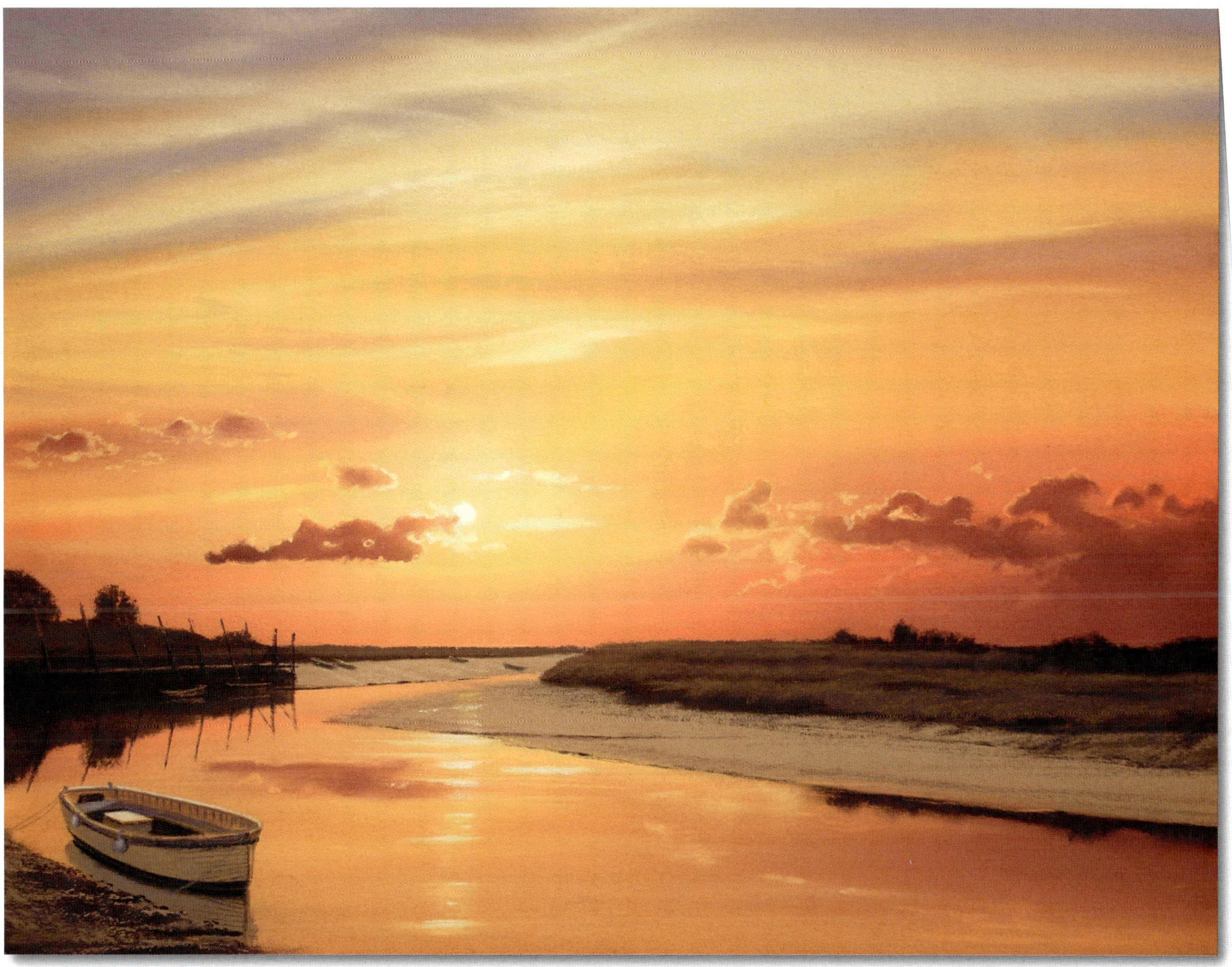

Late Evening, Blakeney.

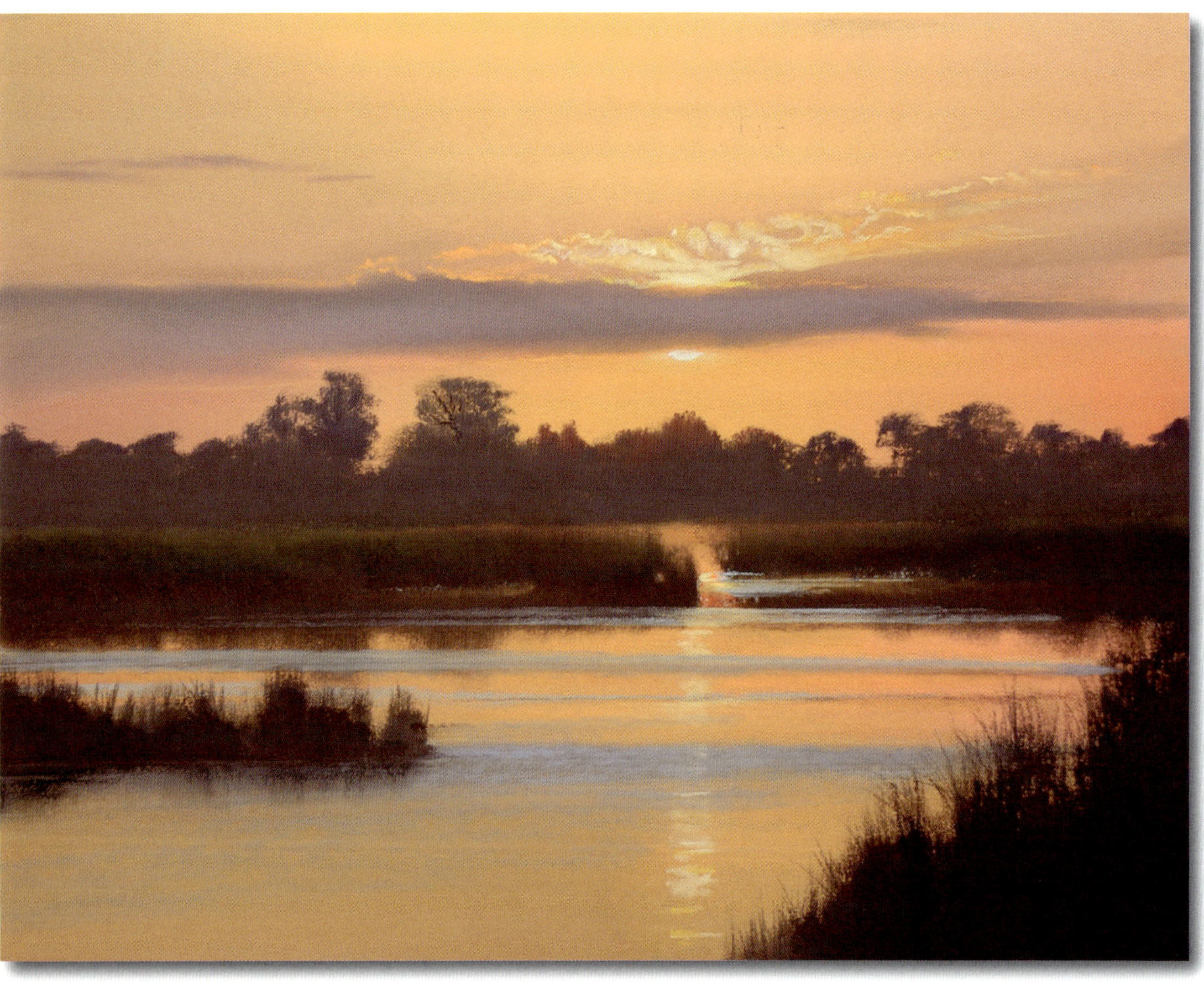

Summer Sun.

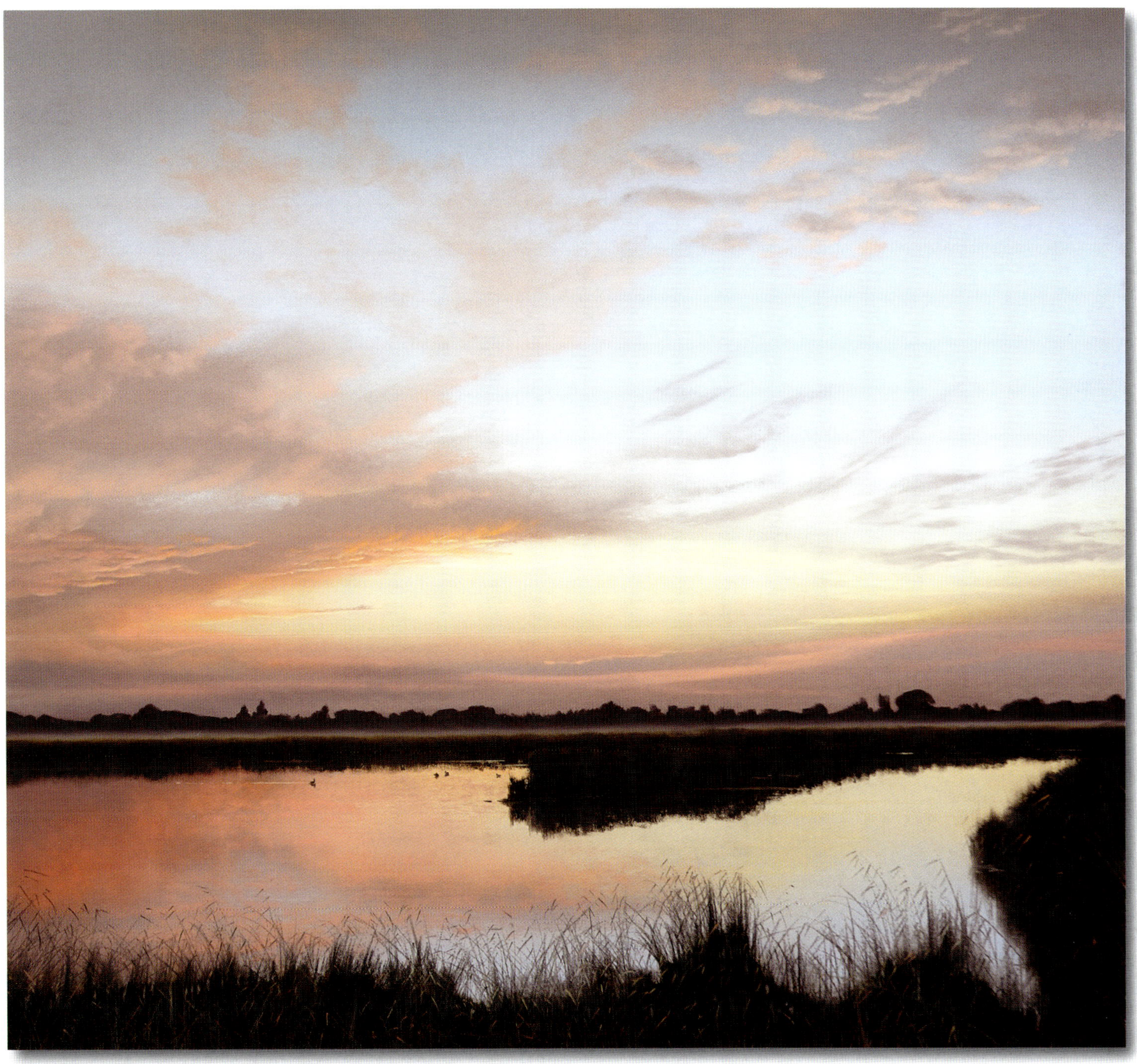

Hickling Broad.

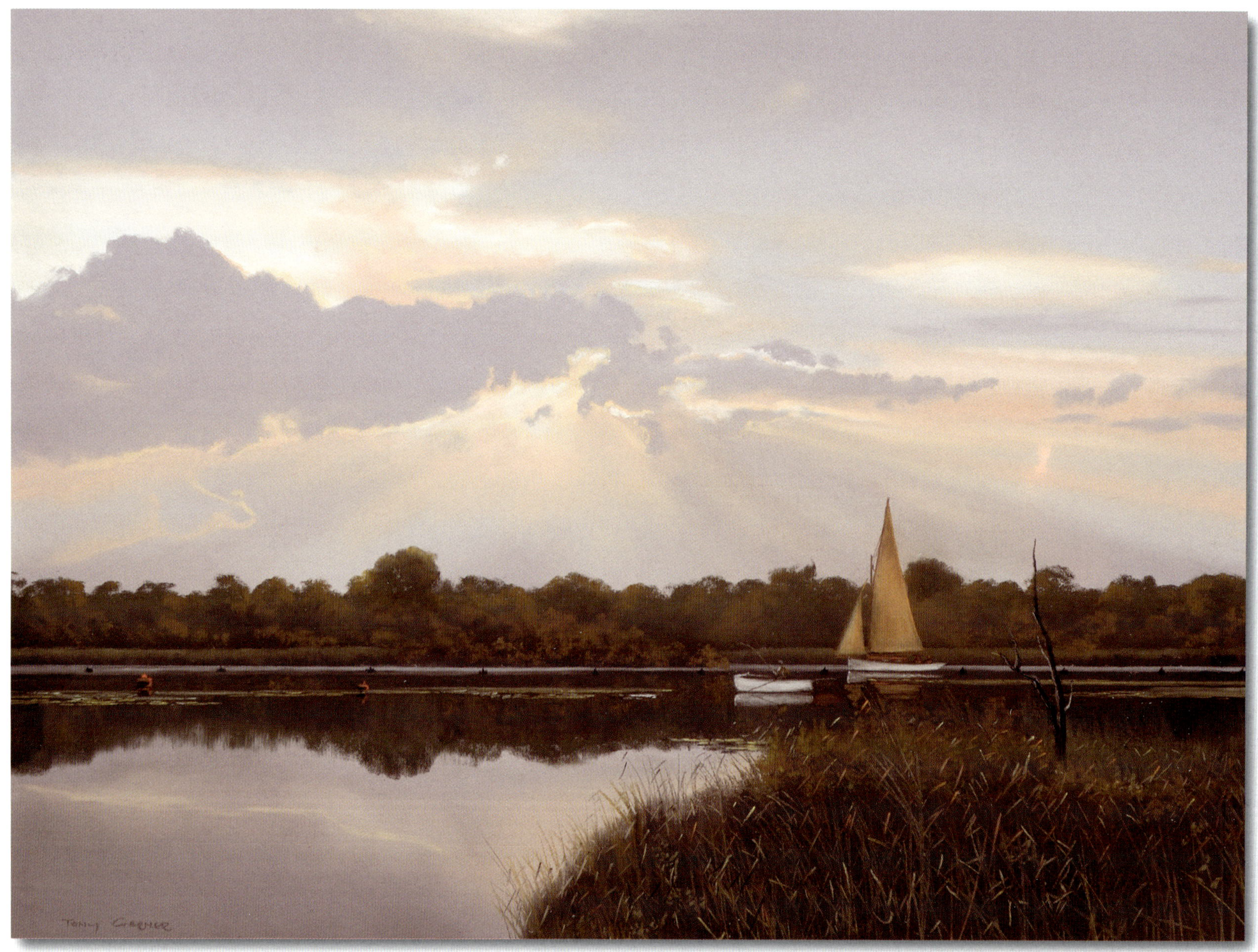

Fishing on Rockland Broad.

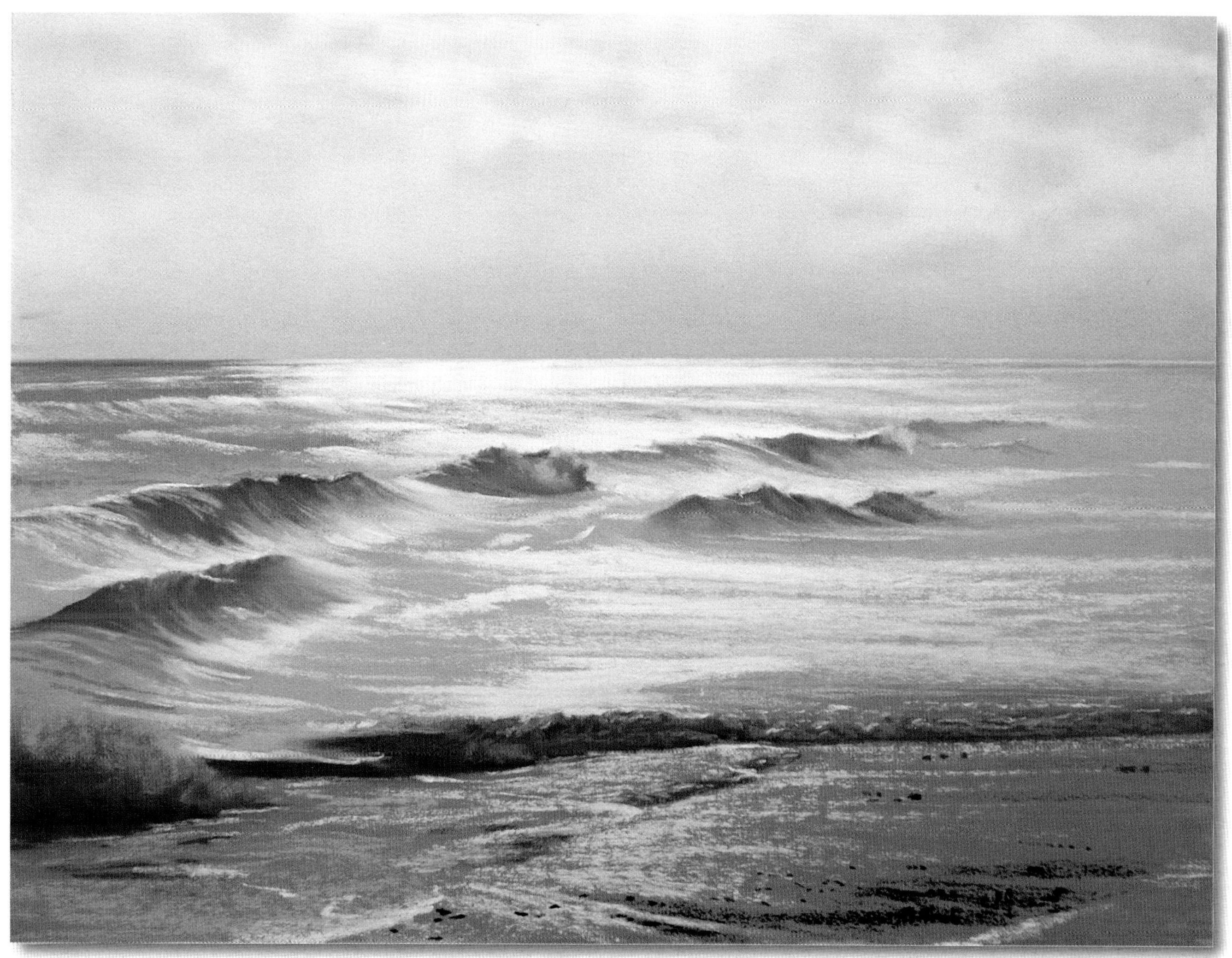

Silver Seas.

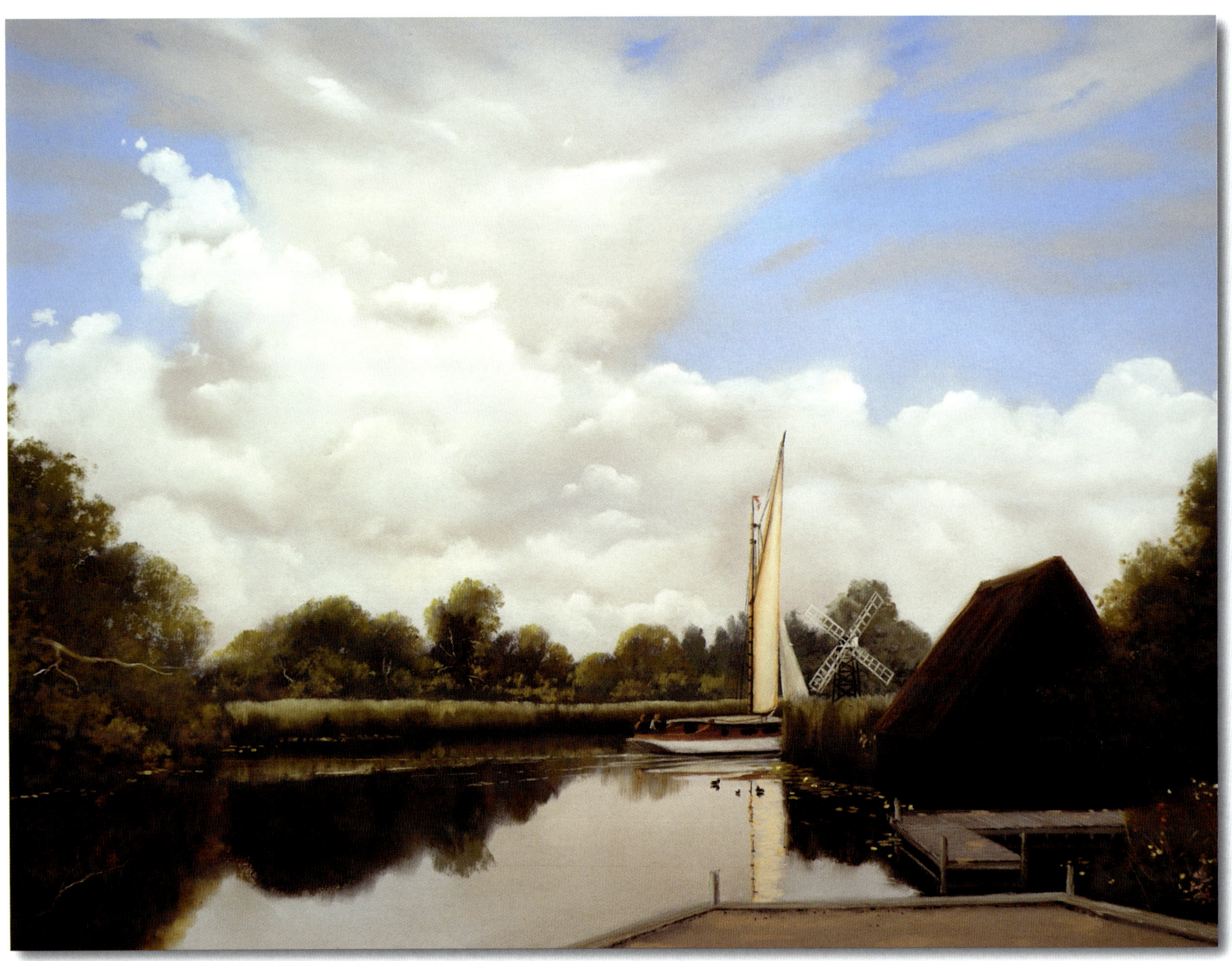

At How Hill.

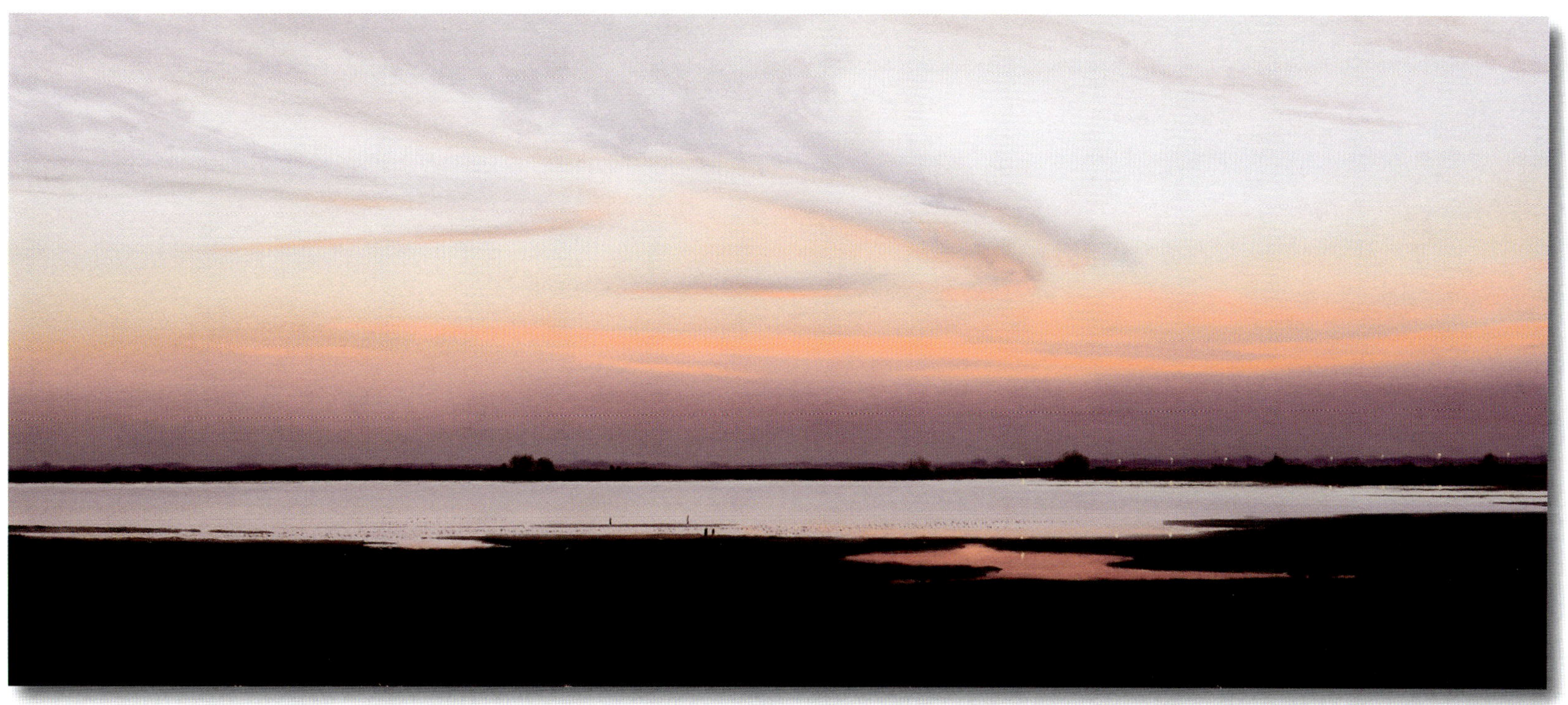

Sundown on Breydon Water.

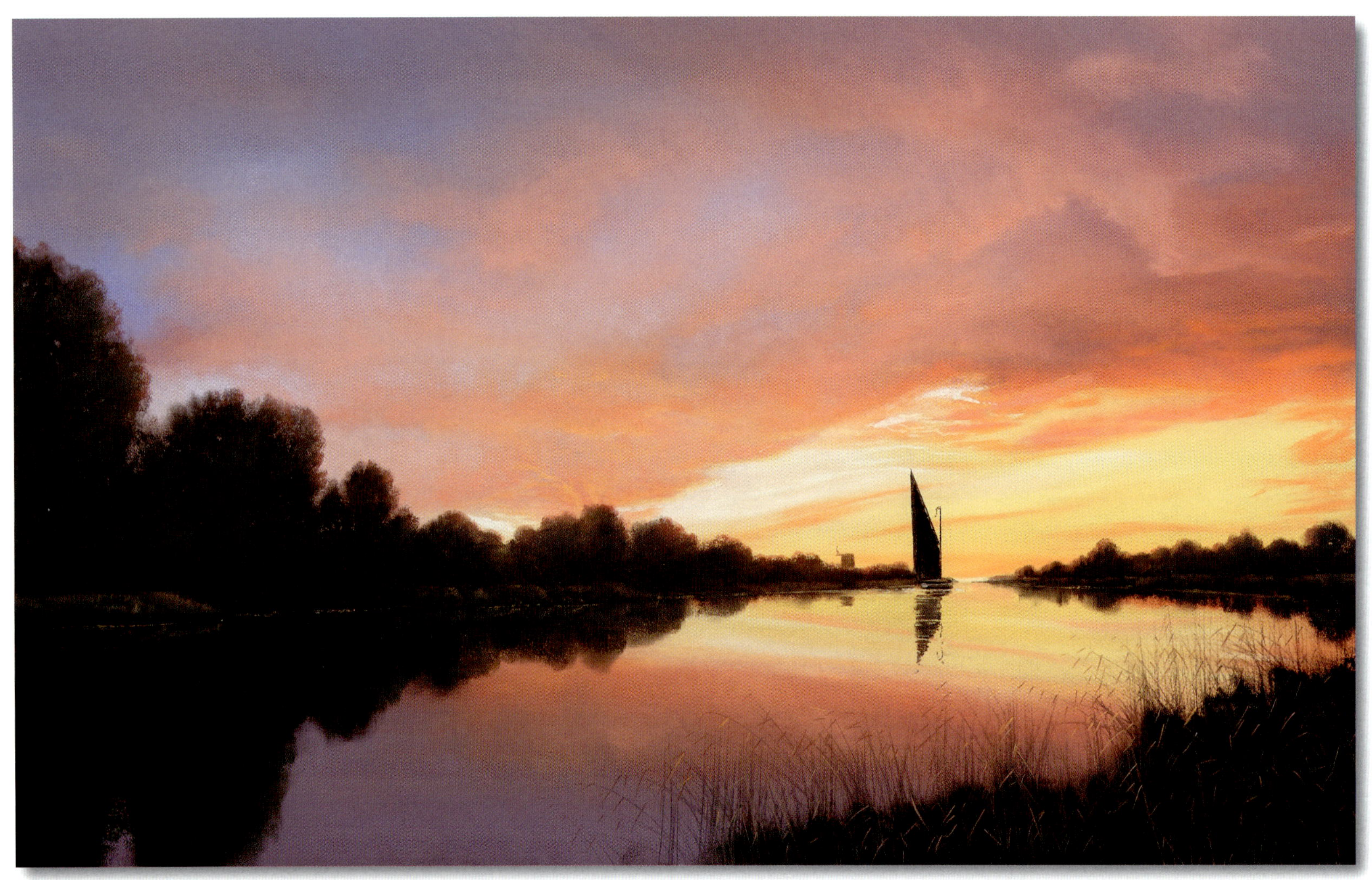

Black Sailed Trader.

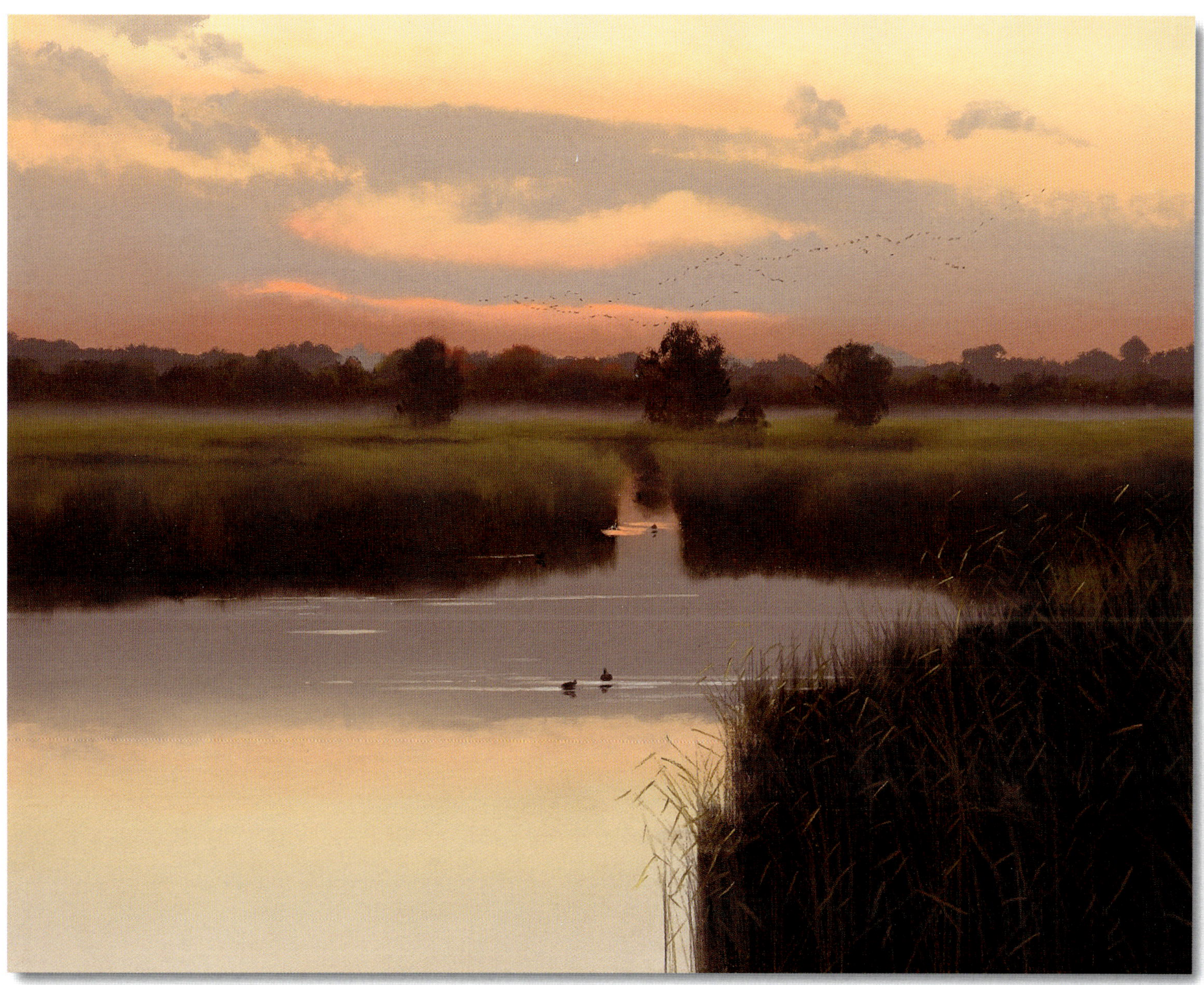

Evening Calm.

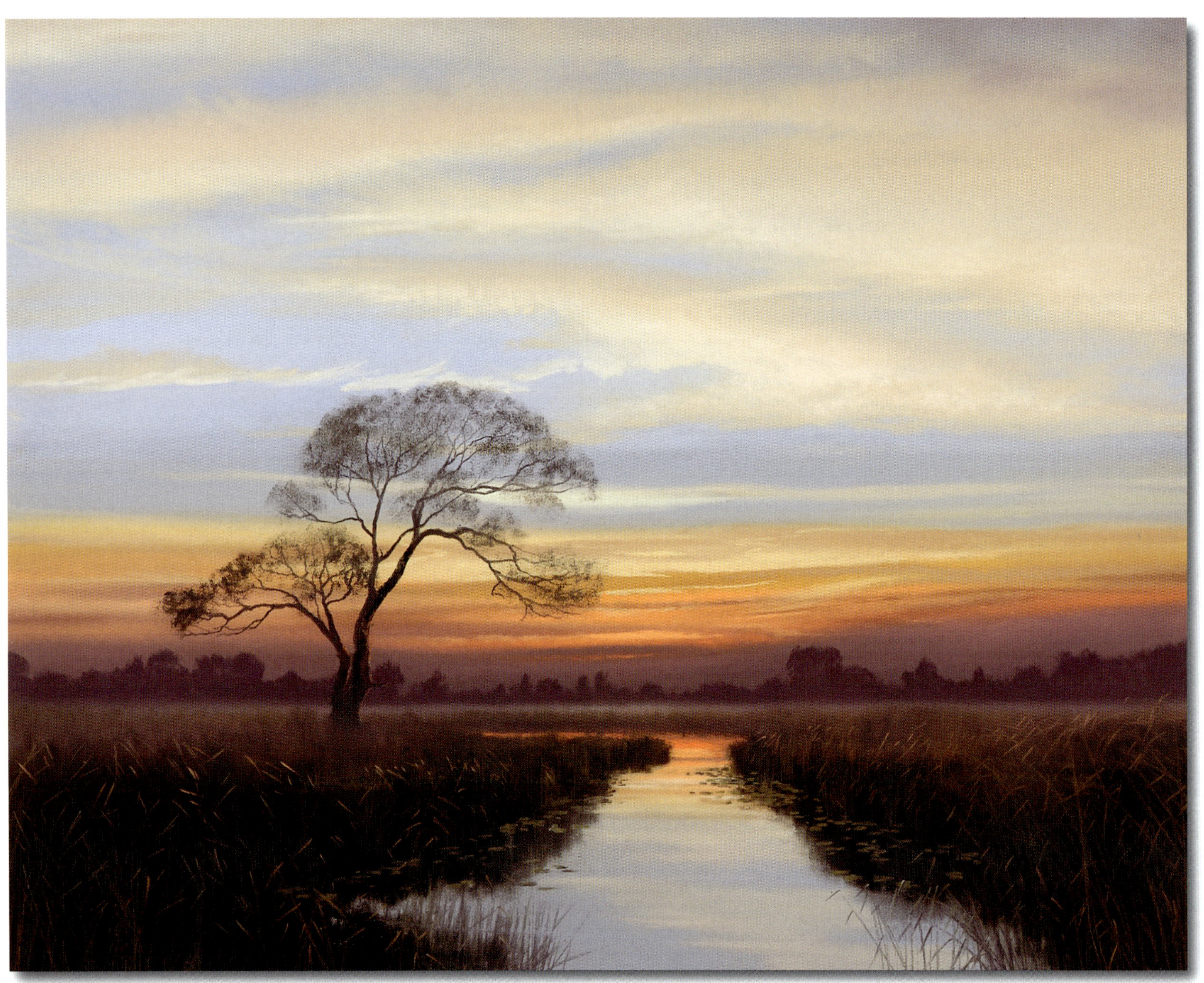

Amid the Reeds.

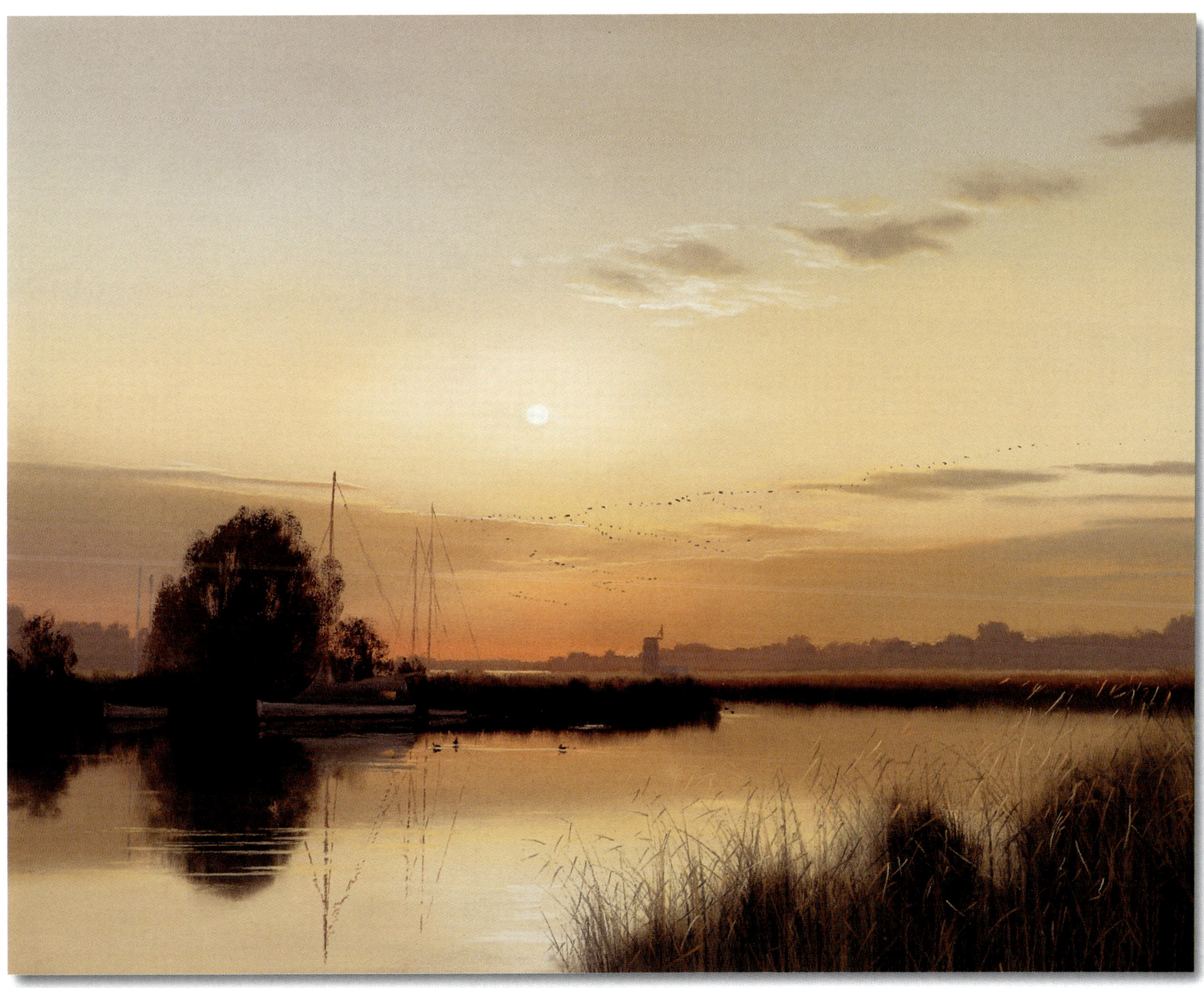

Stillness.

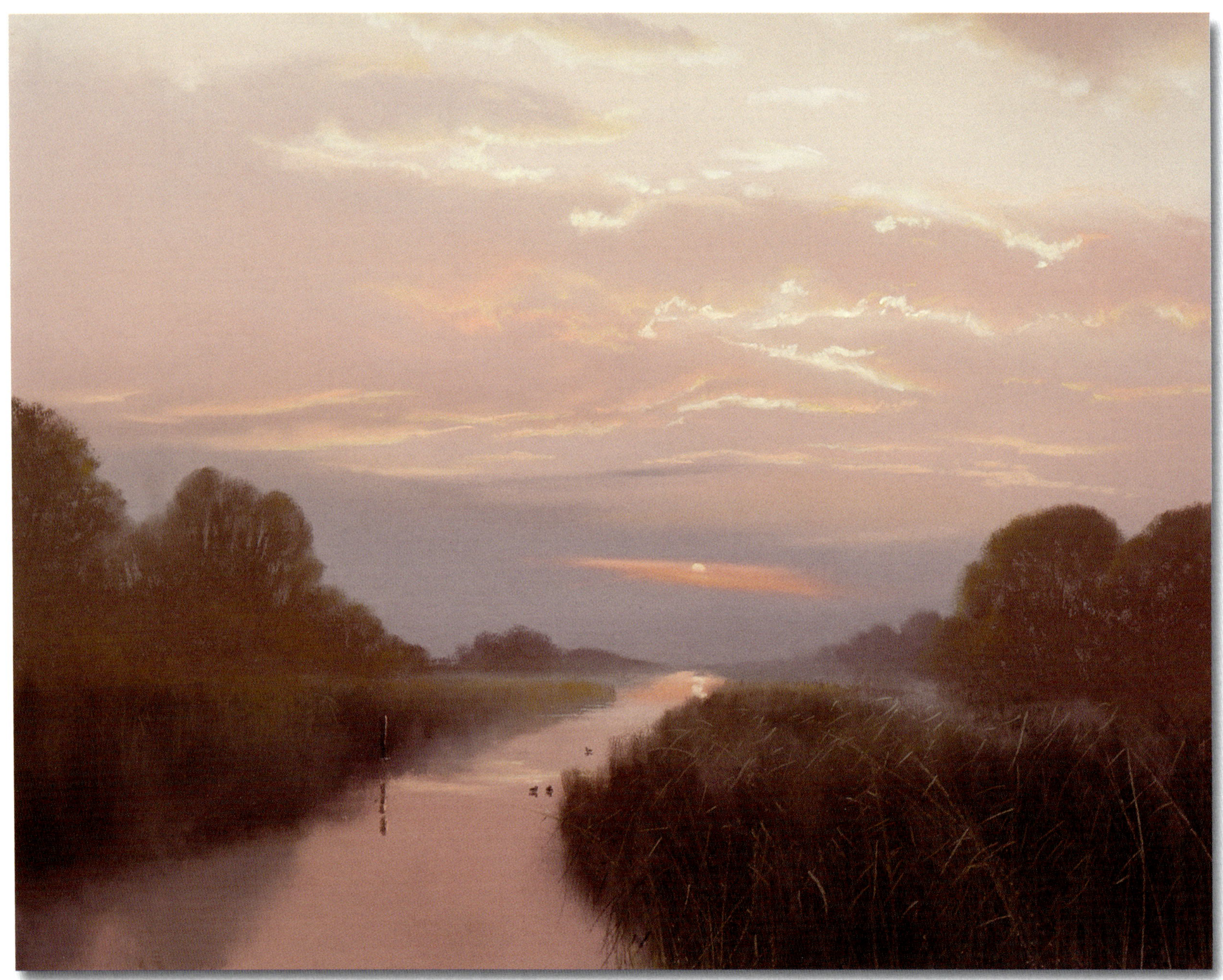

Sutton Remembered.

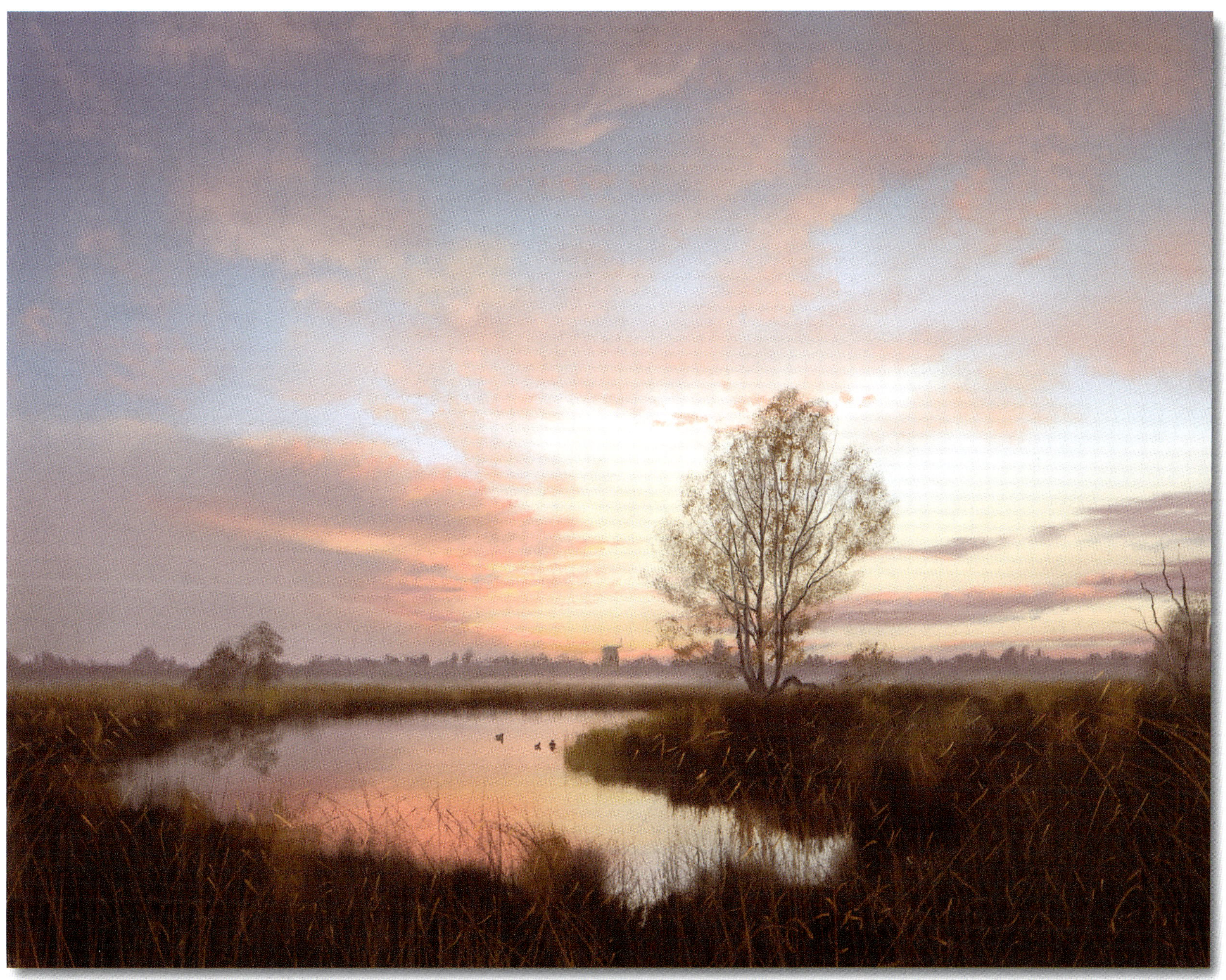

Evening Light.

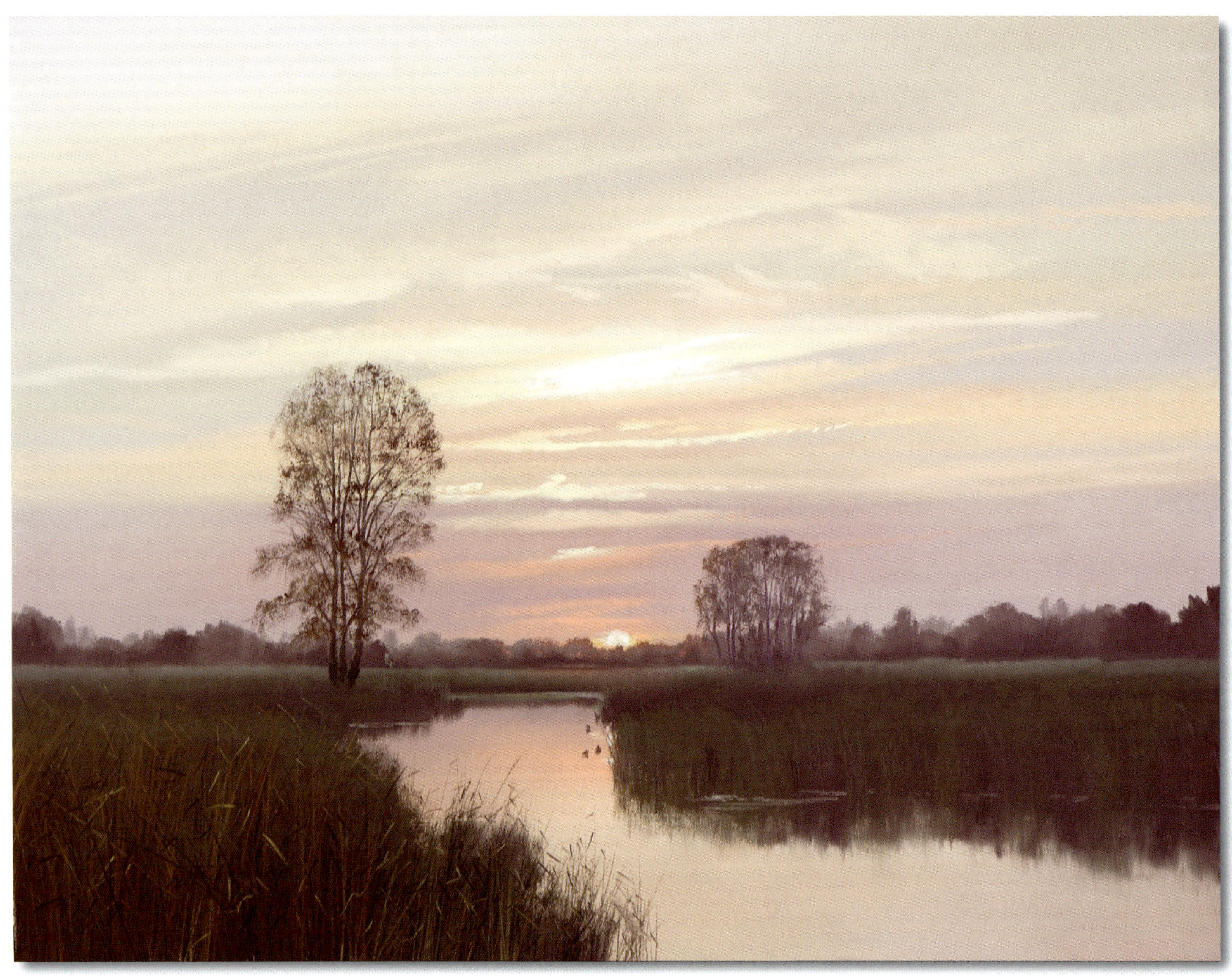

Pastel Skies.

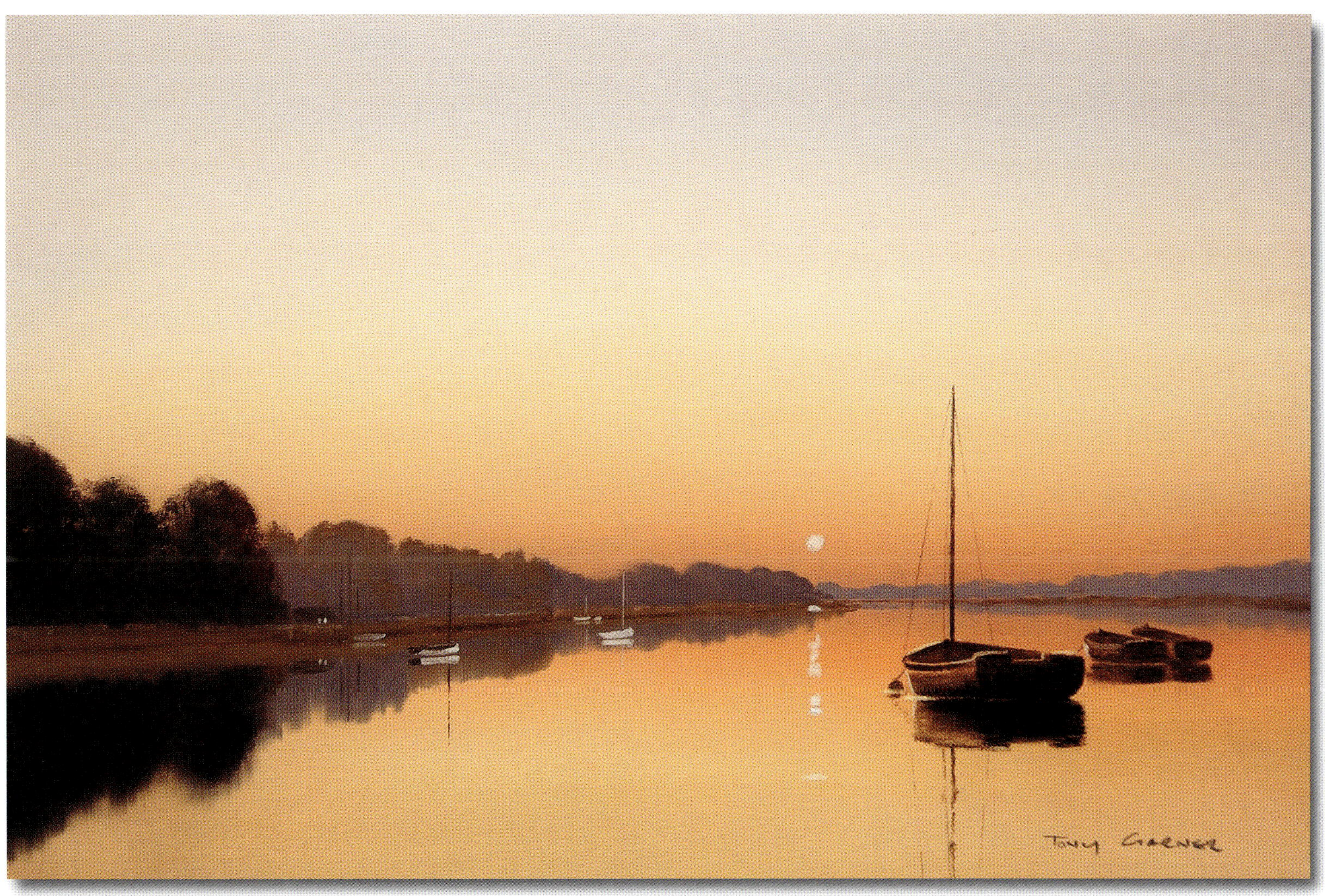

Mellow Glow.

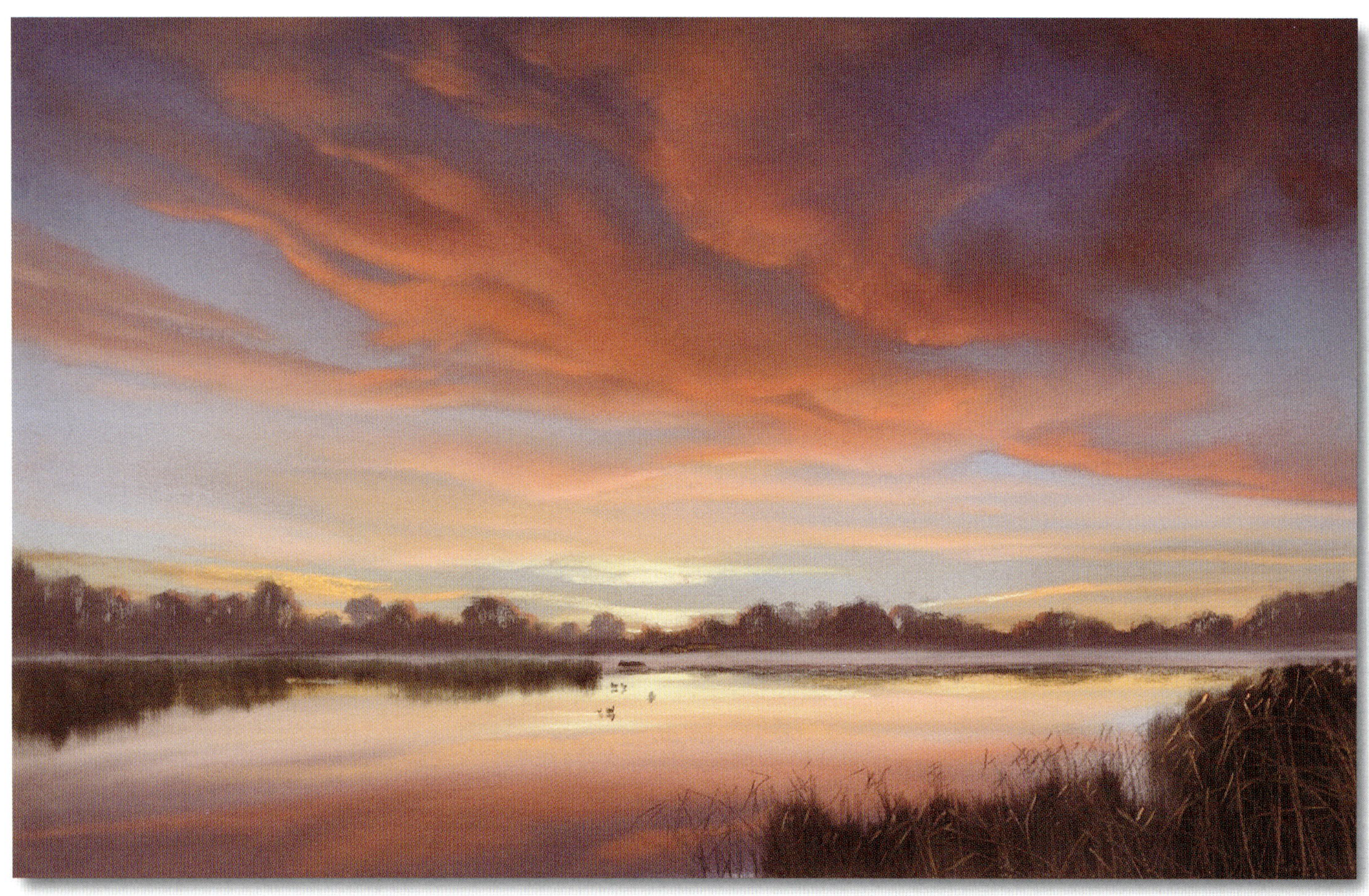

Skies of Fire.

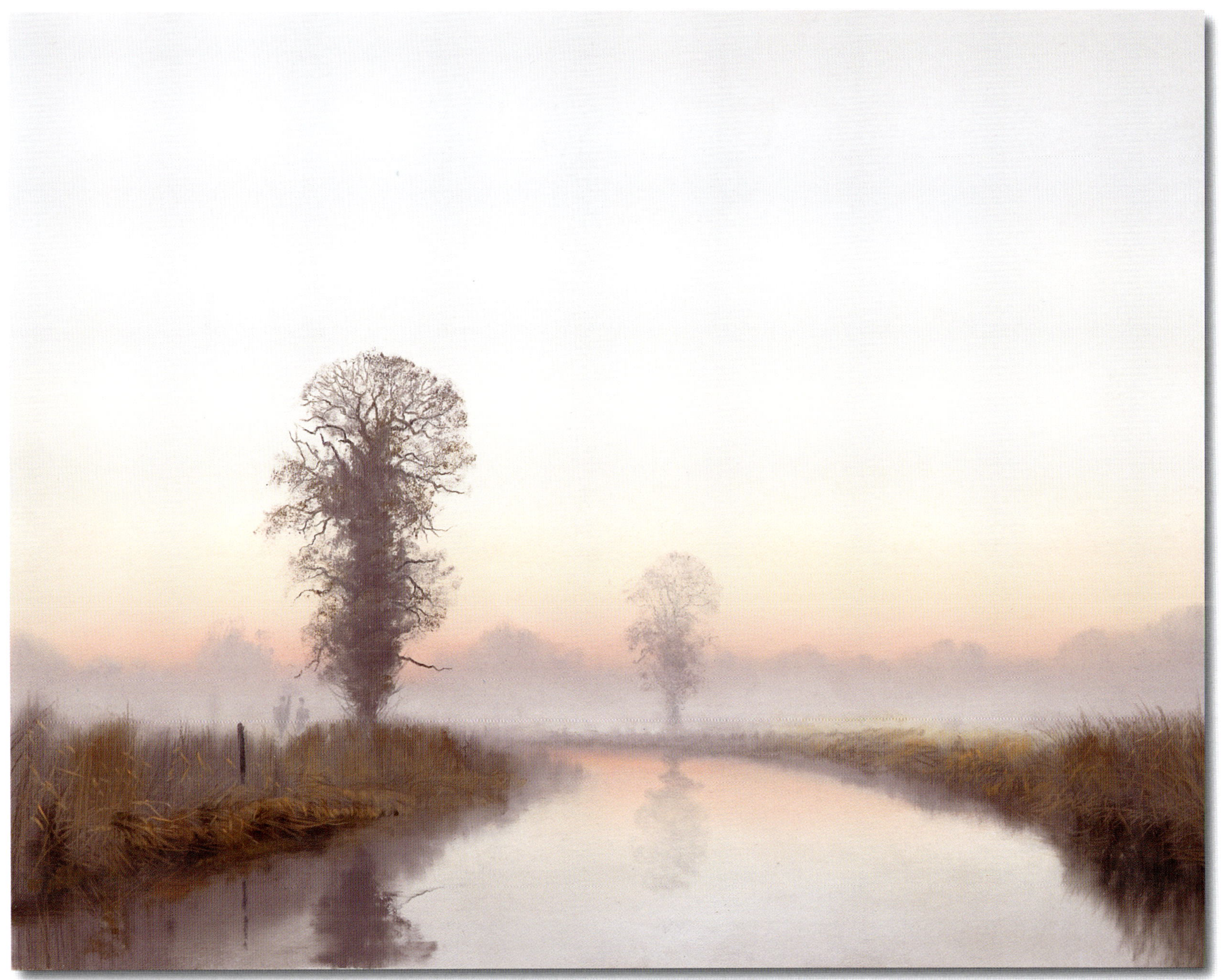

Oaks by the Stream.

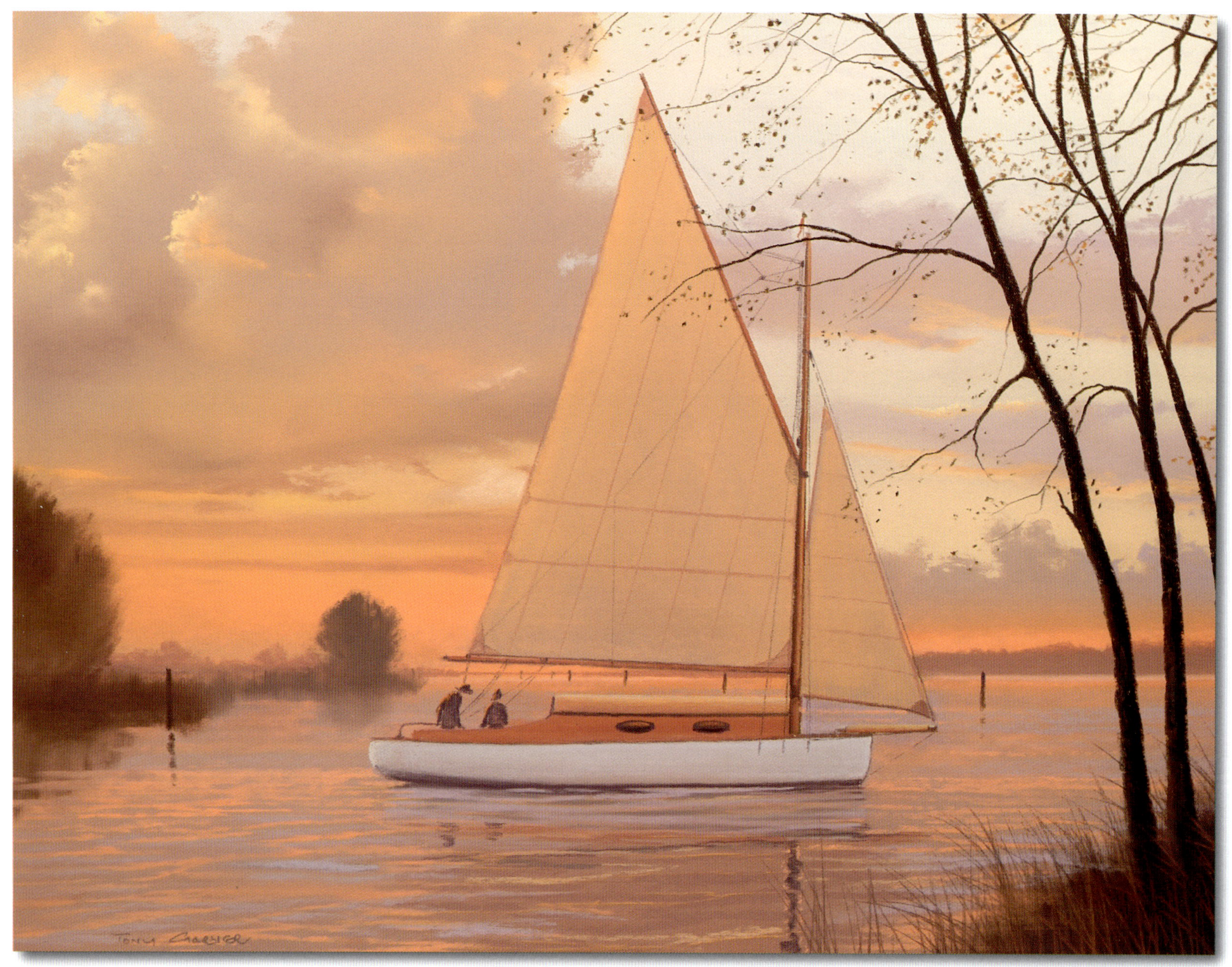

Drifting By.

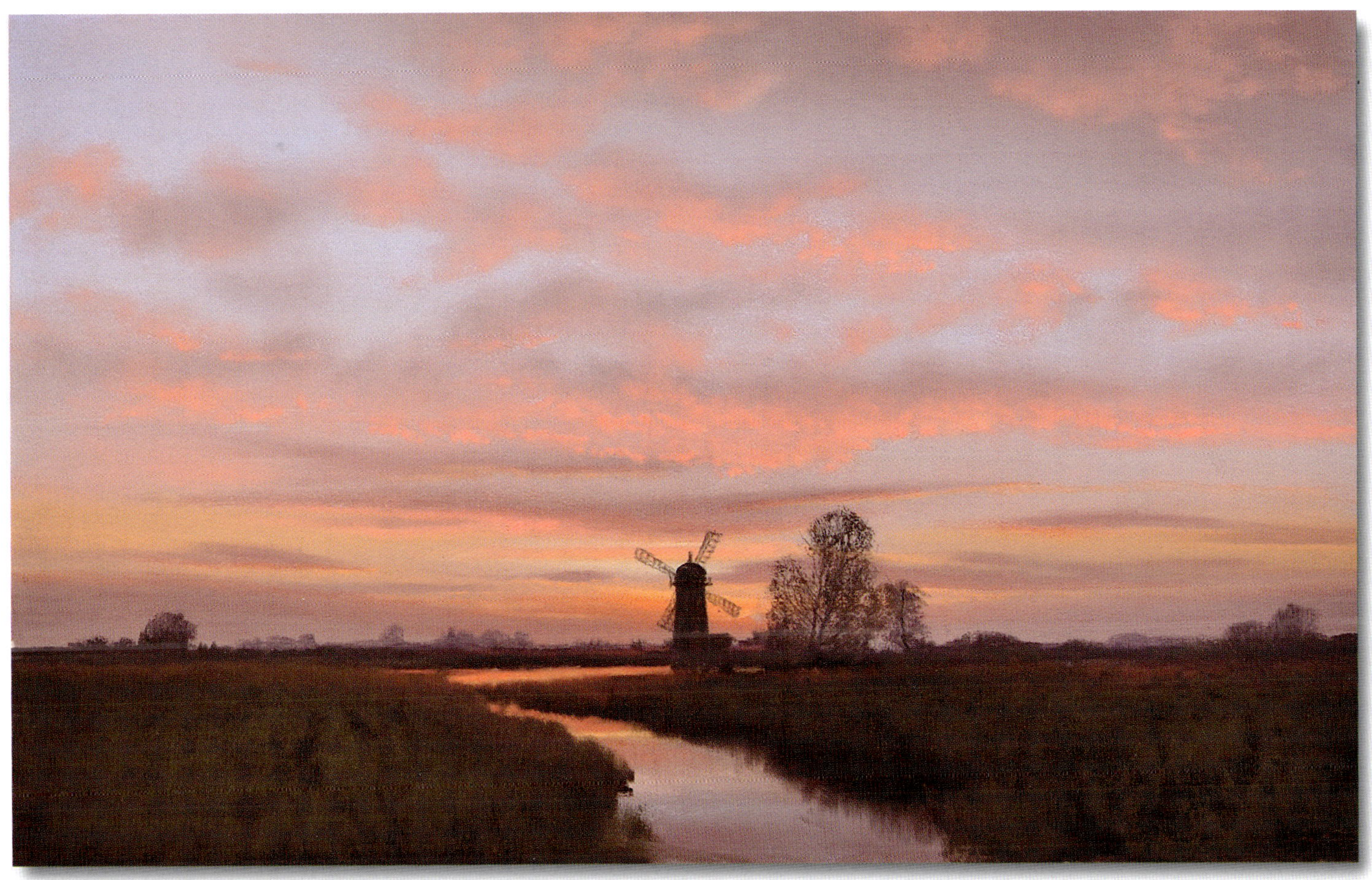

St Bennet's Level.

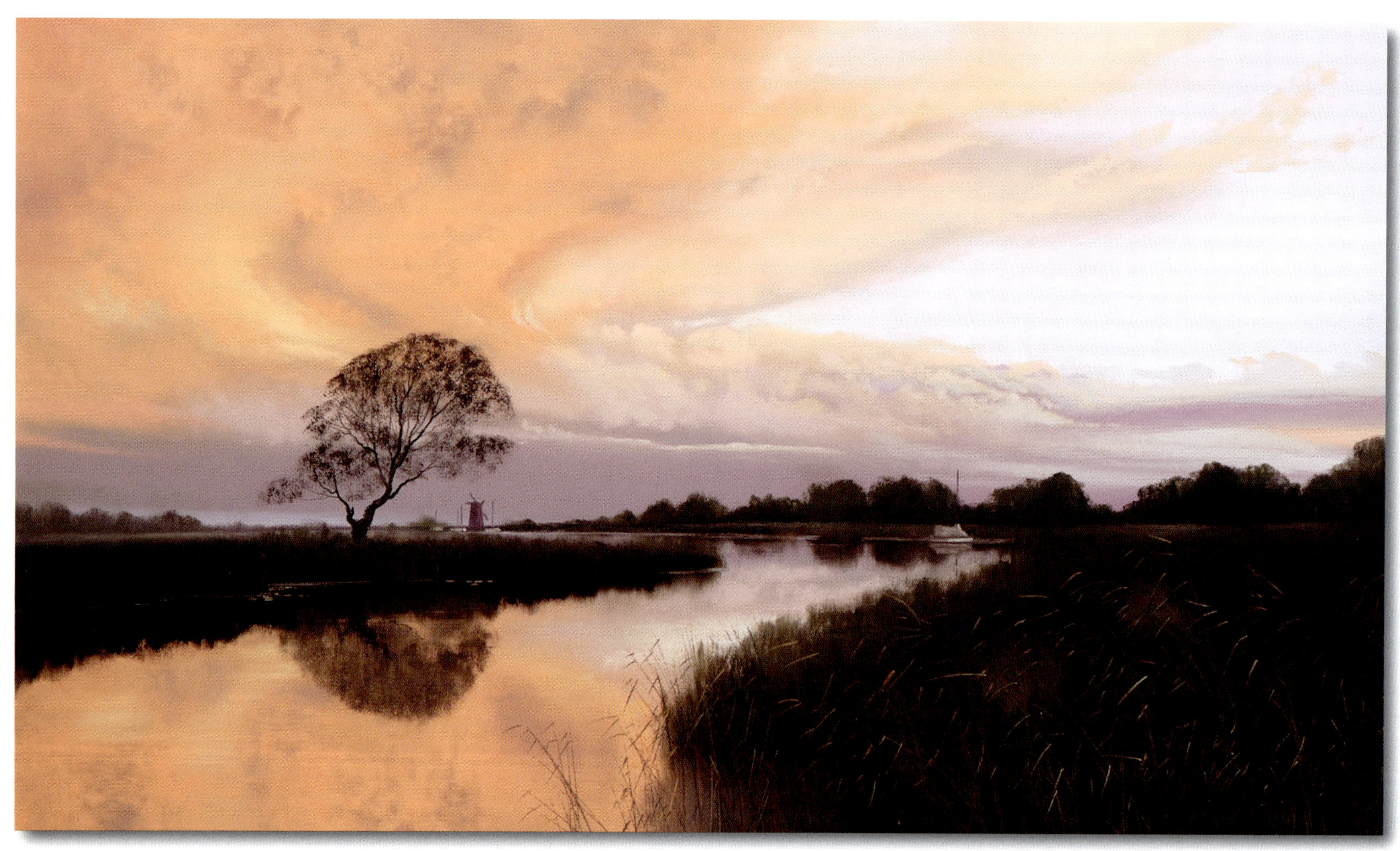

Day's End.

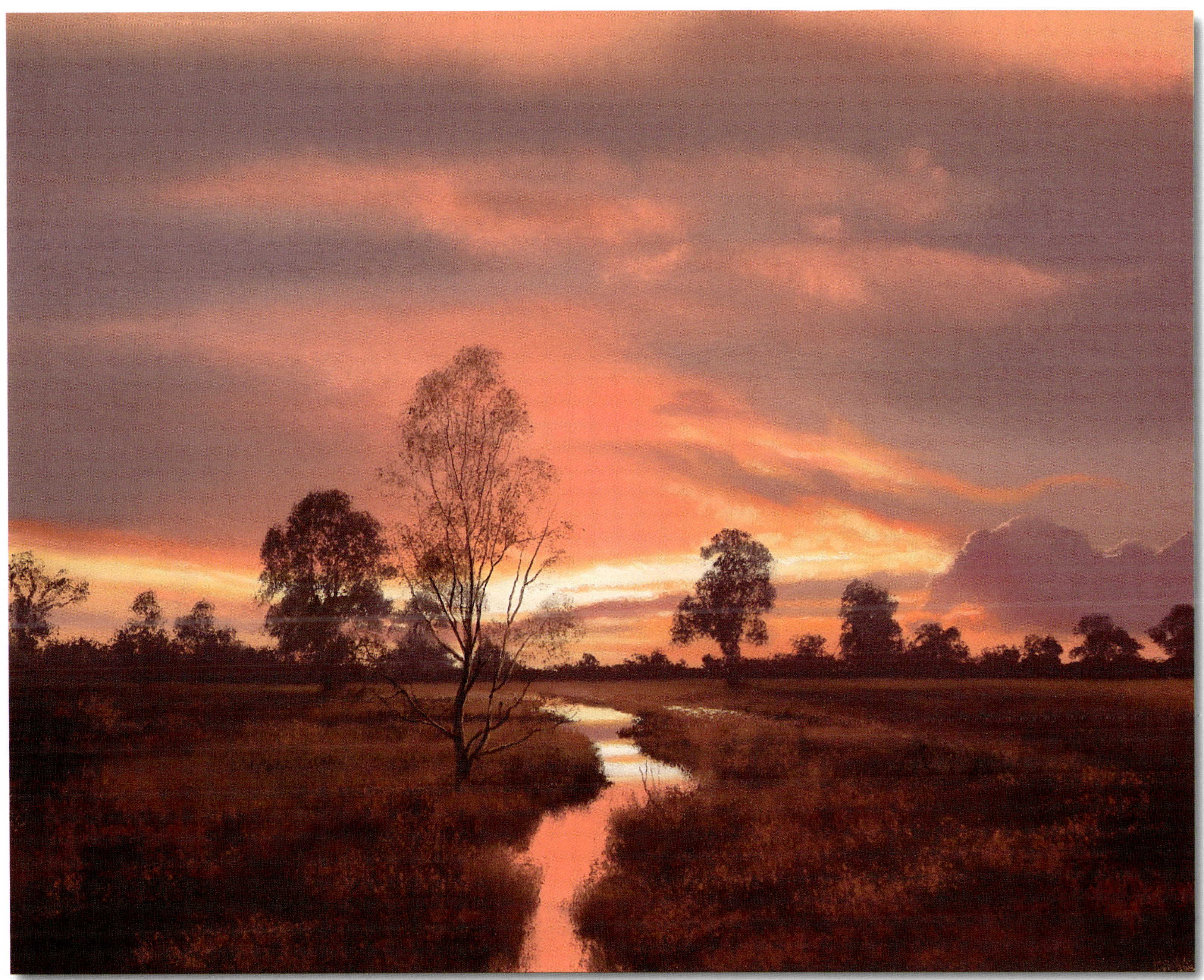

Stream on the Marshes

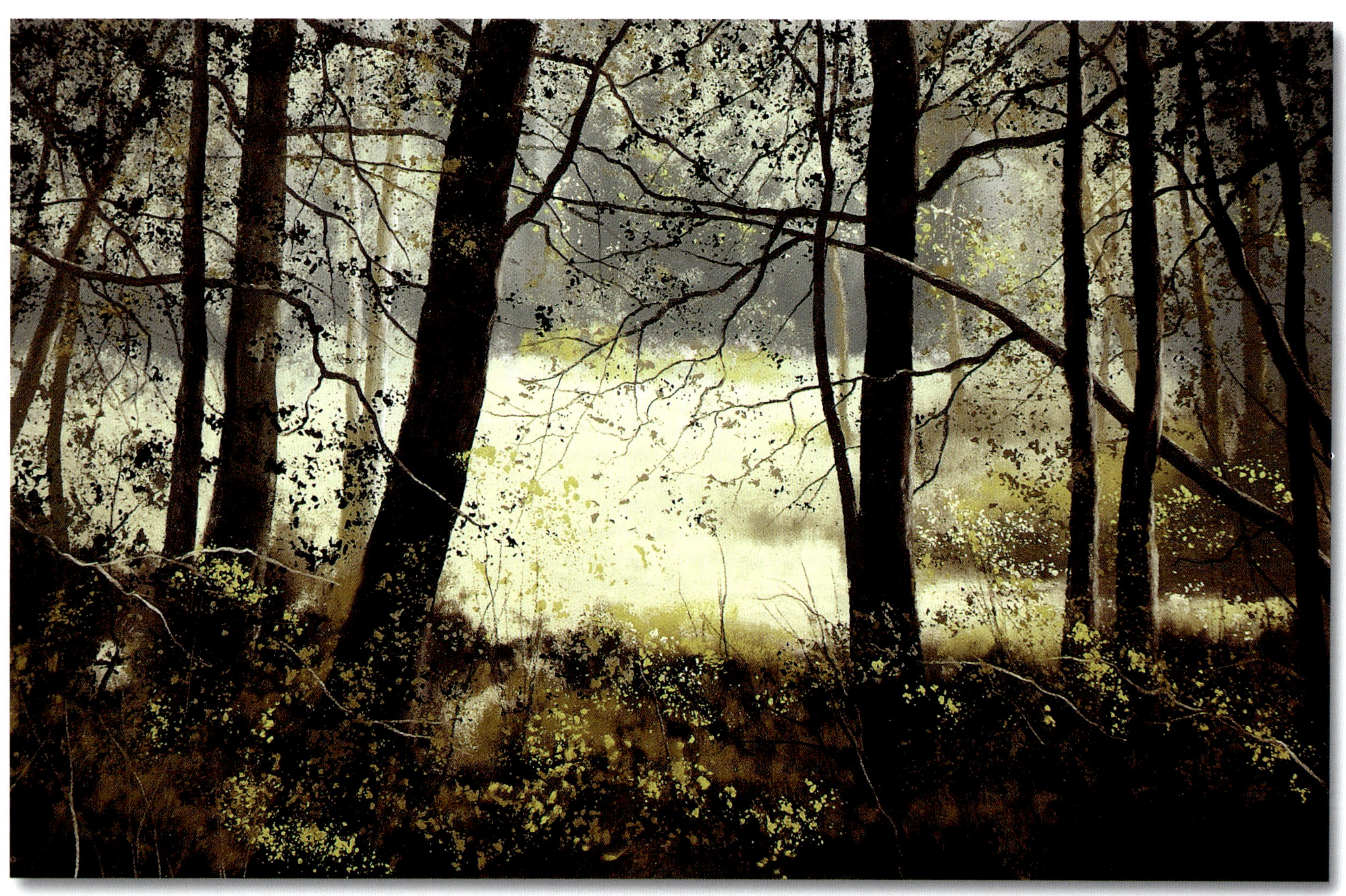

Sunlight and Shadows.

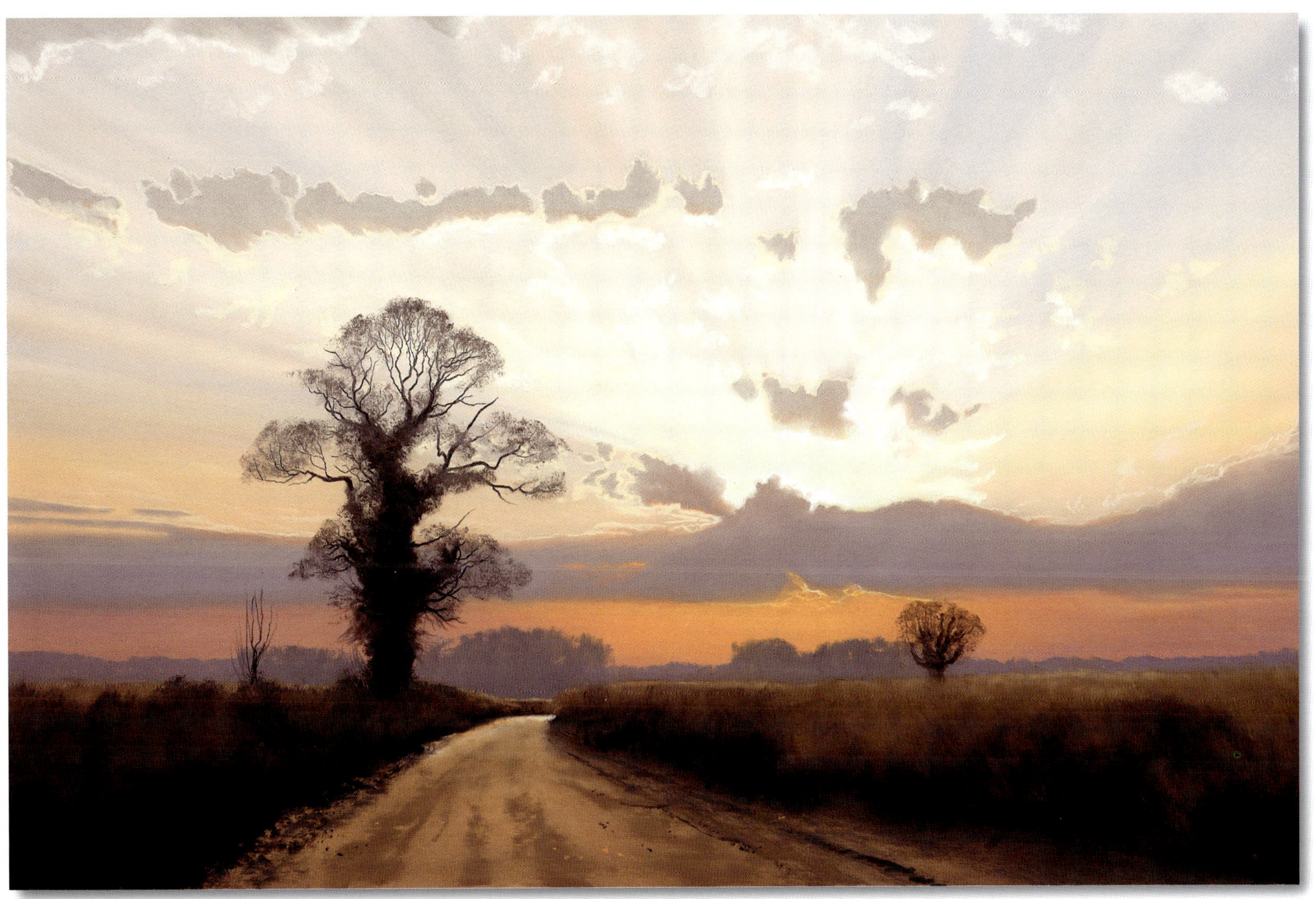

Sunbeams and Silhouettes.

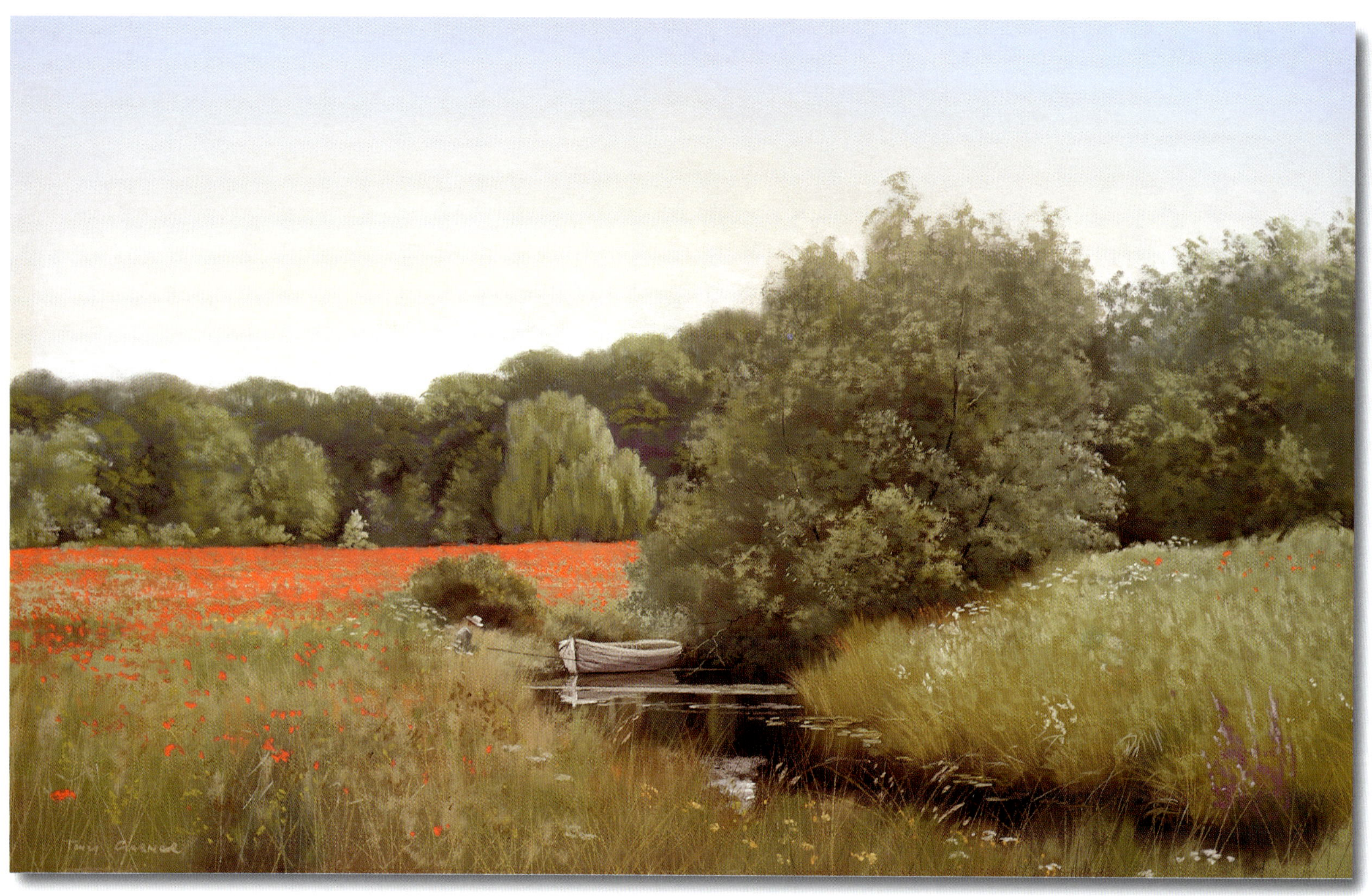

Summer.

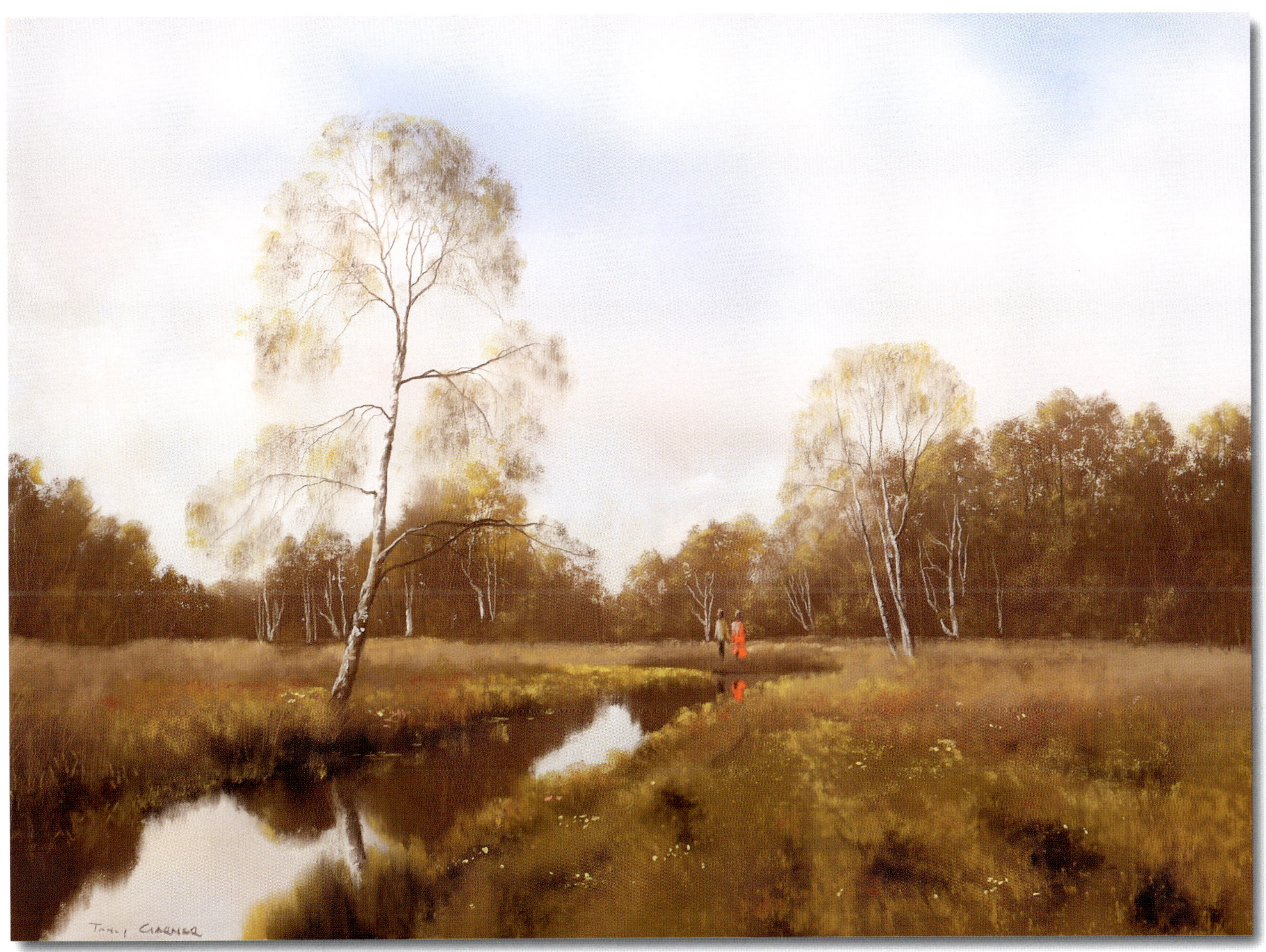

Spring on the Marshes.

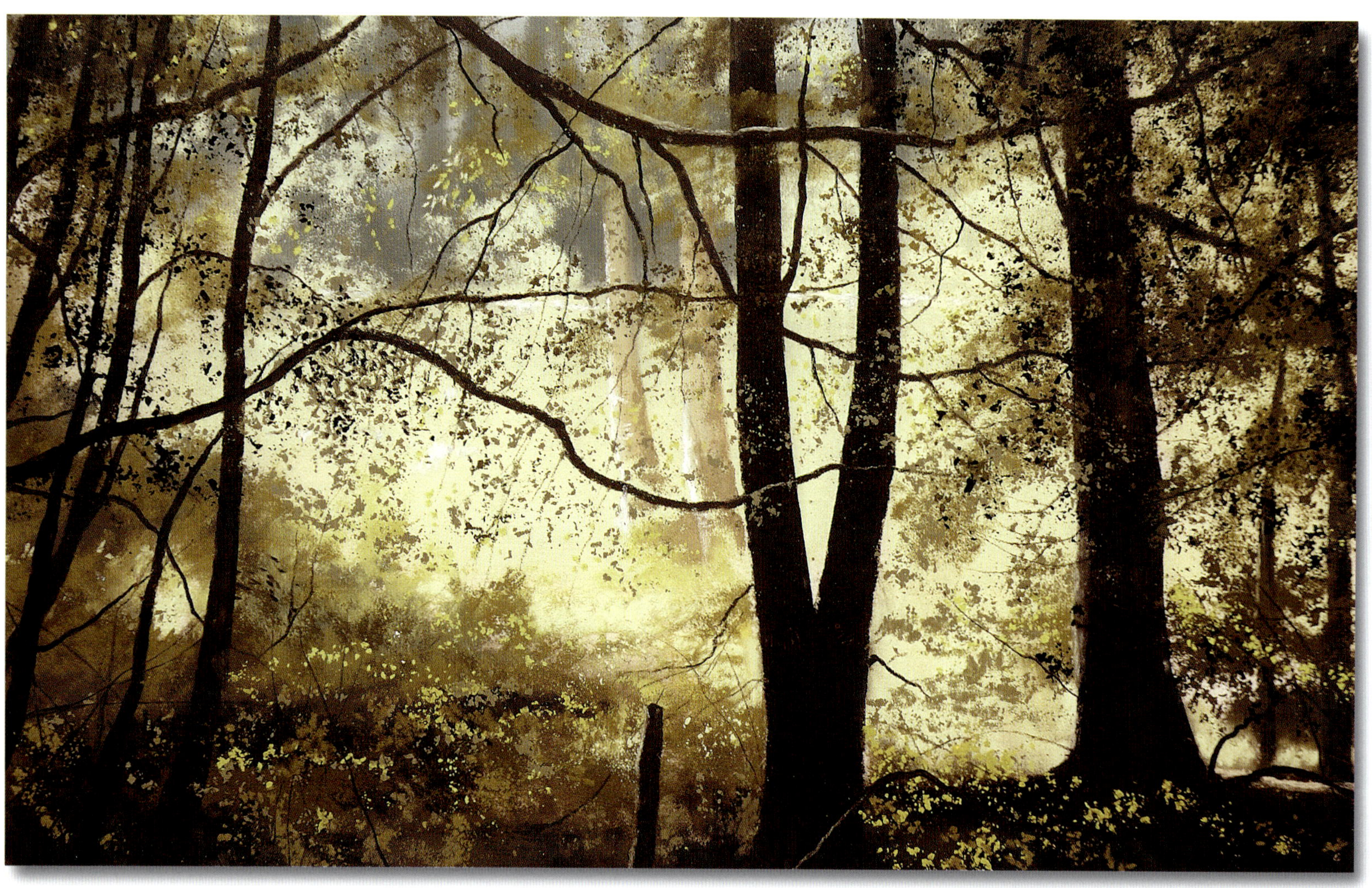

Spring Light.

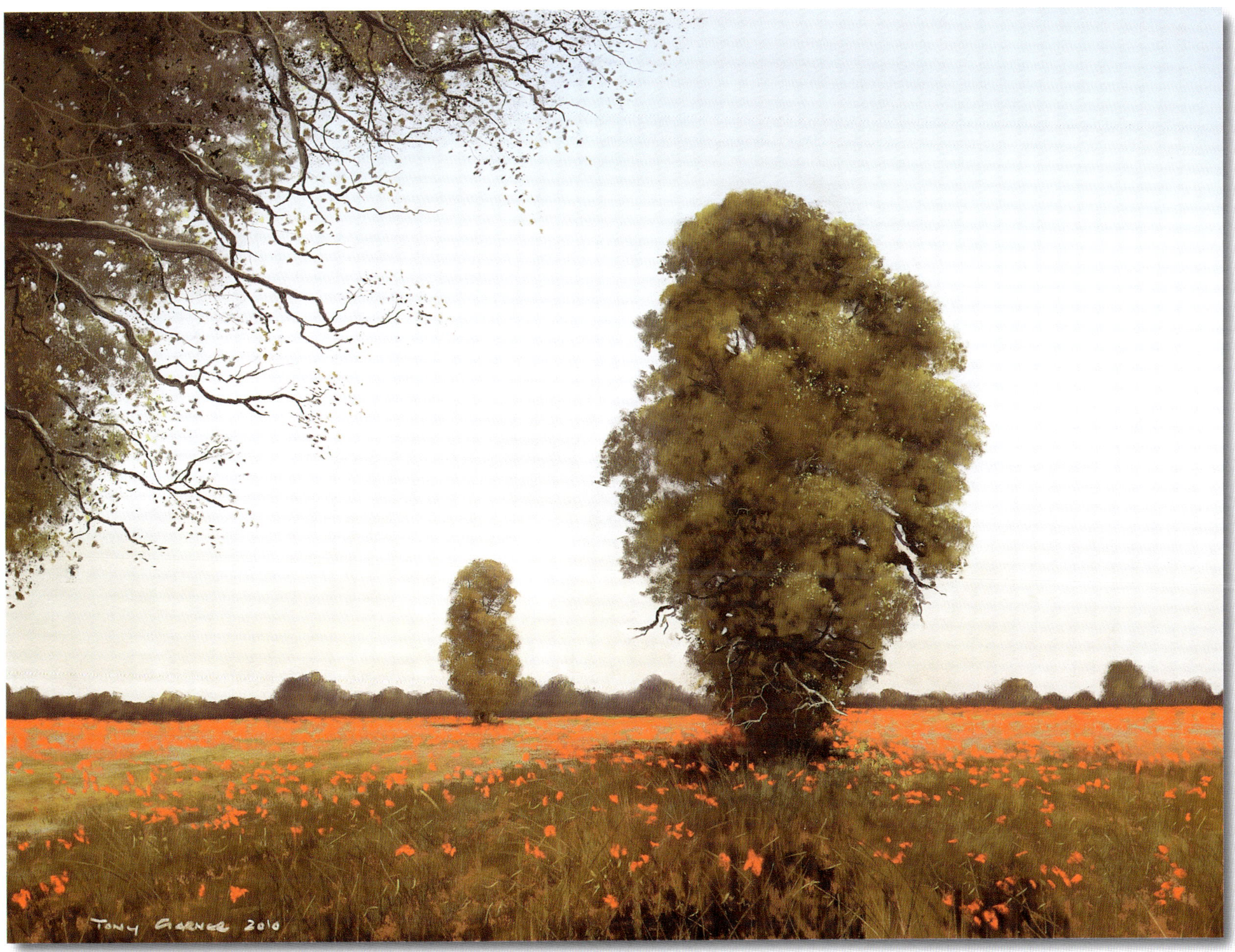

Smiling Faces.

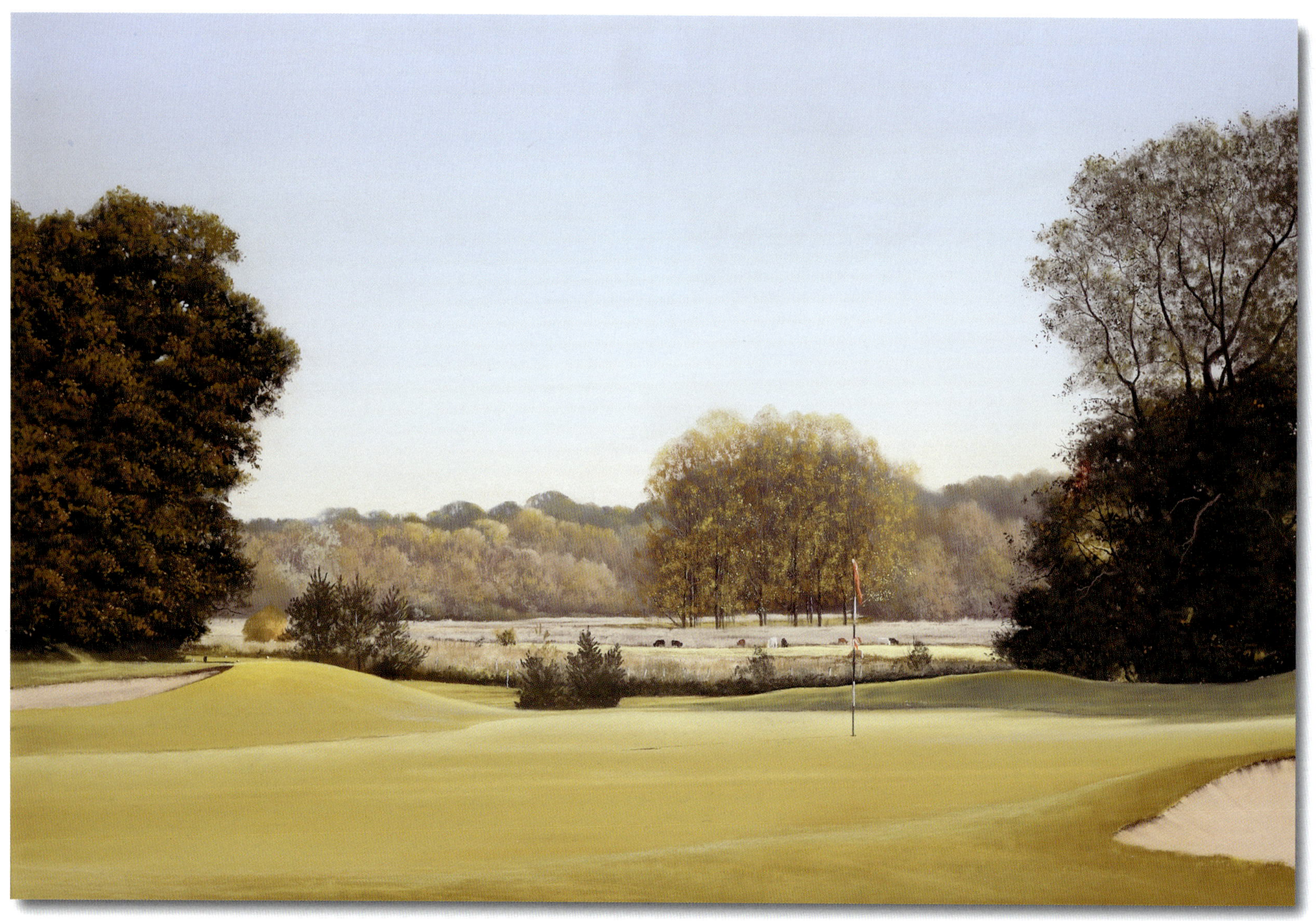

October Morning.
Commissioned by Eaton Golf Club for their Centenary, 2010

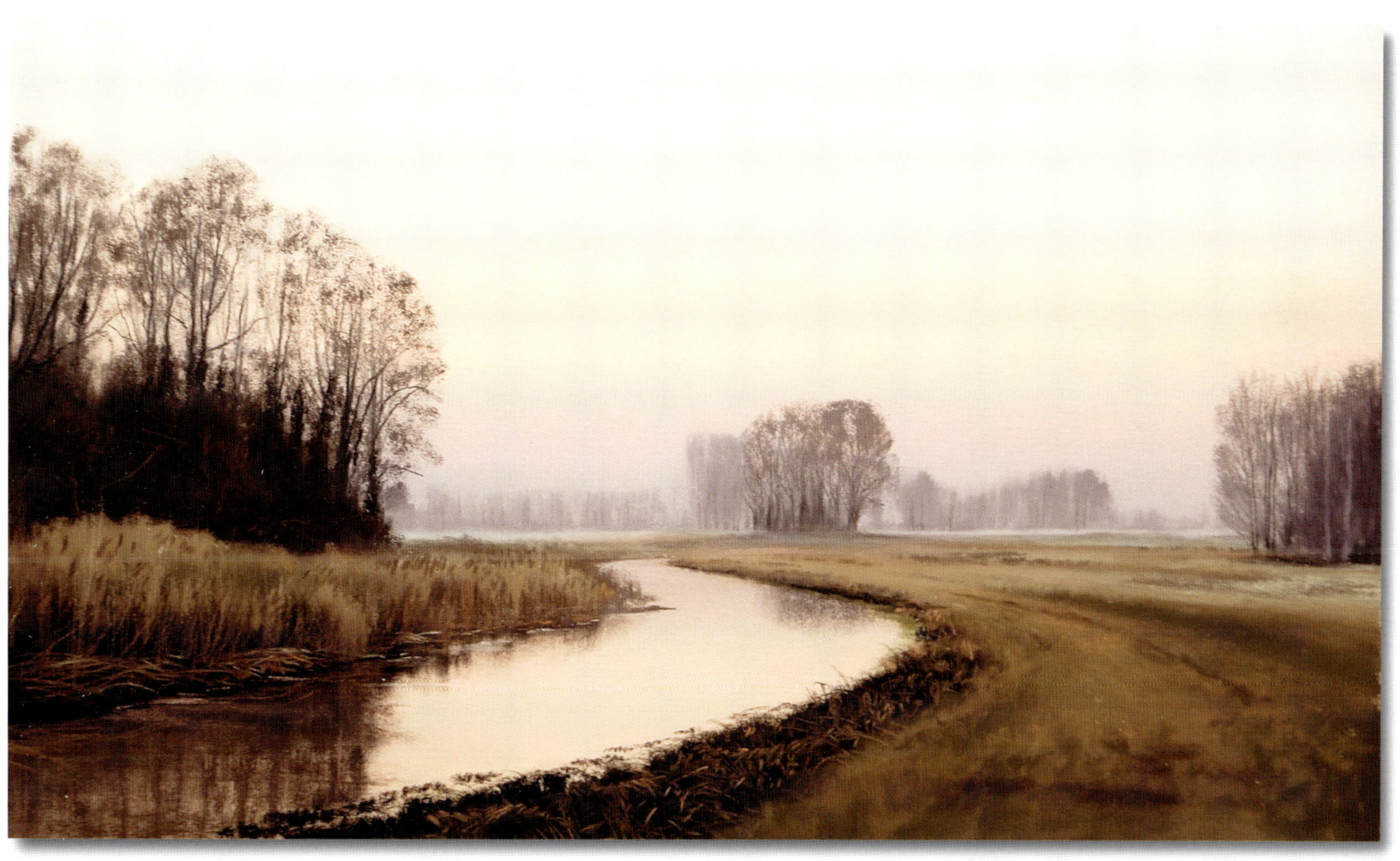

Fading Light.

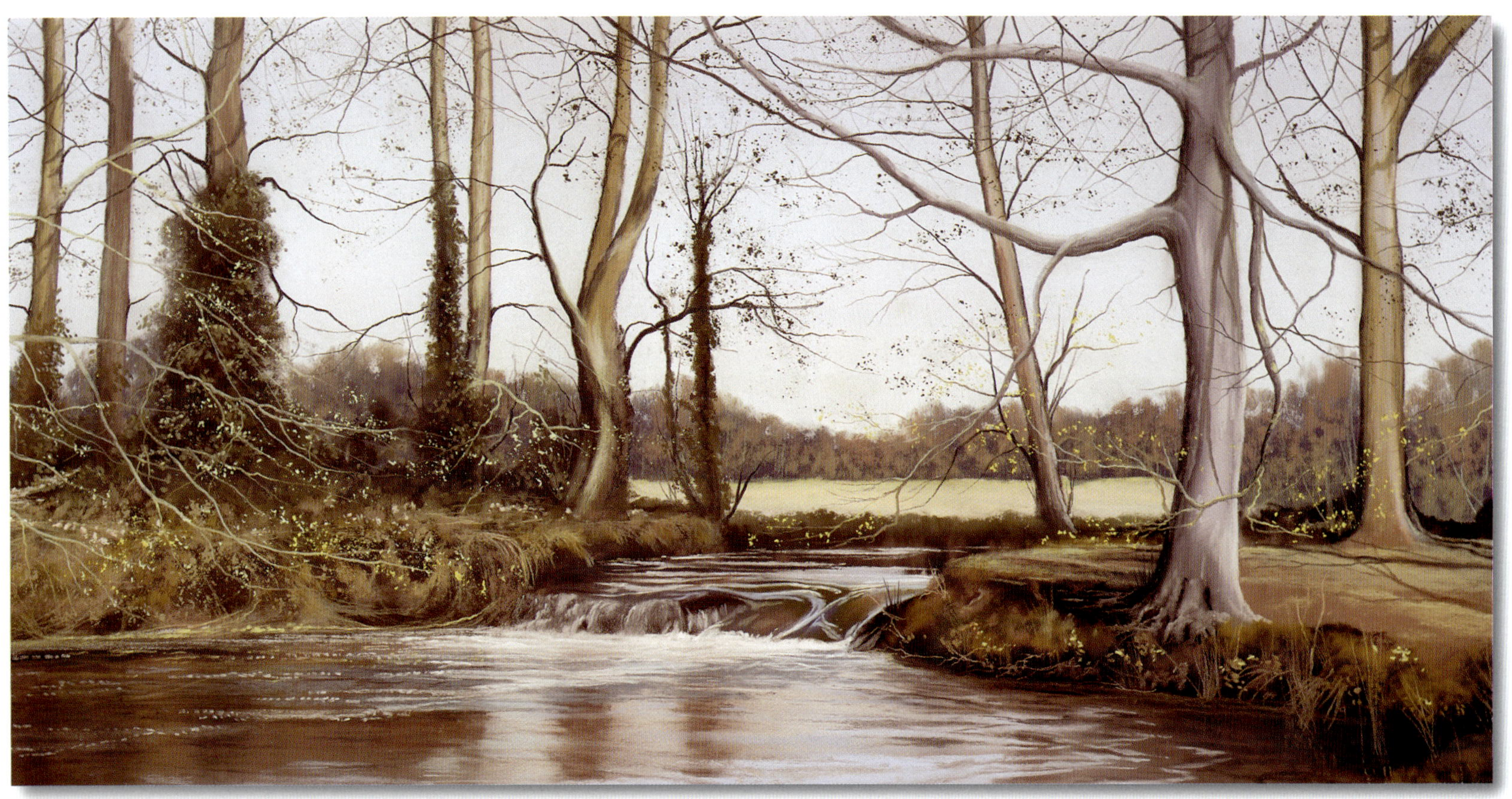

Wensum Weir.

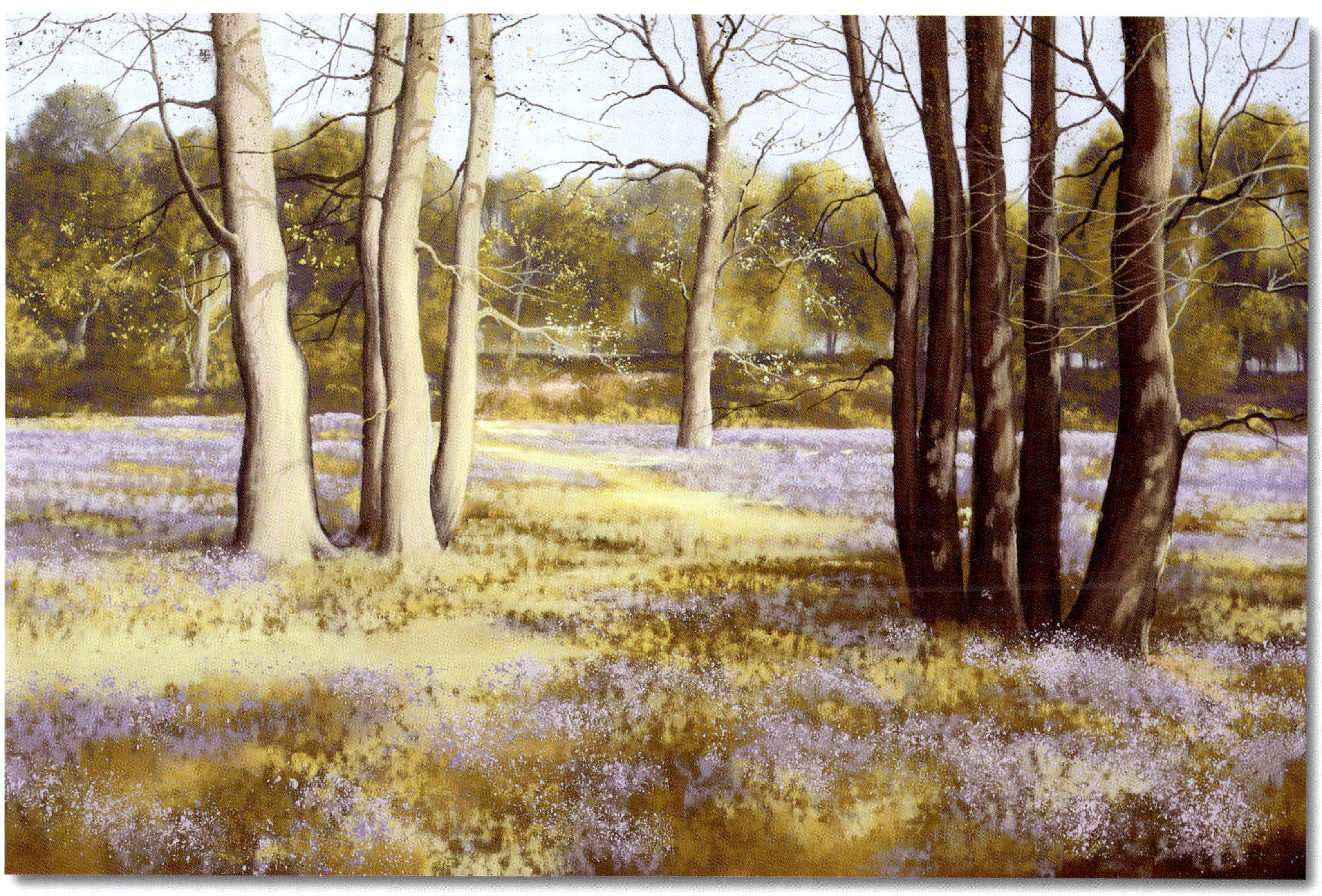

Bluebells.

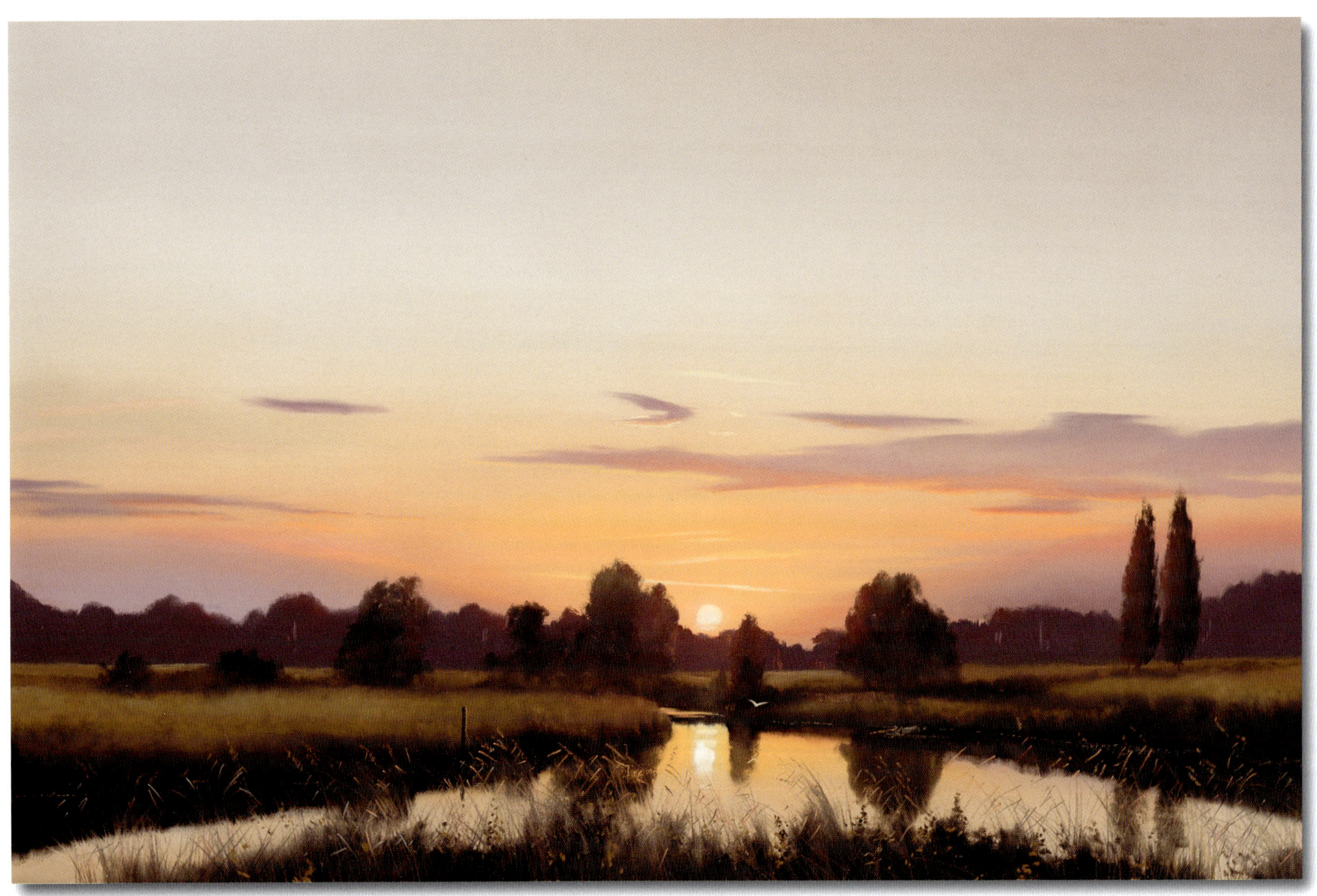

Watersmeet.

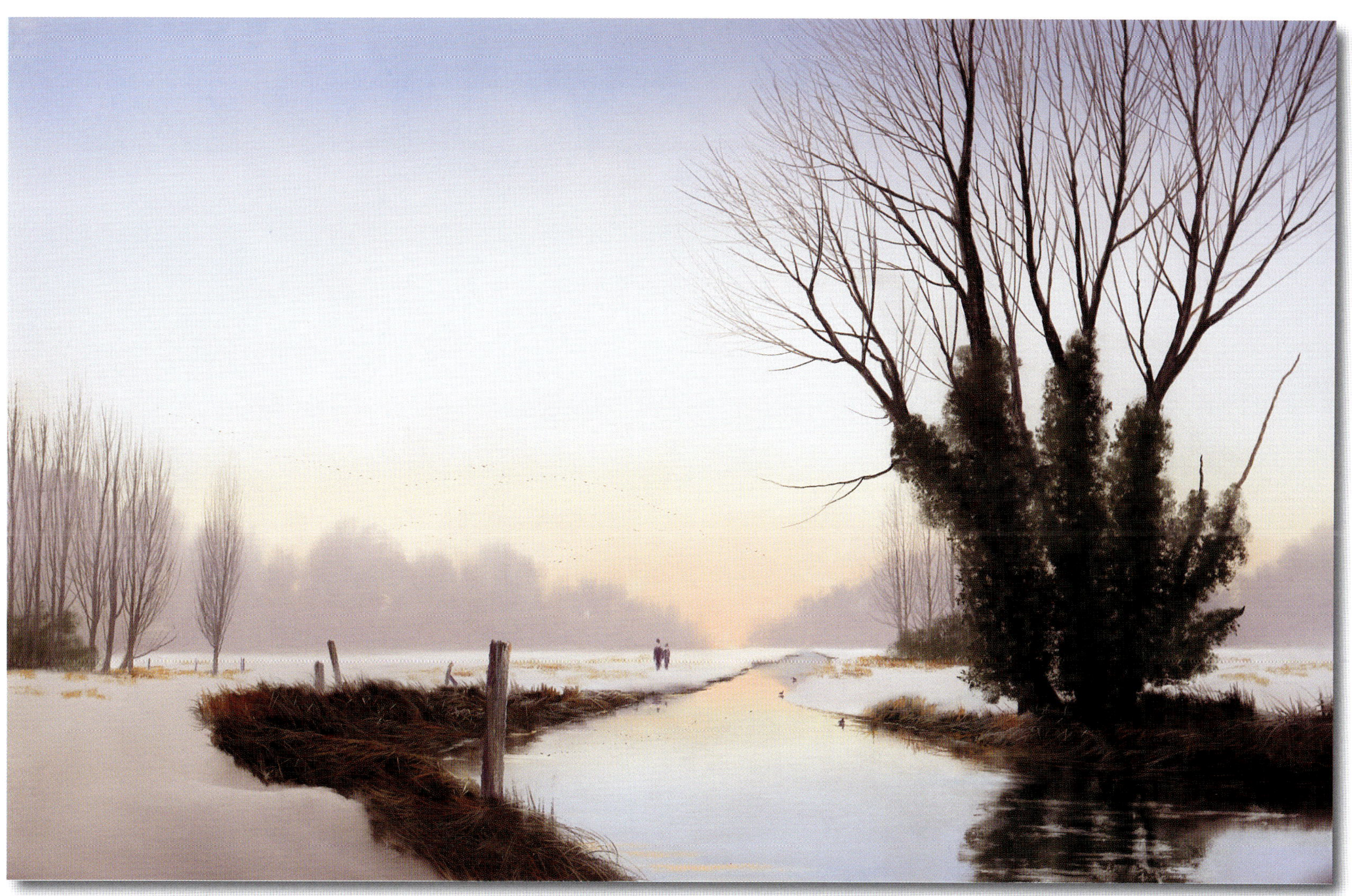

Early Winter Snow, Buxton.

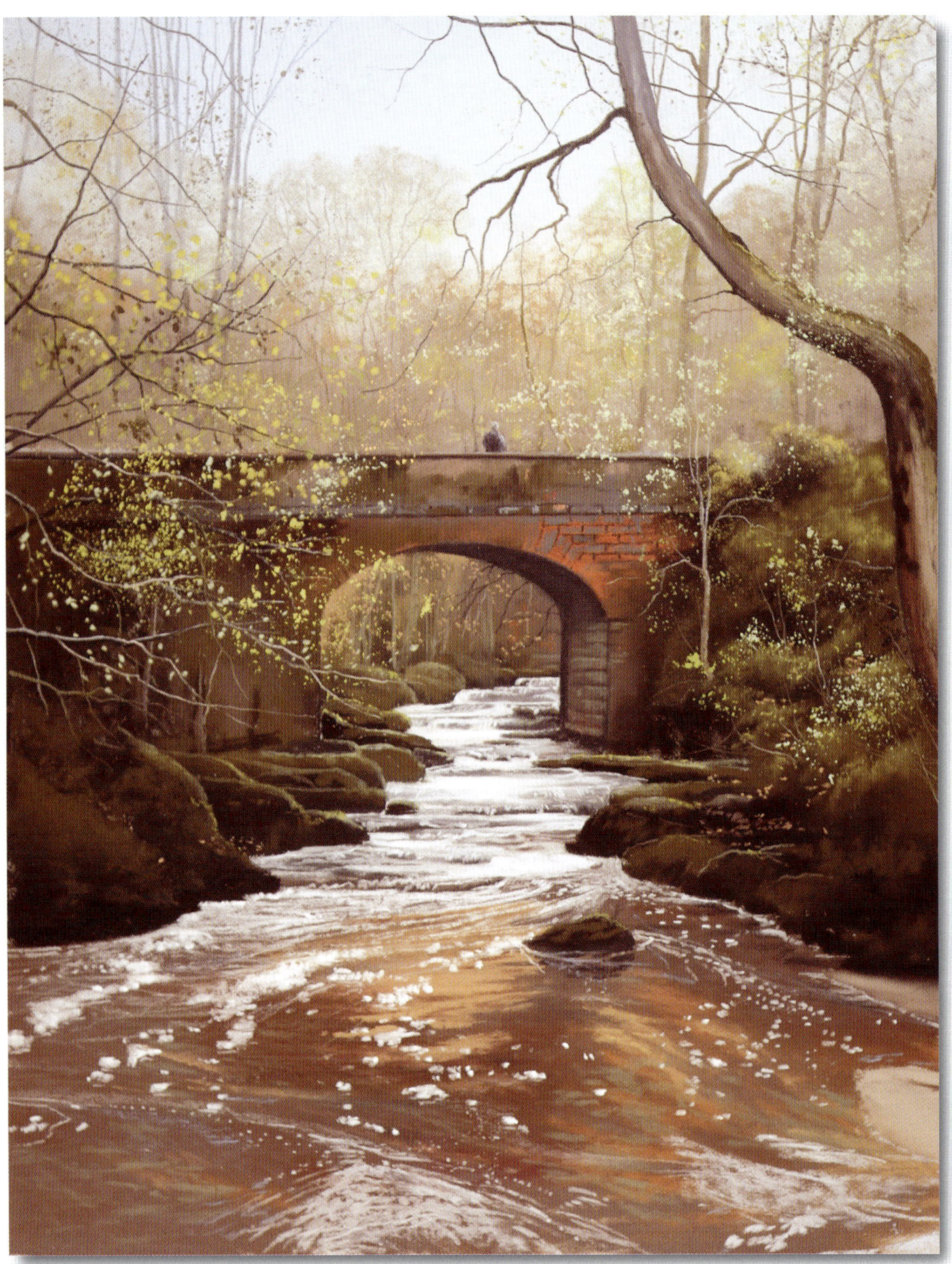

Tumbling Stream, Whitby.

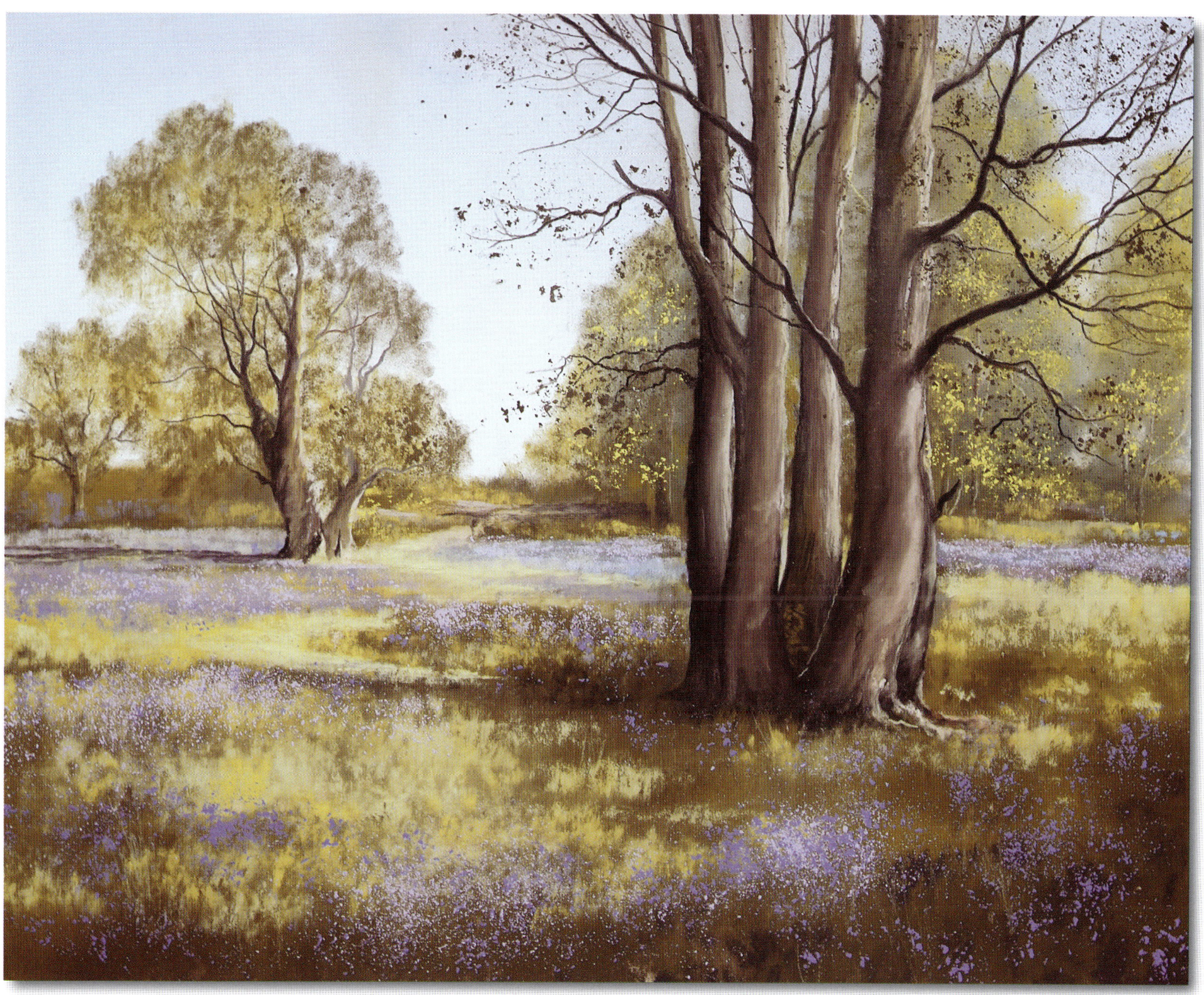

Carpet of Blue.

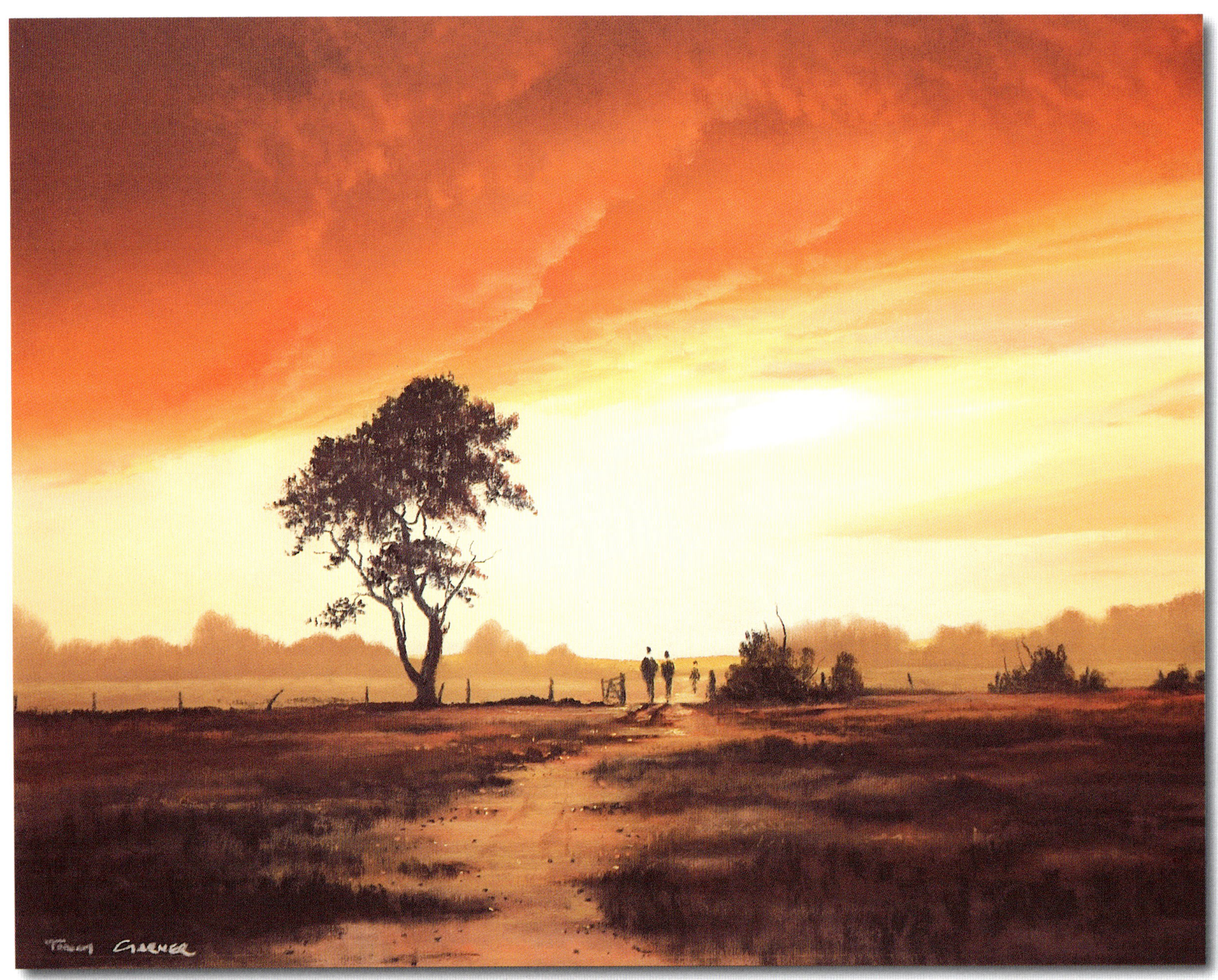

Come On, We'll Be Late.

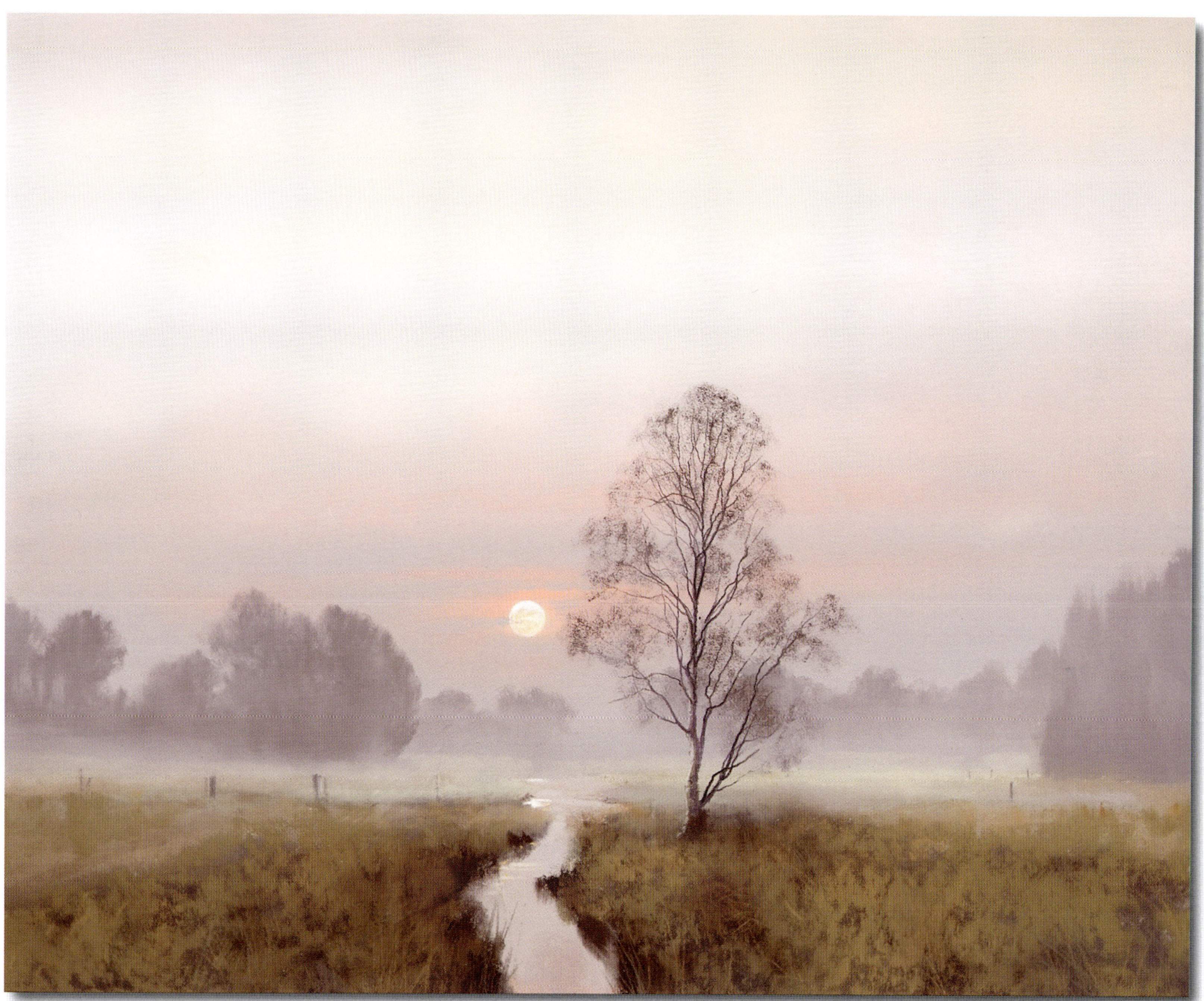

Serene Moments.

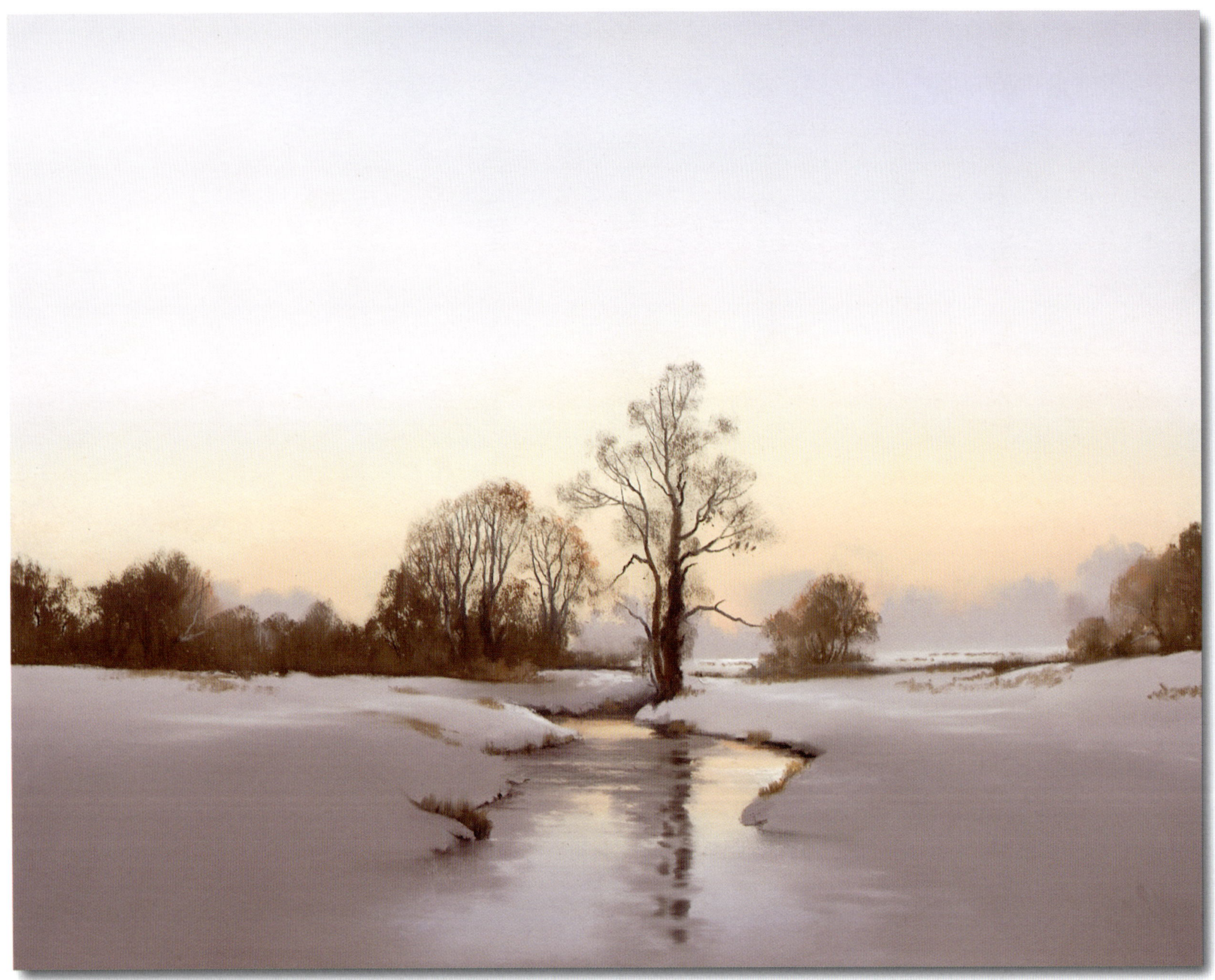

Snowfall at Sunset.

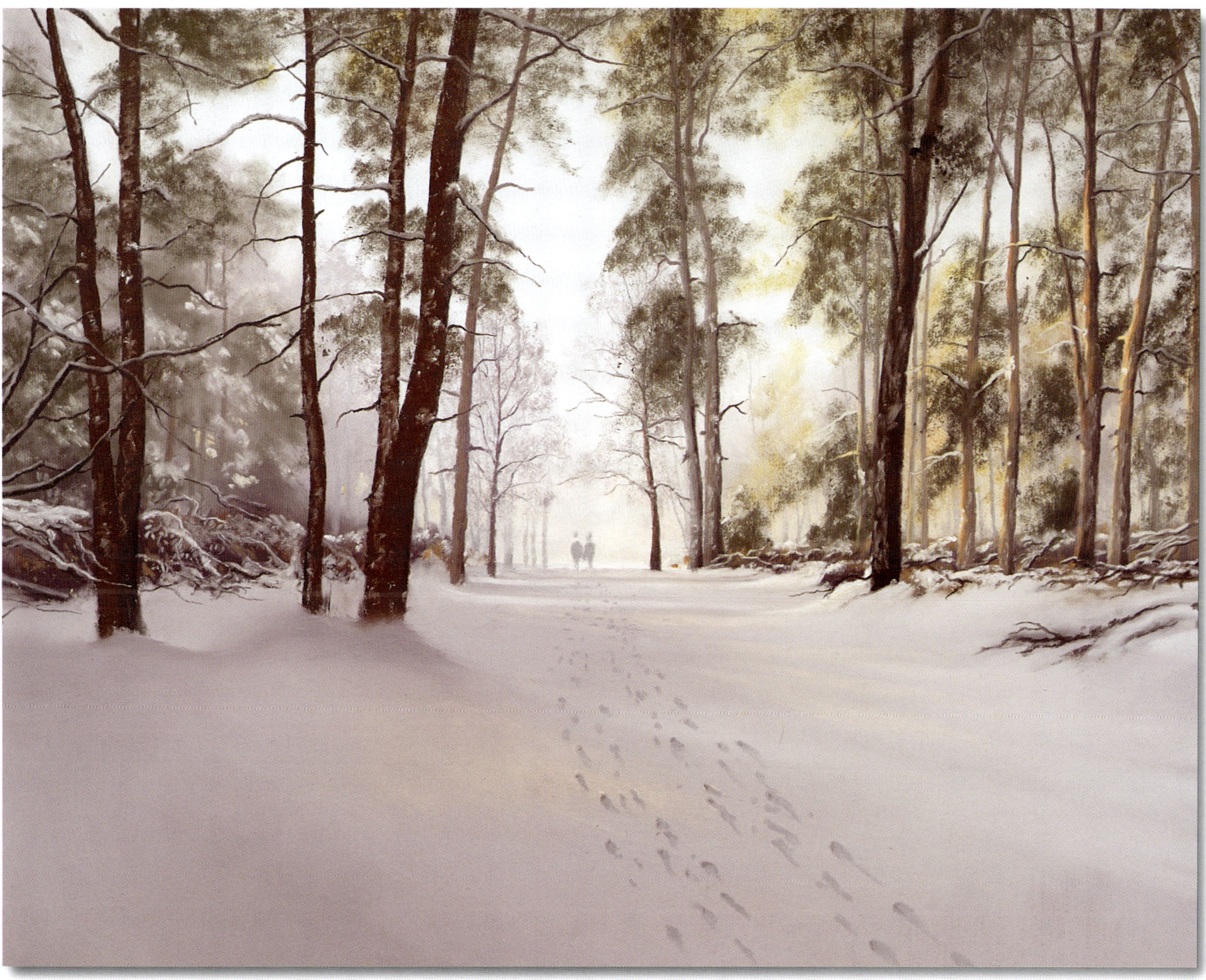

Footprints.

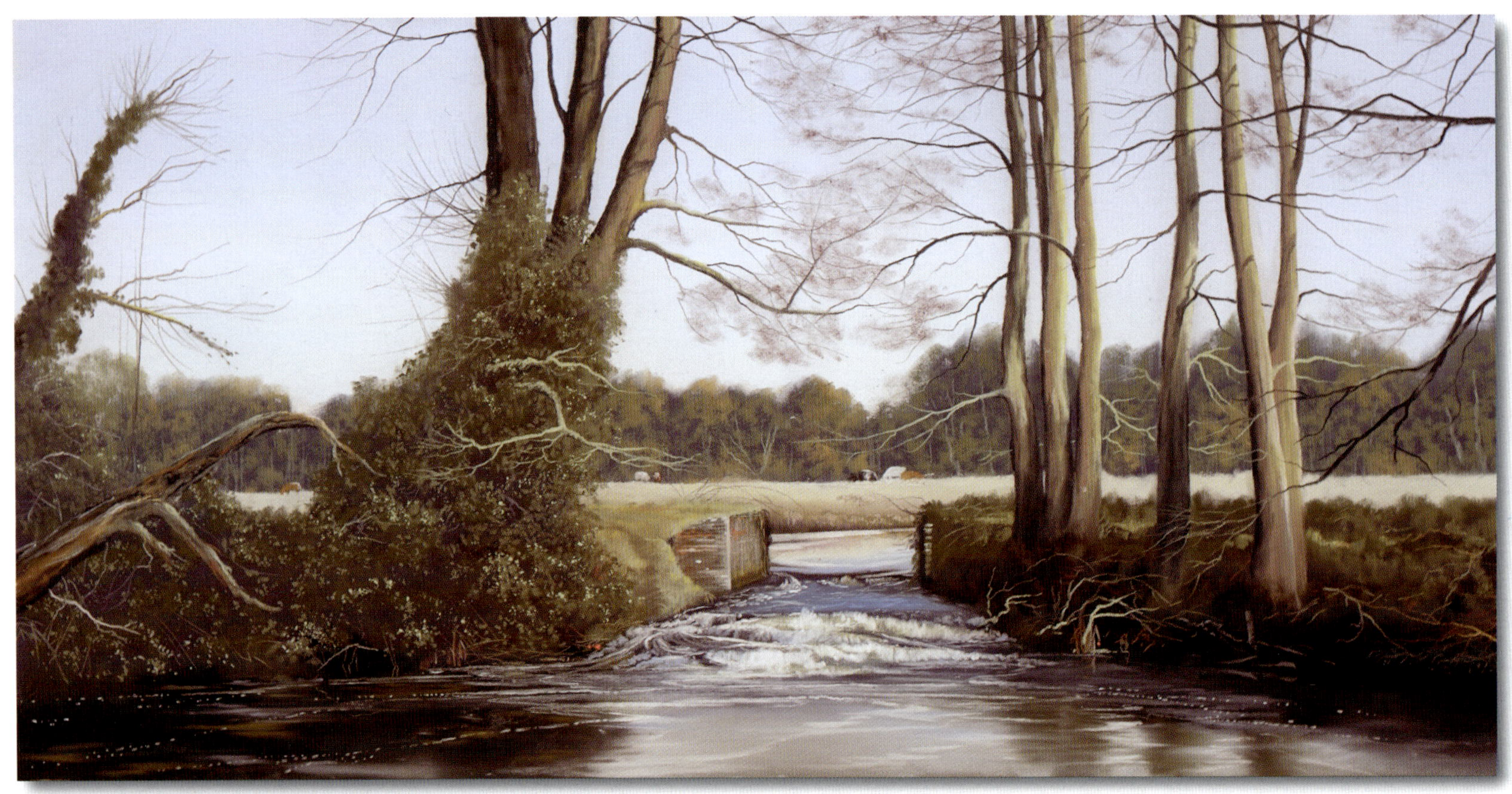

Winter Sun, River Wensum.

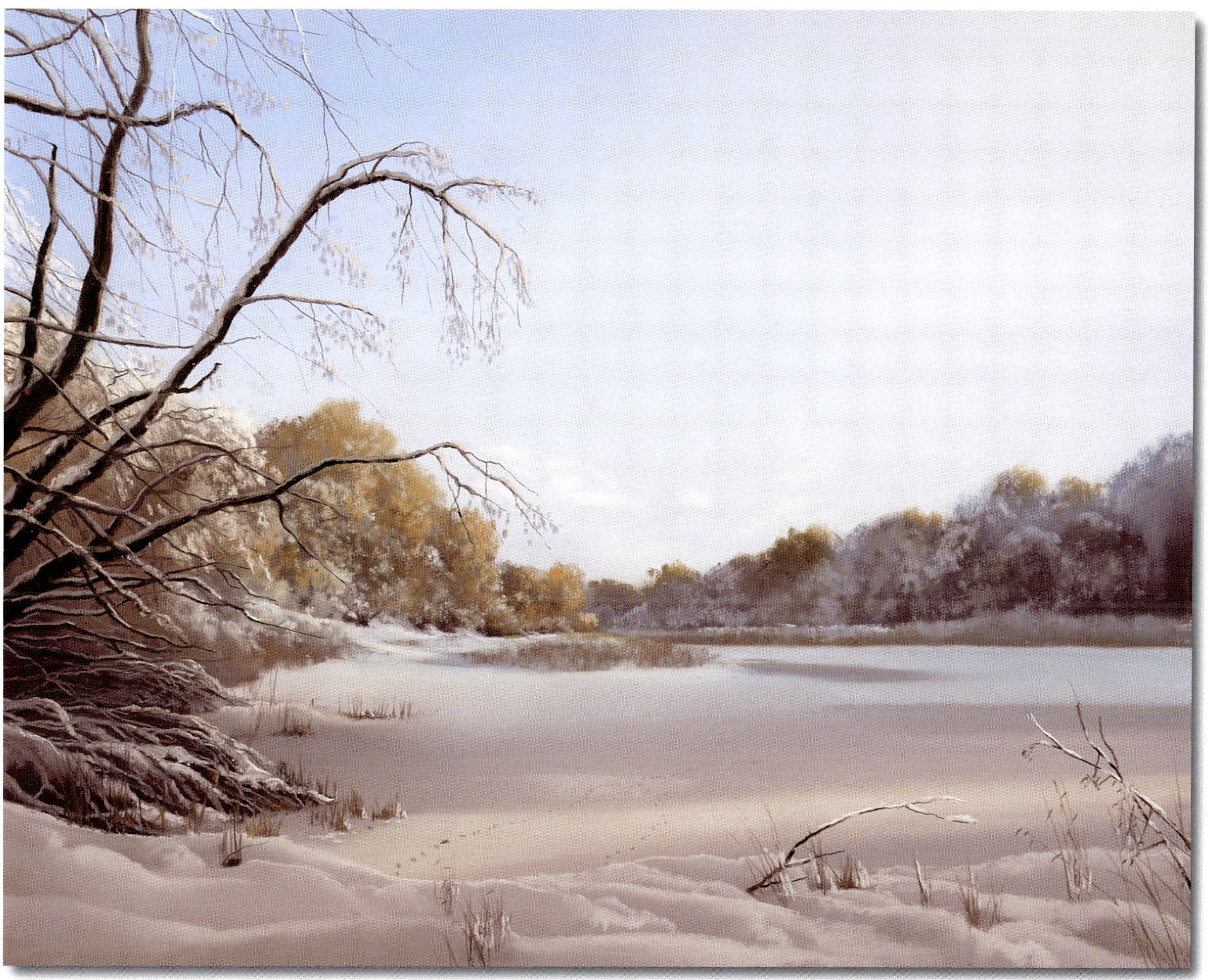

"I Wonder Who Made Those Tracks?"

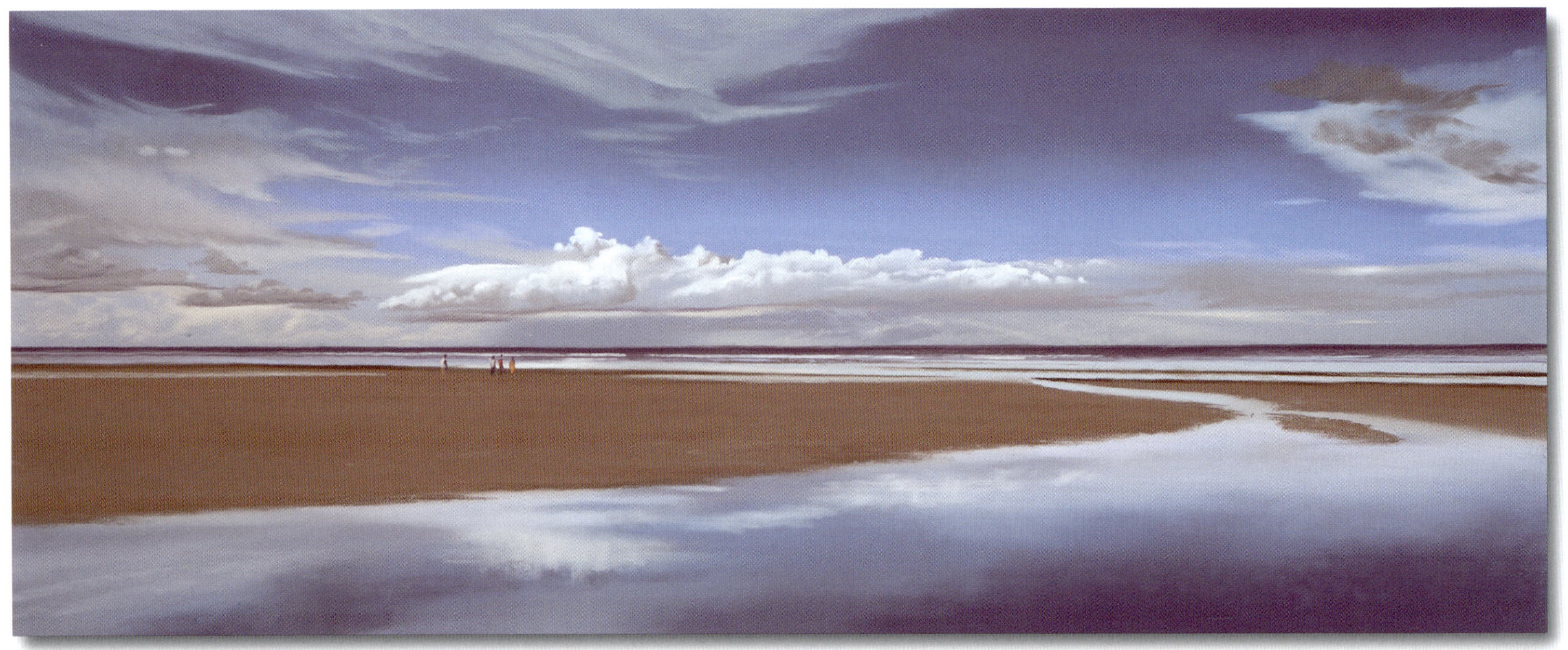

Low Water.

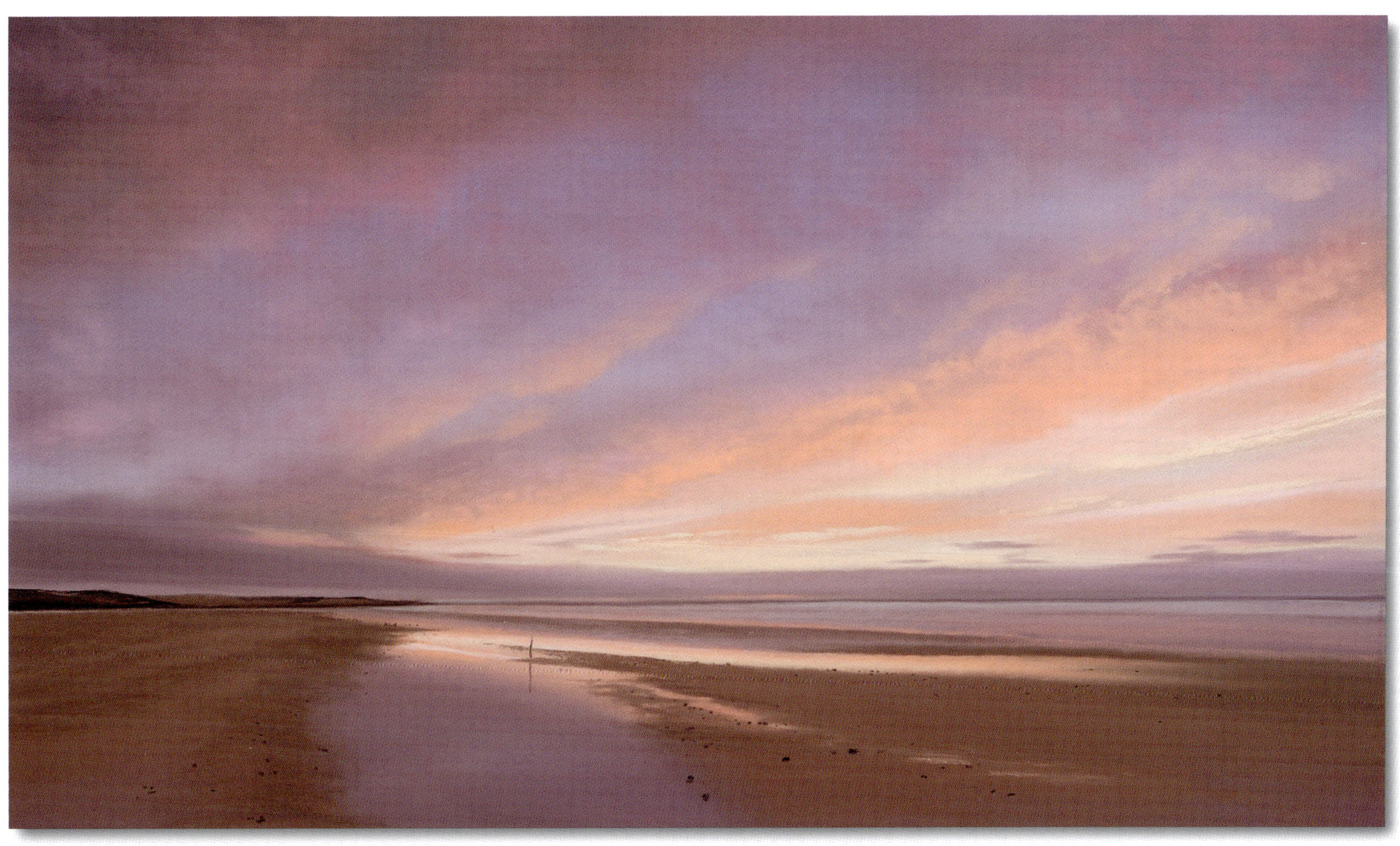

Coastal Dawn.

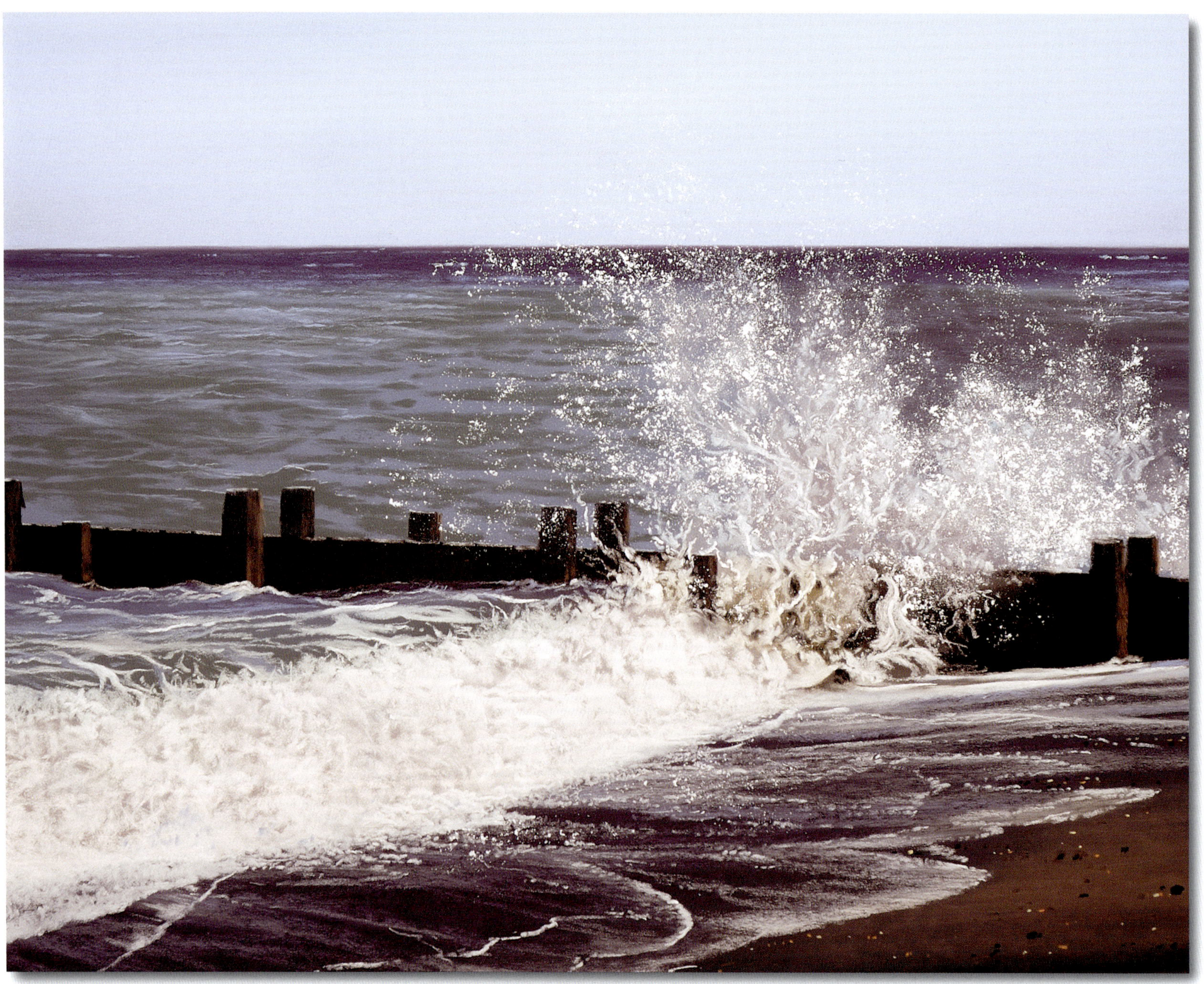

At High Water.

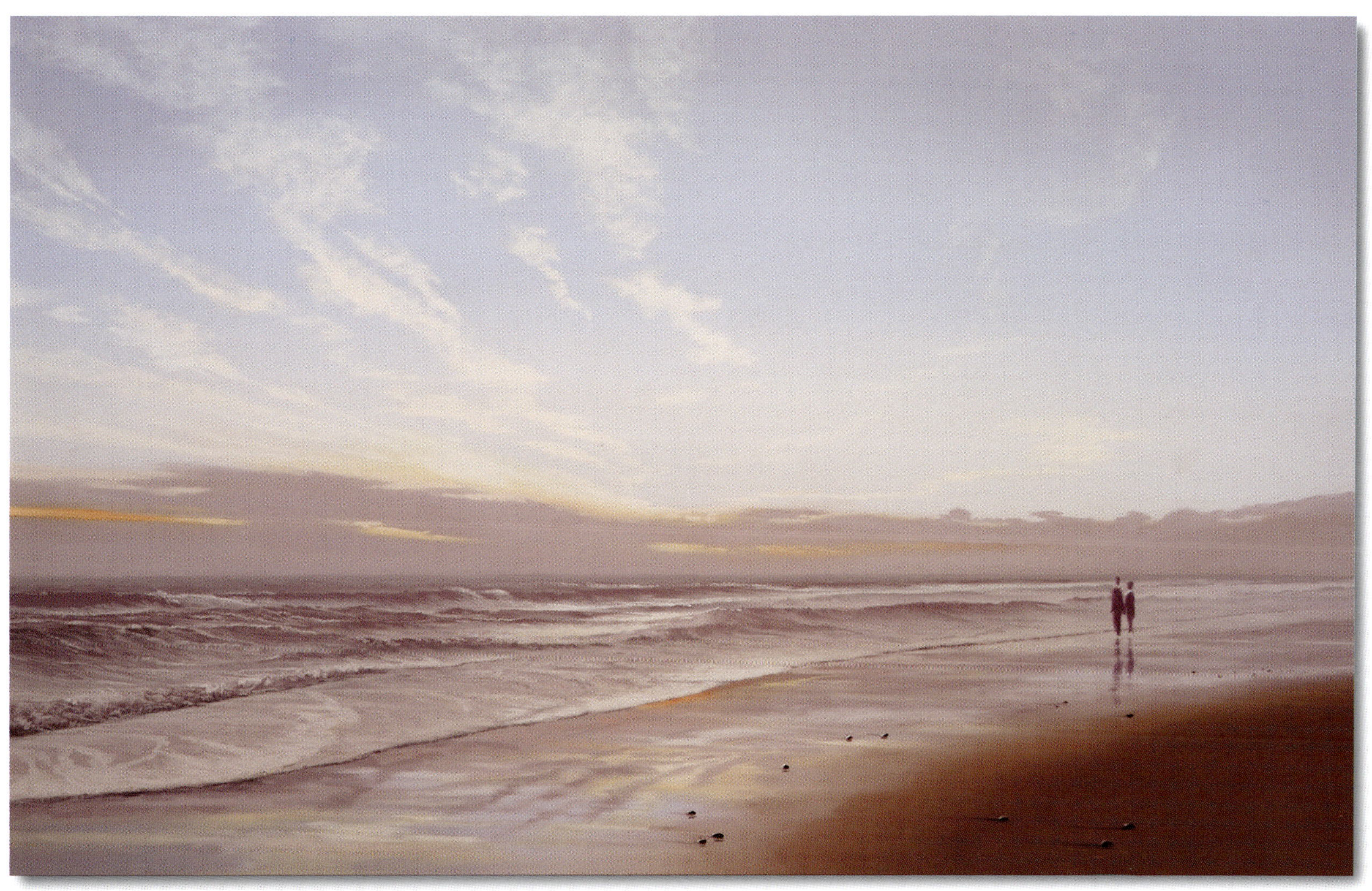

Don't Come to Close.

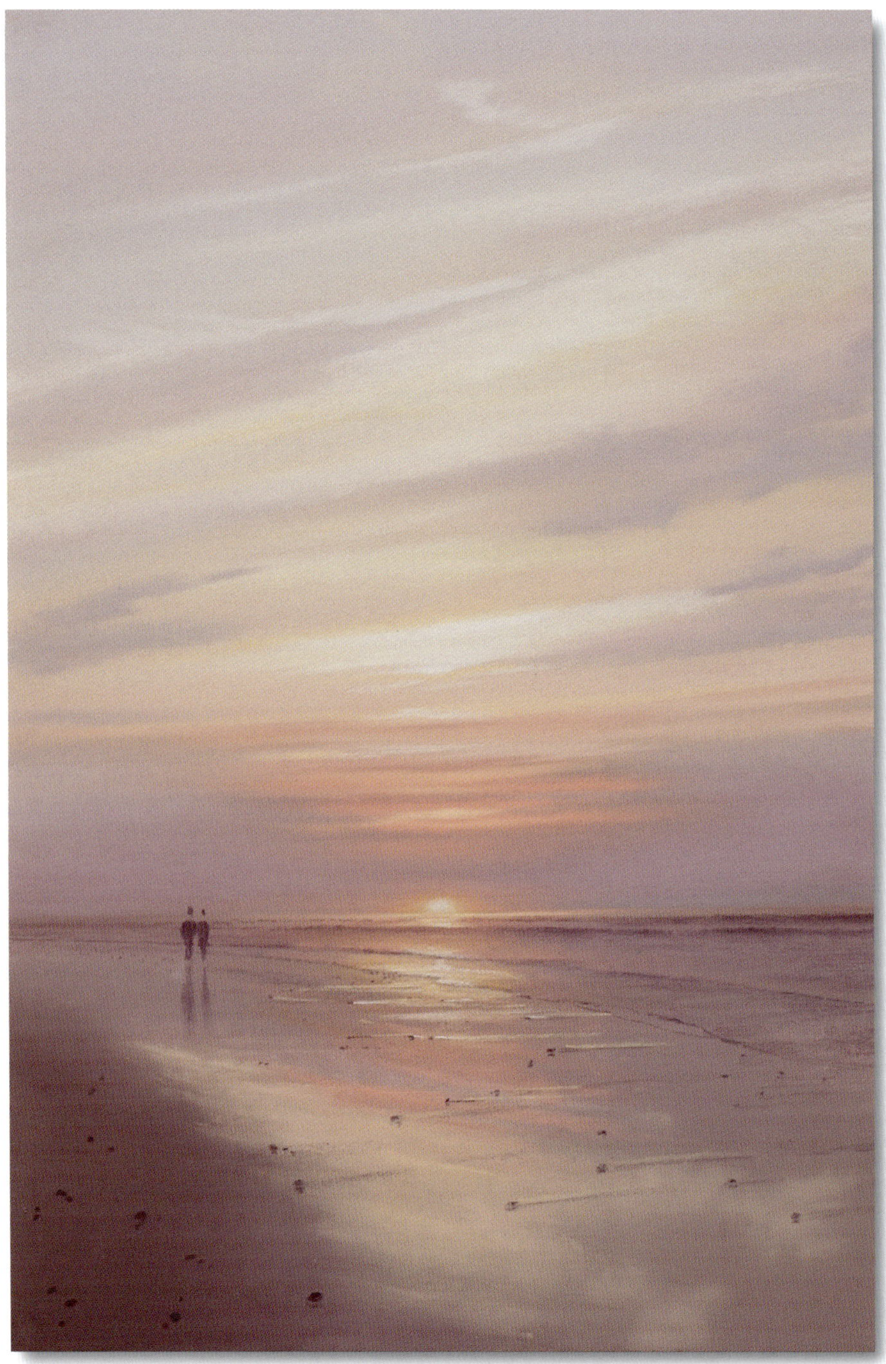

Just the Two of Us.

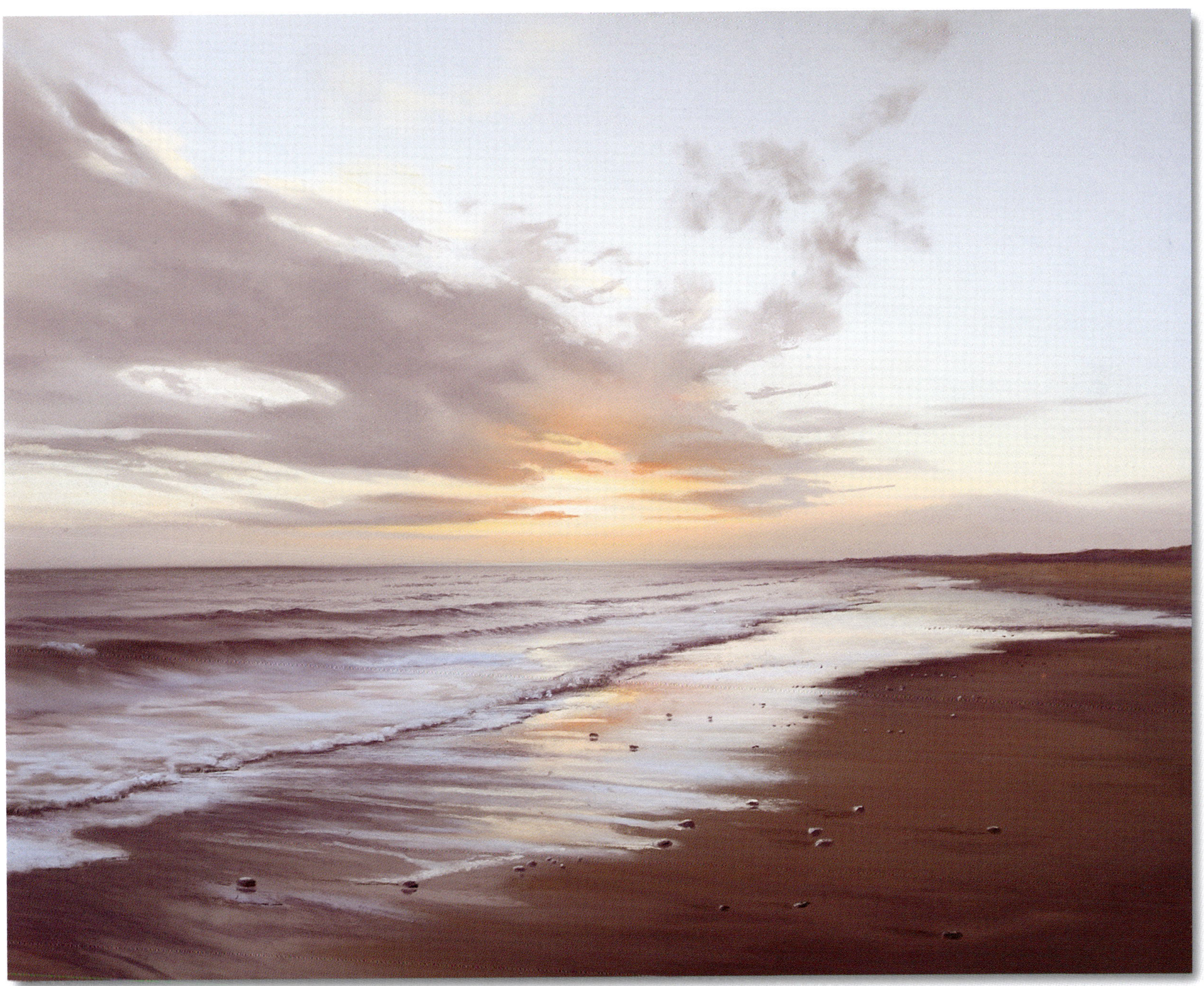

Winter Sunrise.

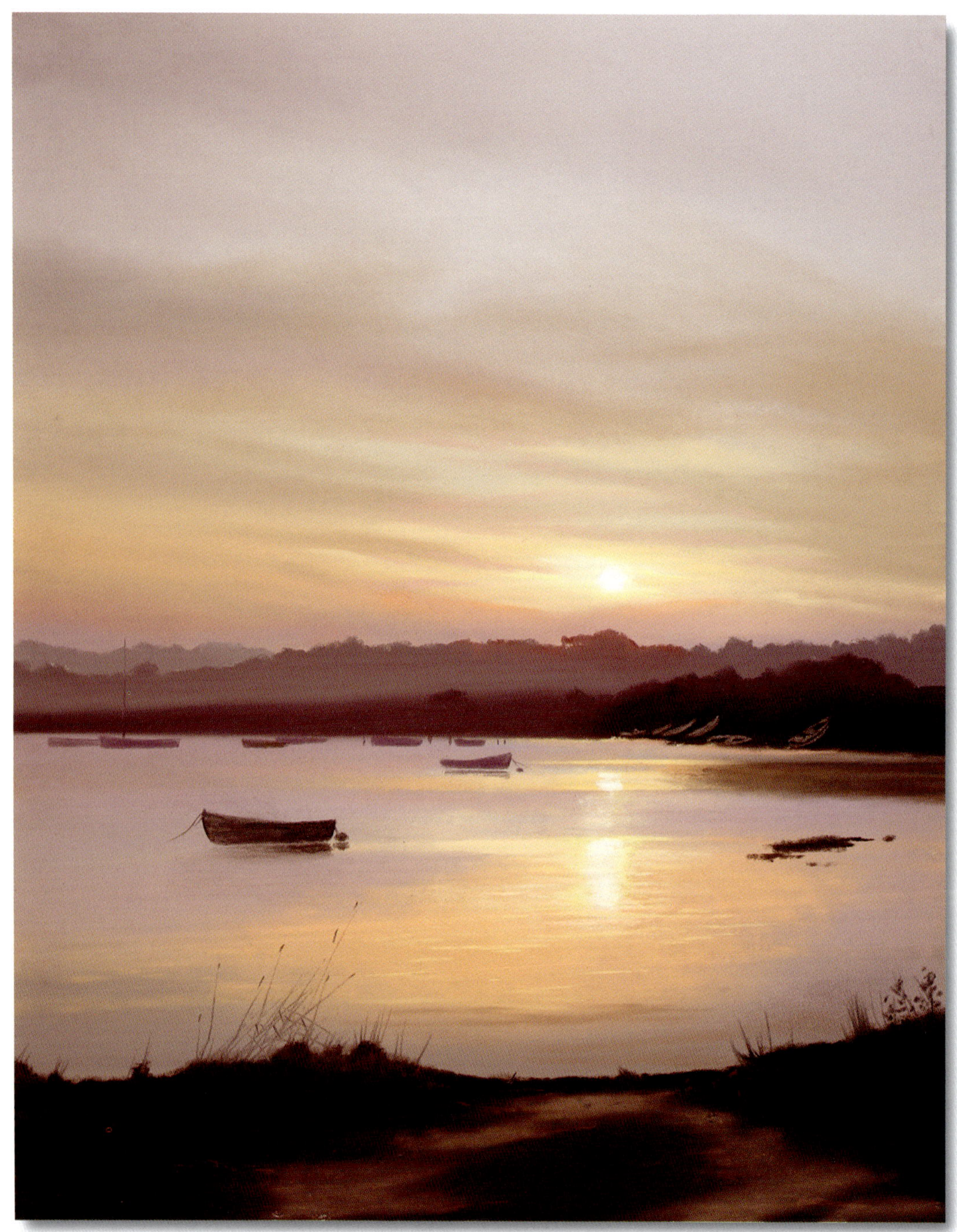

Rising Tide, Morston.

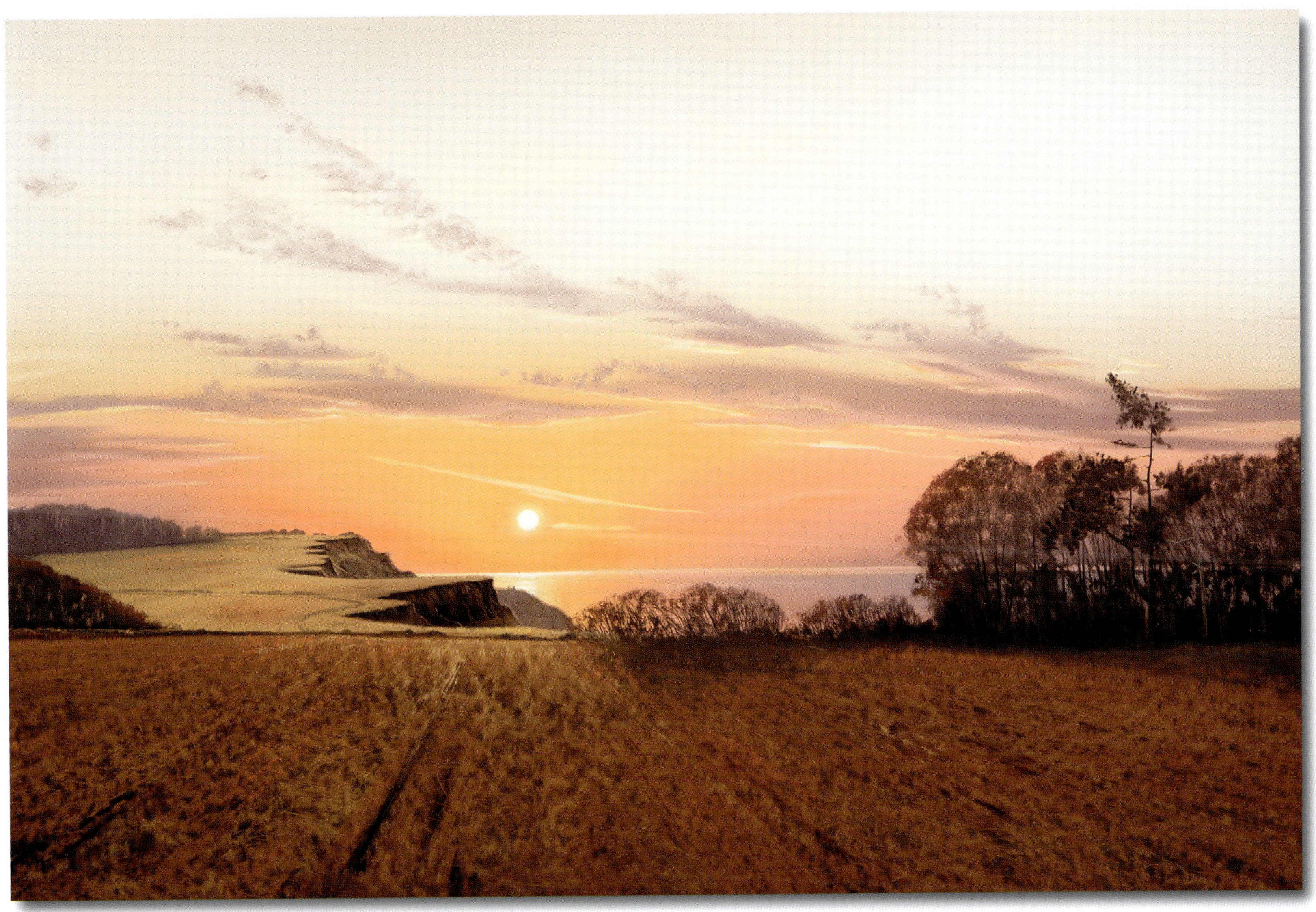

Sunset at Seven.

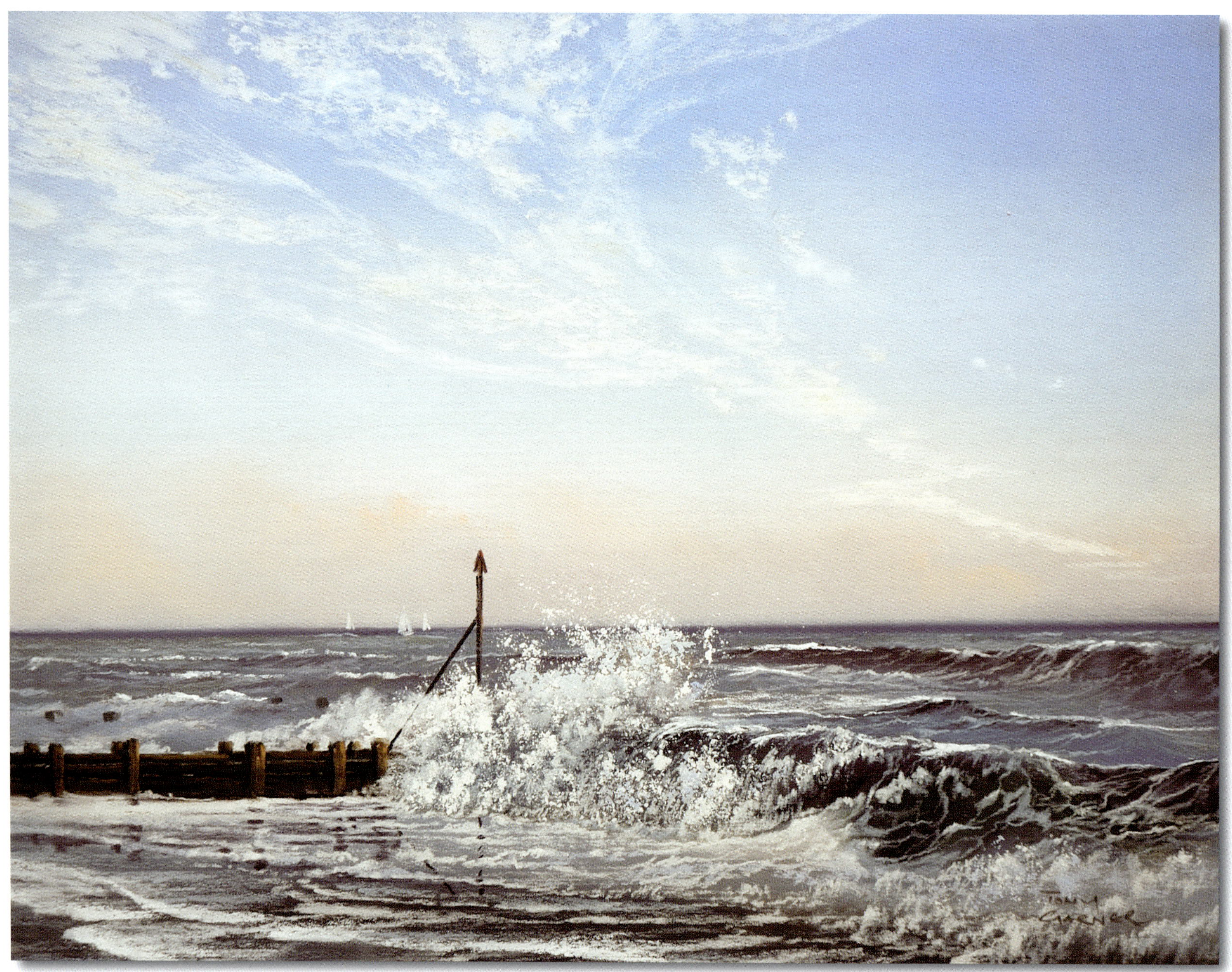

Distant Sails.

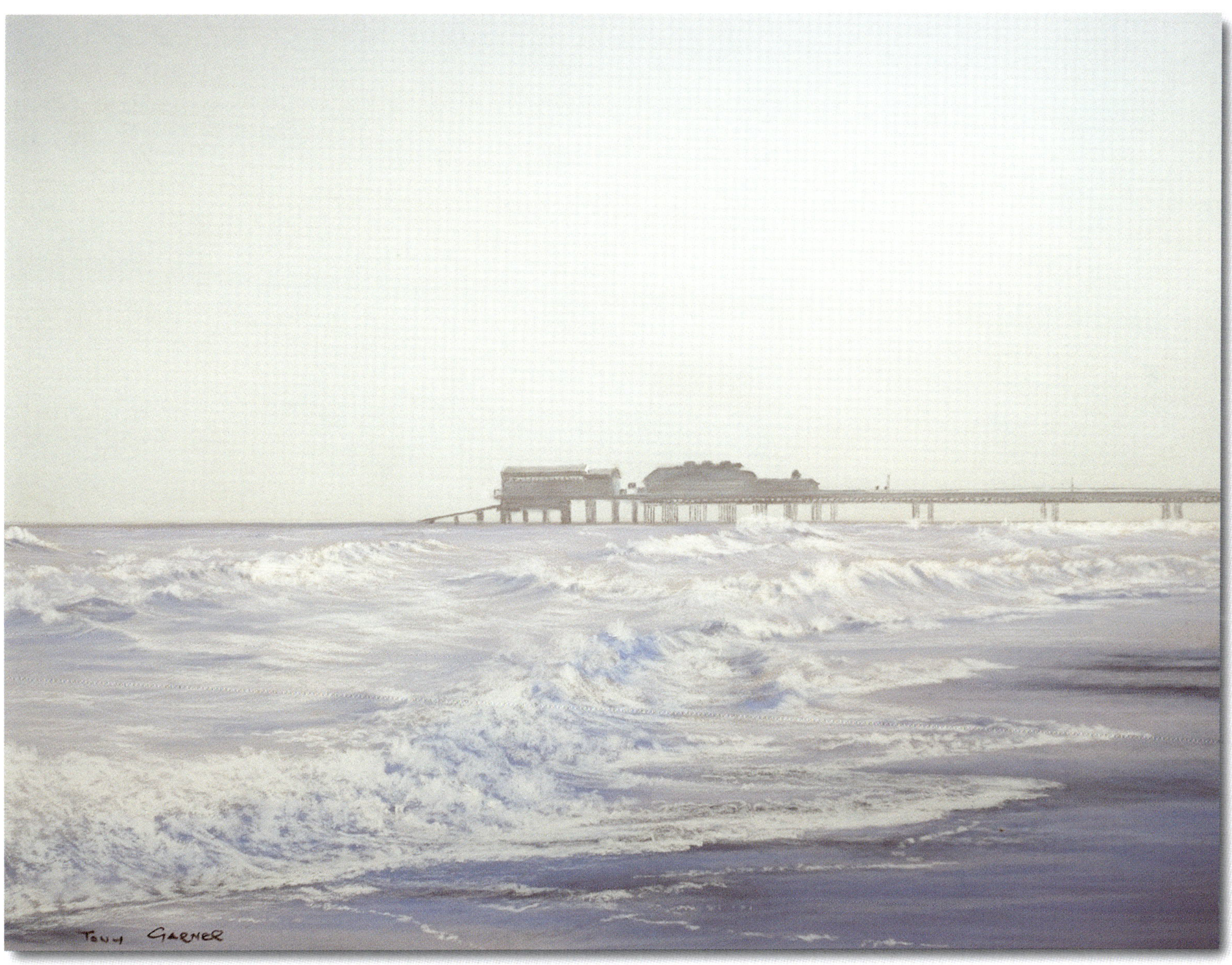

Hazy Day.

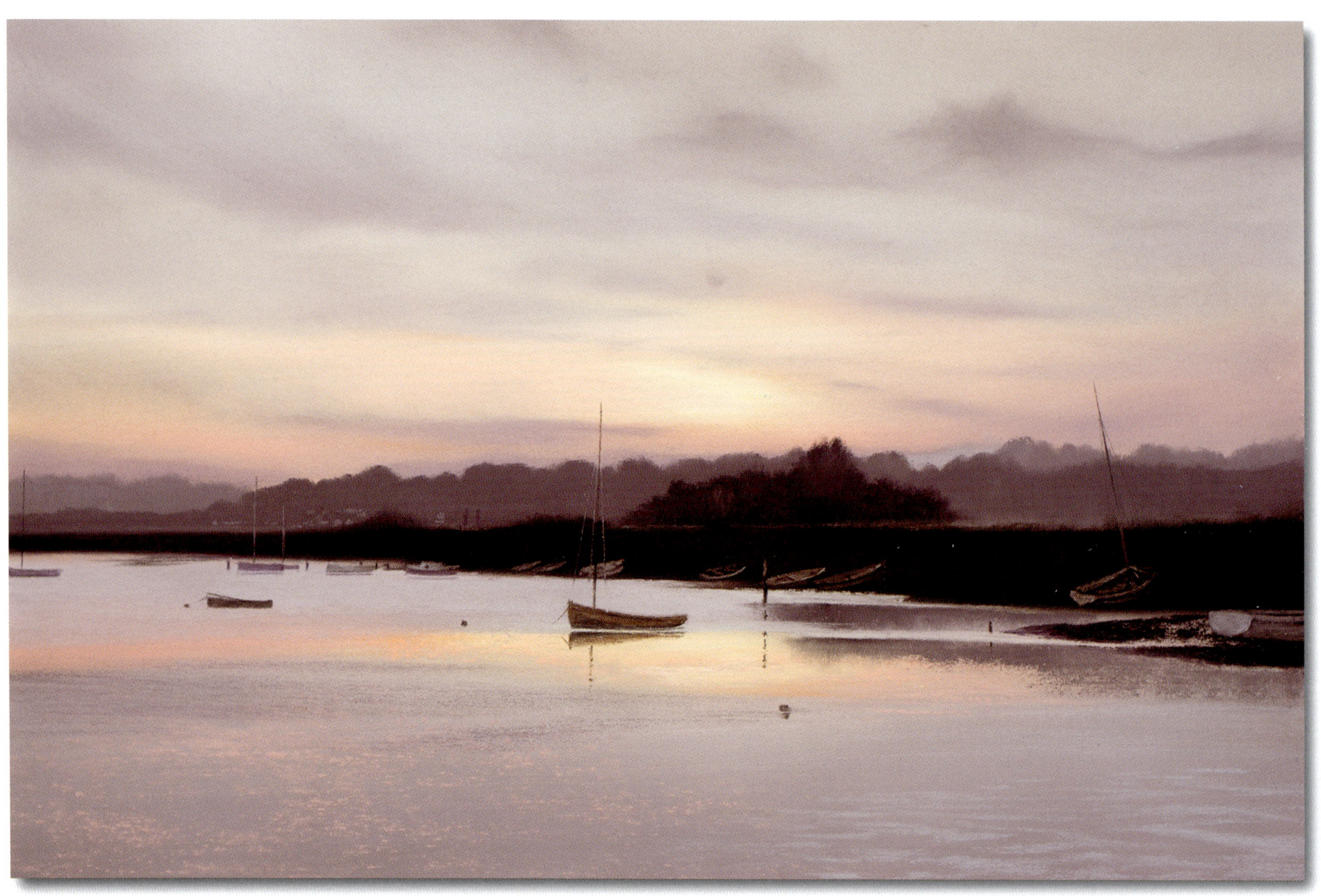

Morston Dawn.

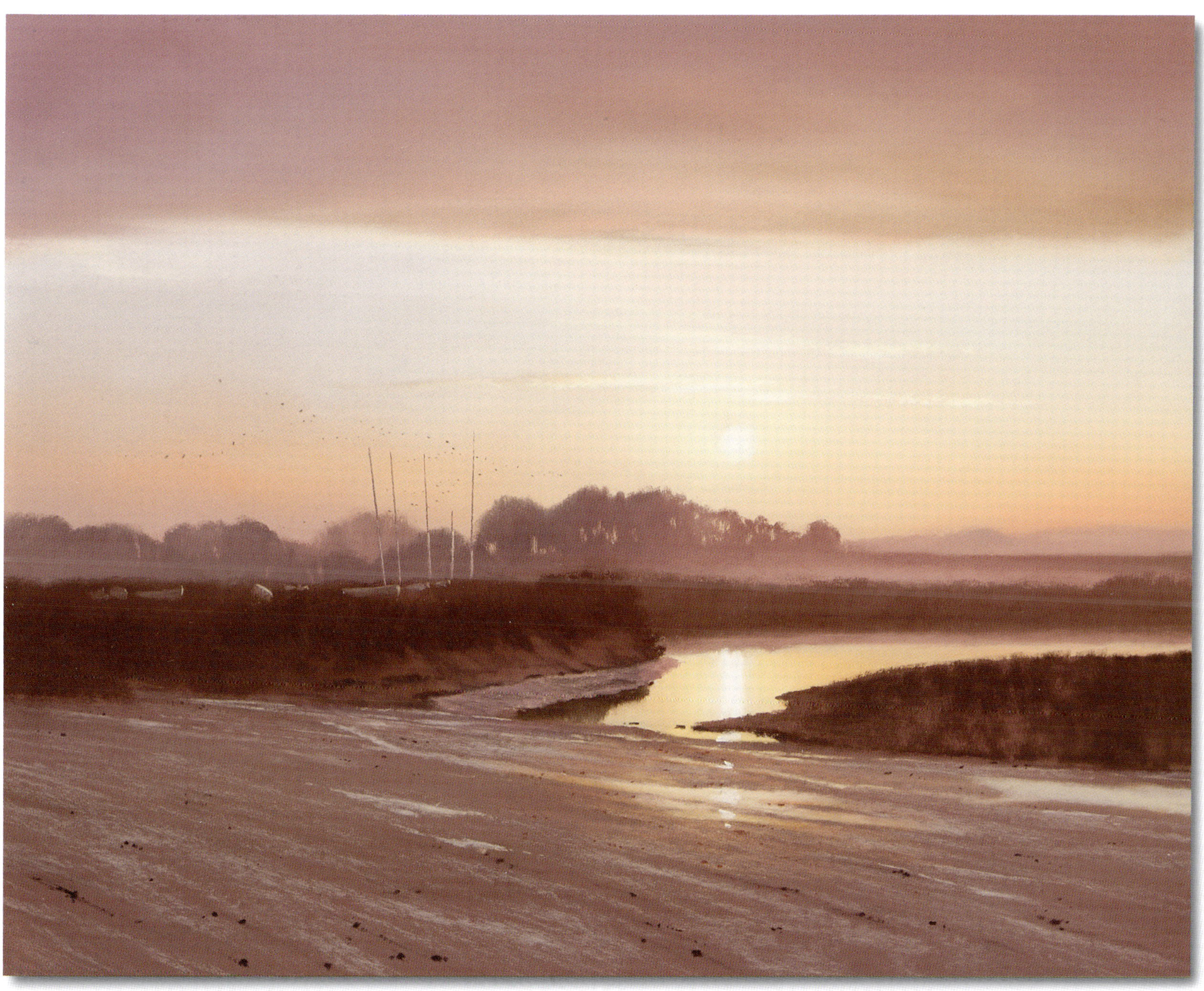

Morston Mist.

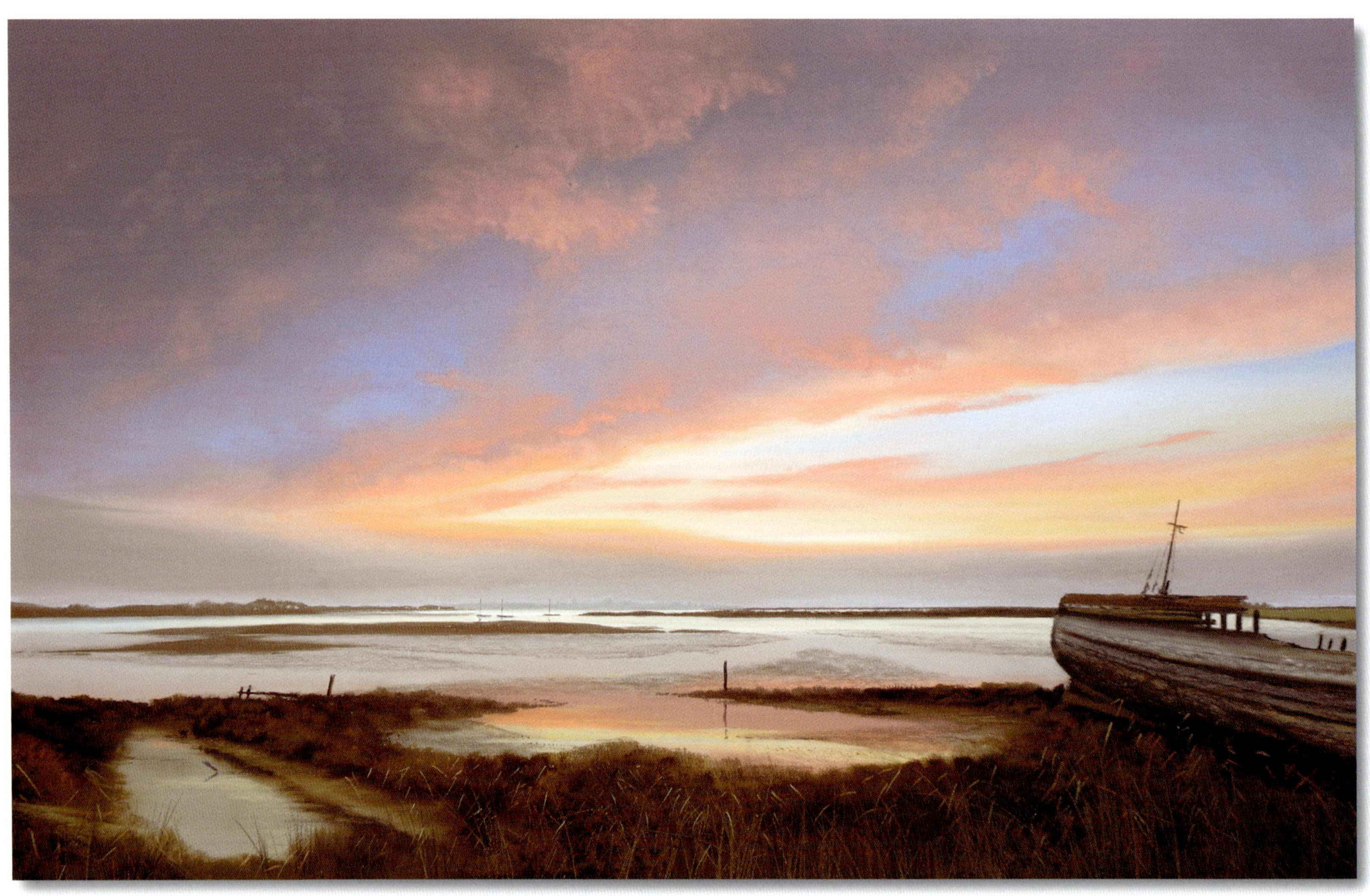

Coastal Dawn.

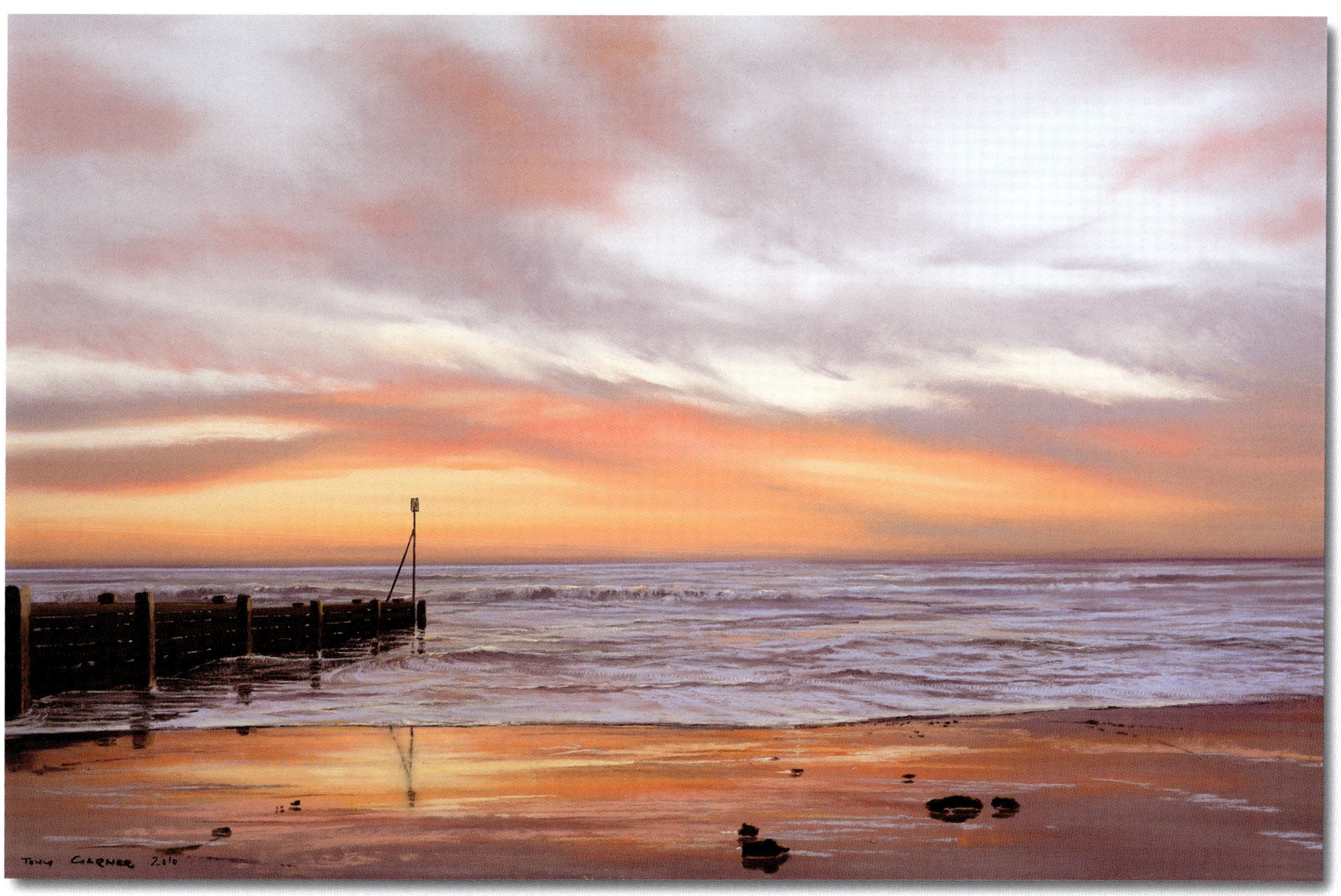

Summer Sunset.

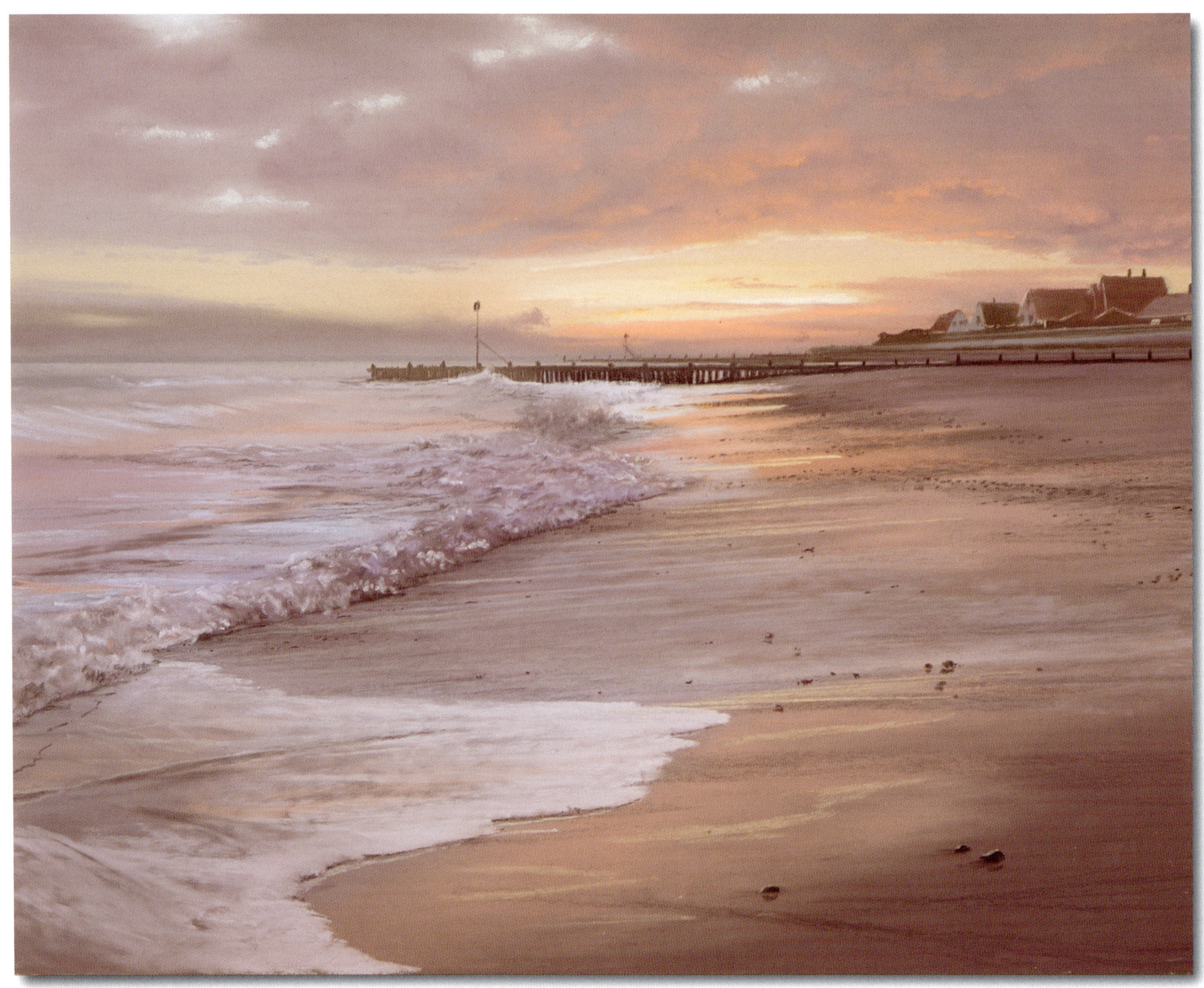

Fiery Dawn, Walcott.

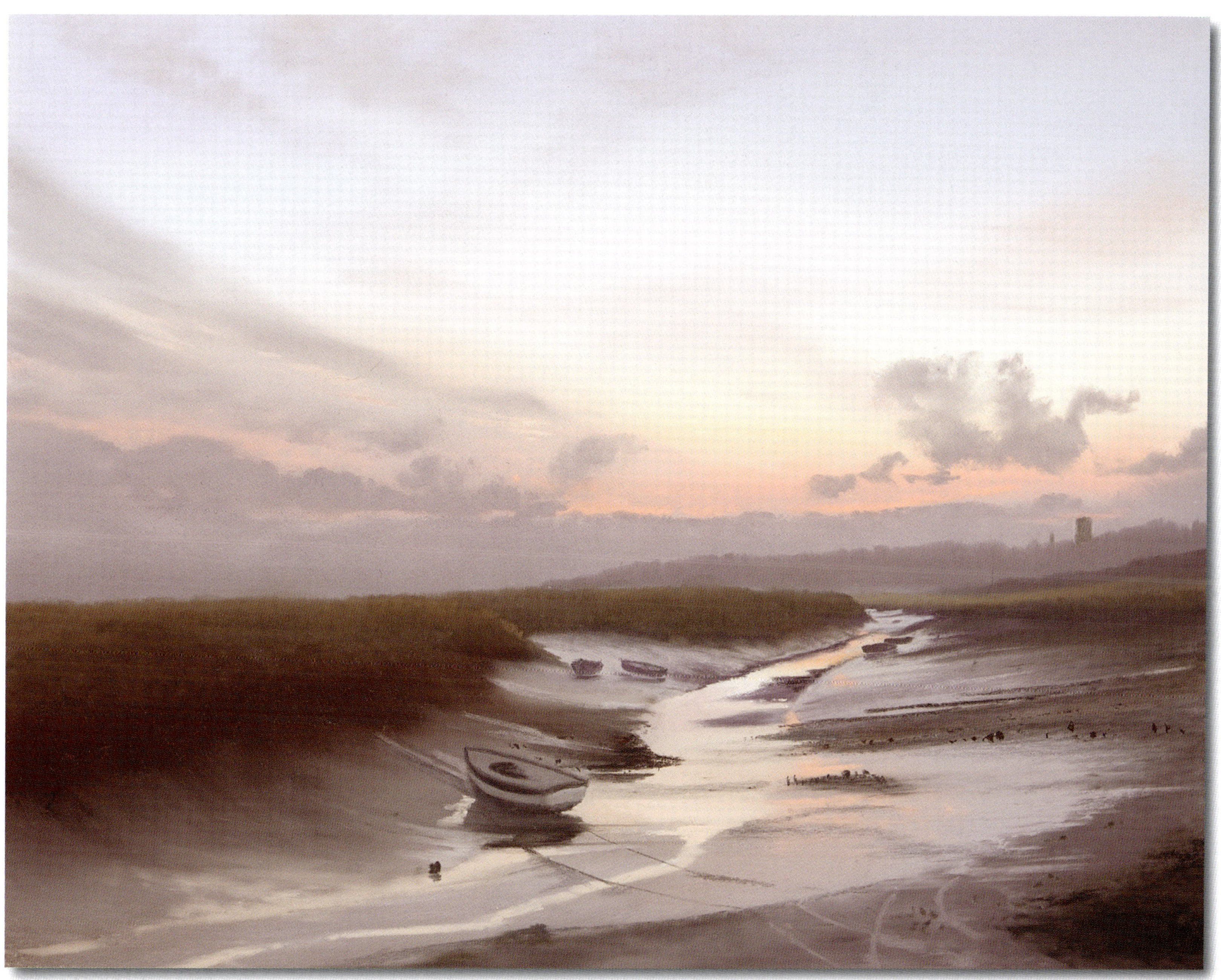

Mist Over Morston.

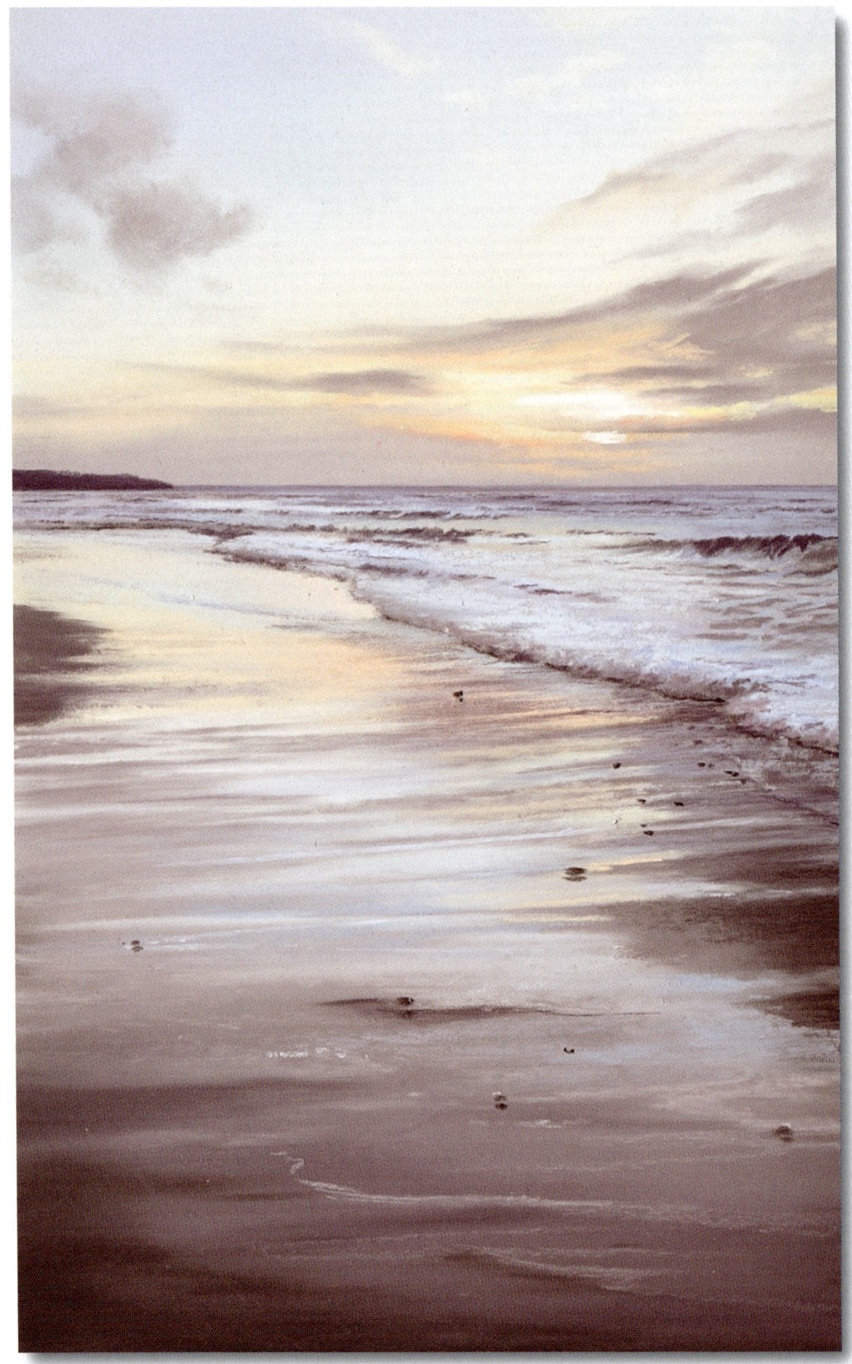

Early Riser.

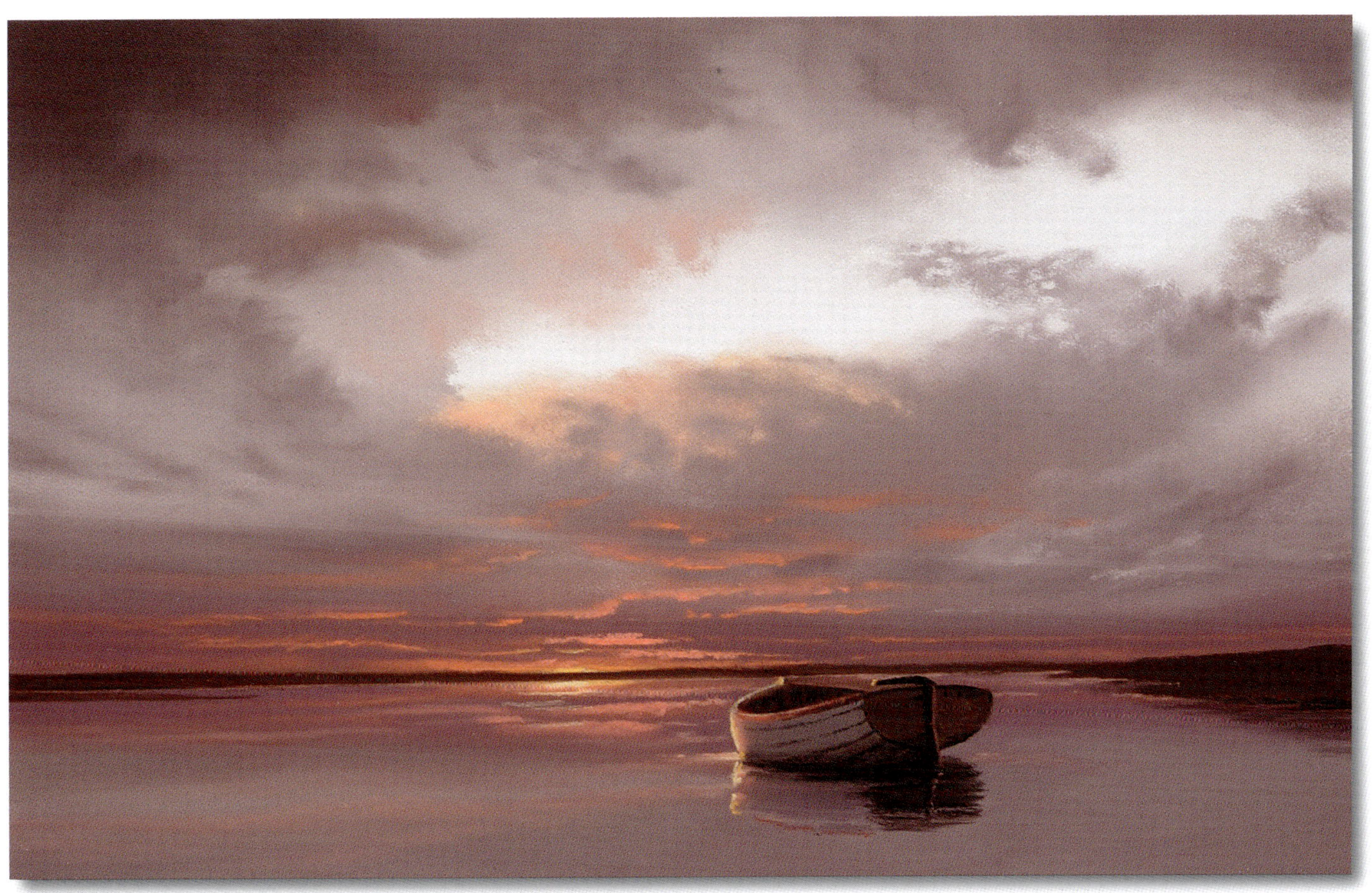

Dying Embers.

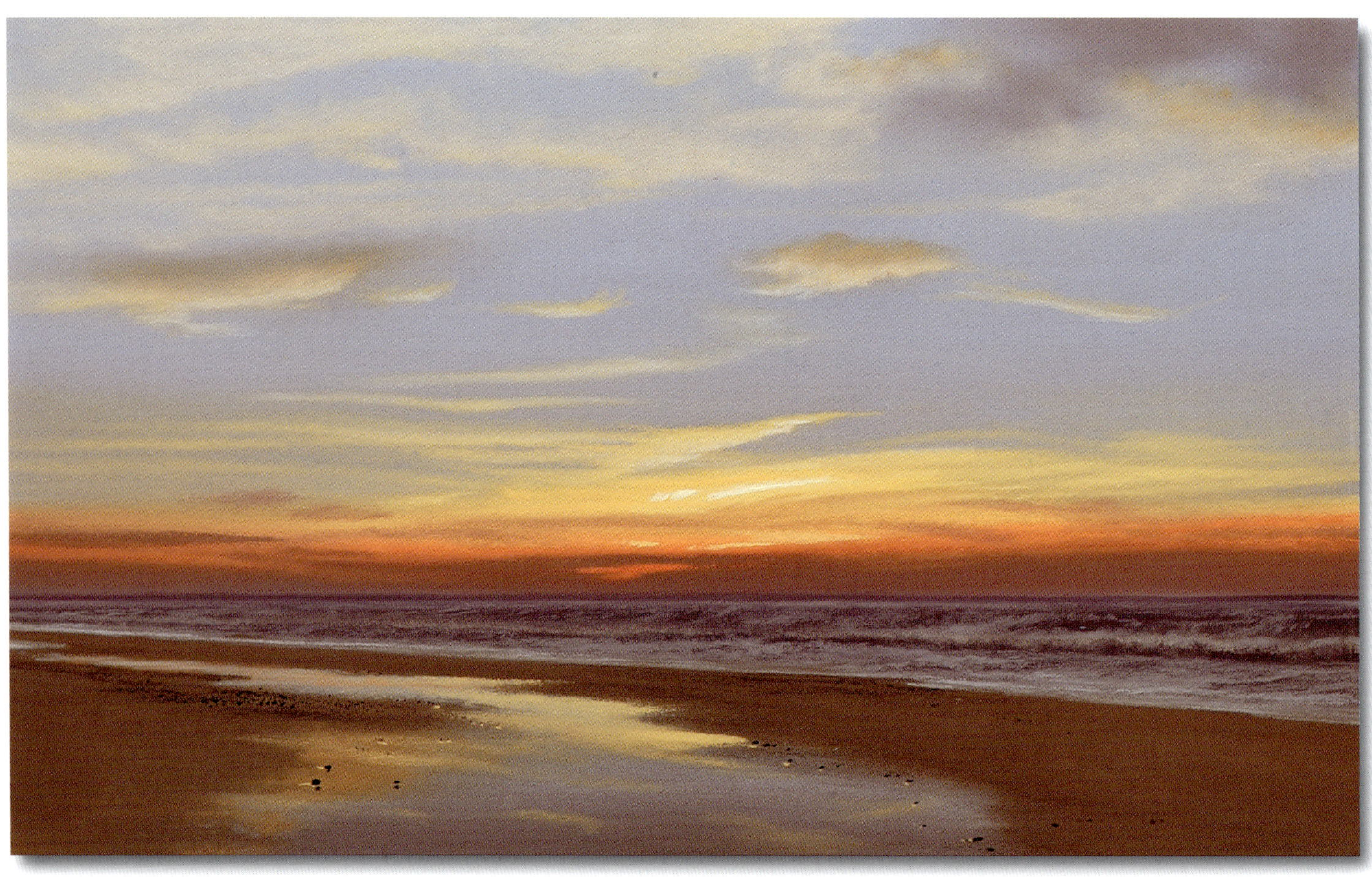

Colours of Dawn.

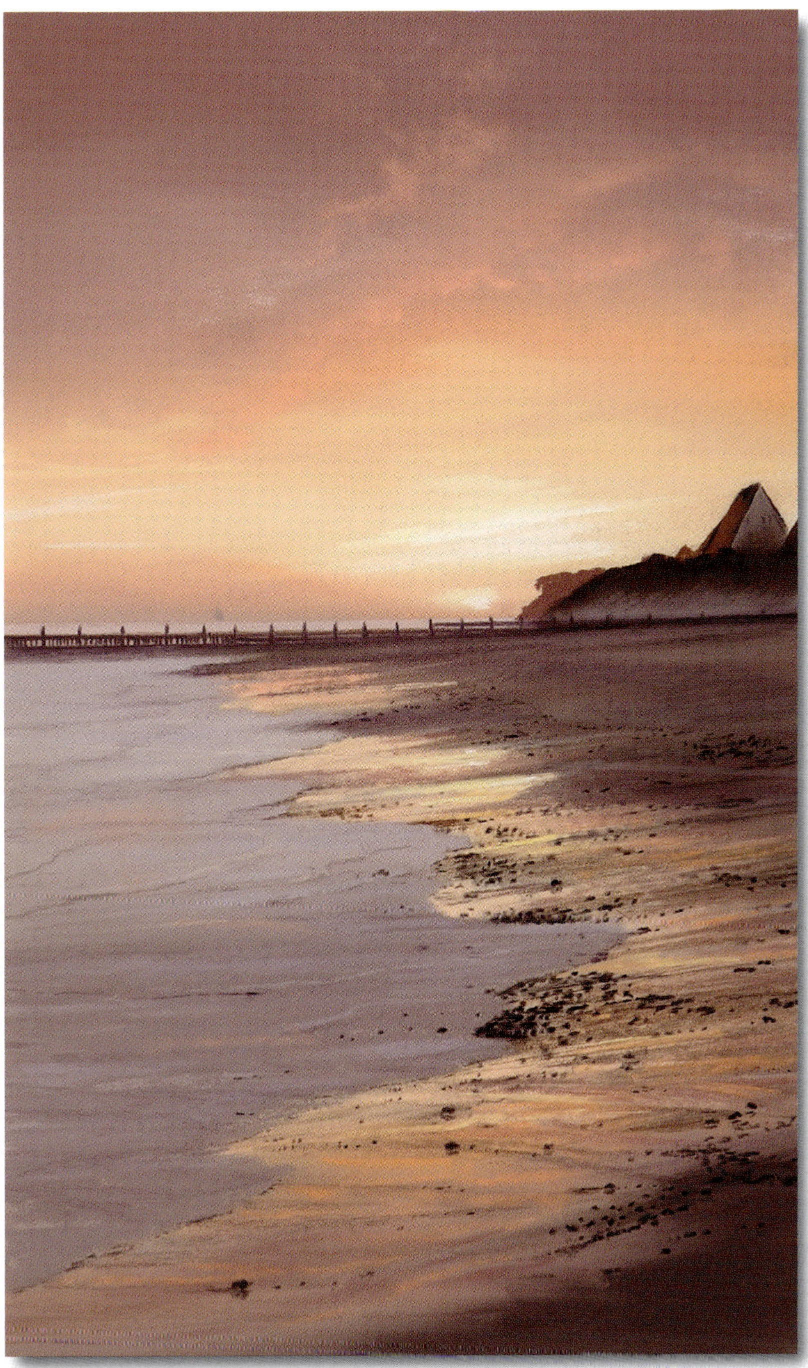

Incoming Tide.

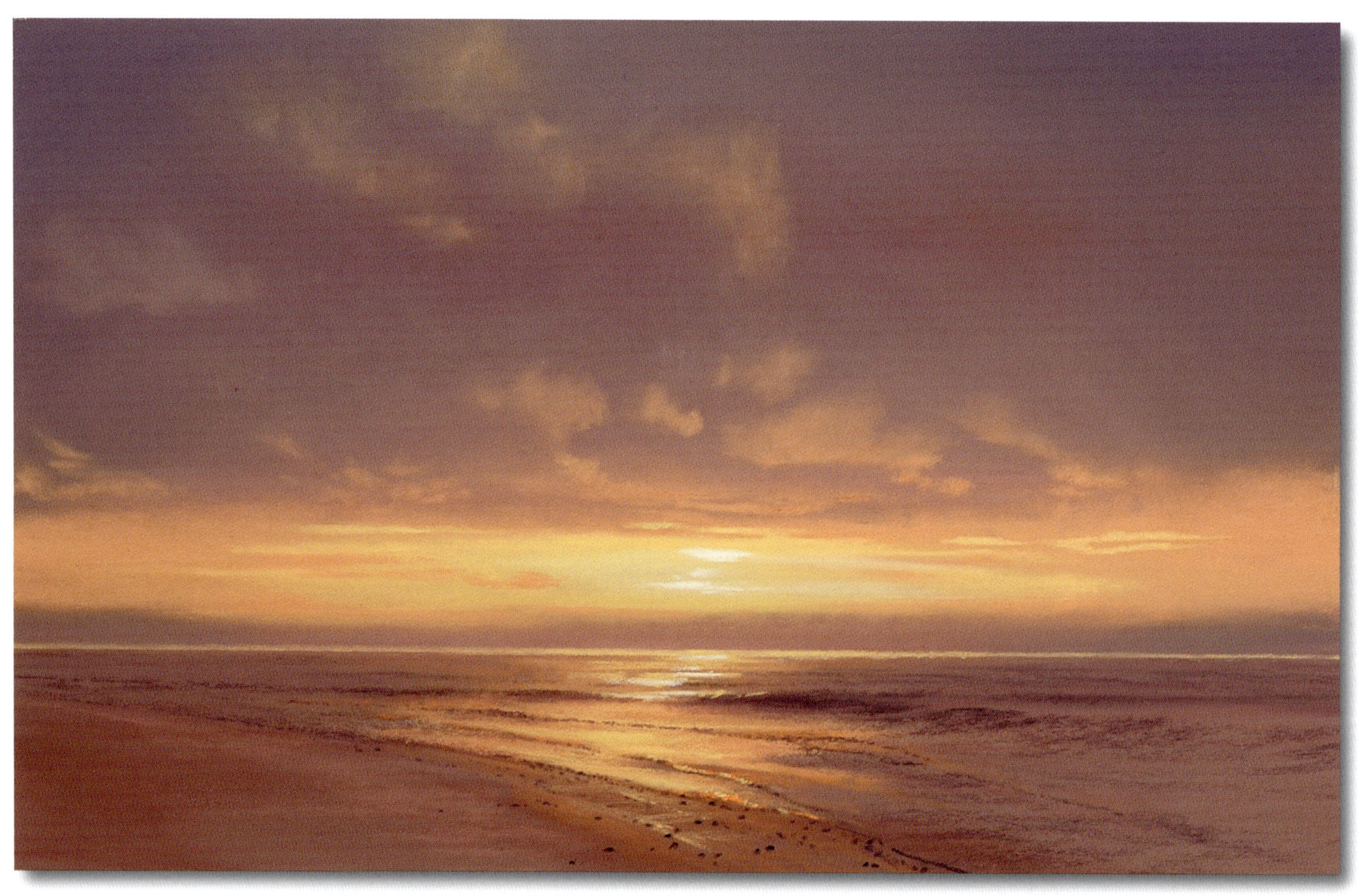

Evening Skies Over the Wash.

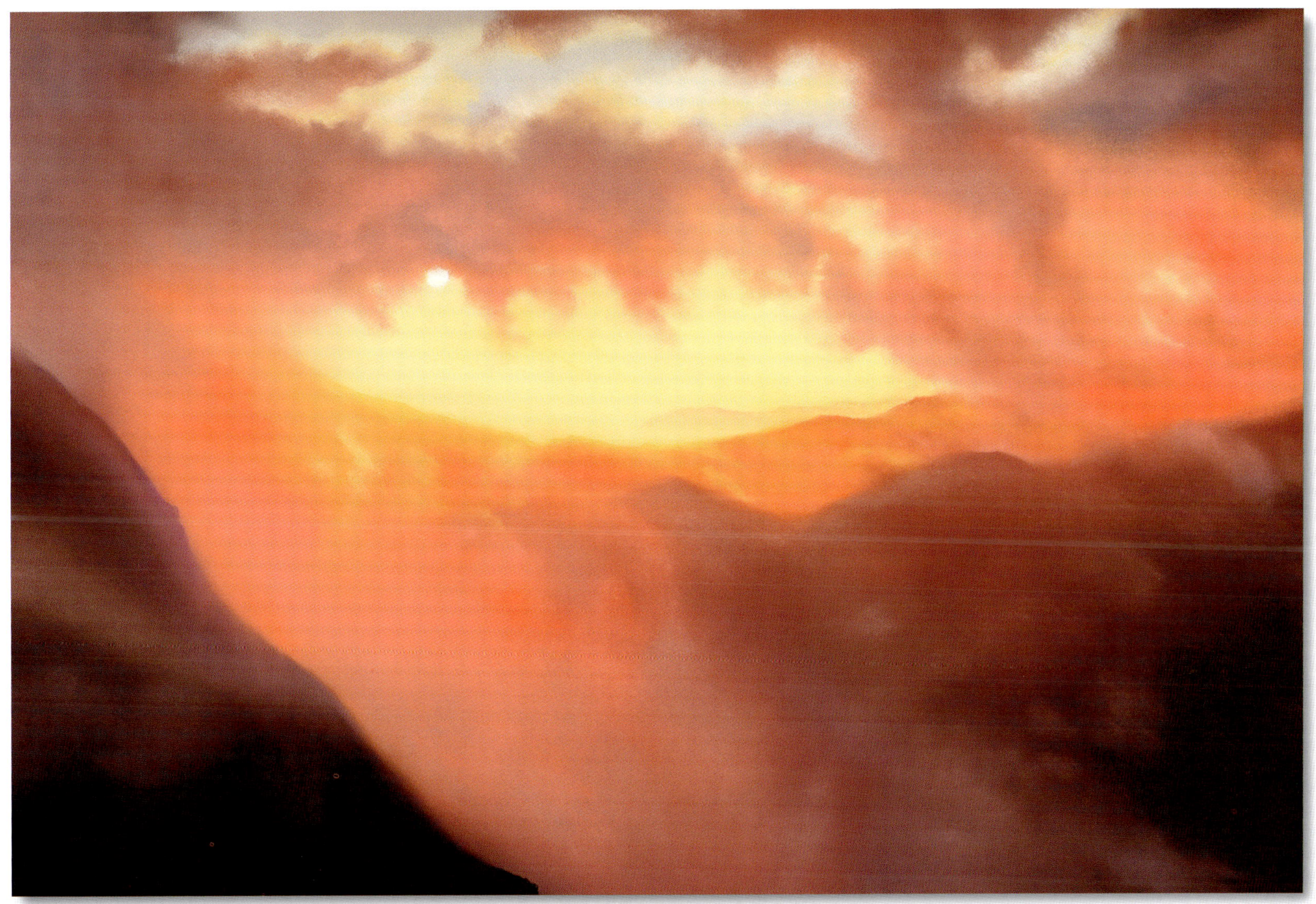

Skyscape.

CHRONOLOGY OF MAJOR AND SOLO EXHIBITIONS

1999	Simpsons of Norwich	First Solo Exhibition
2000	Simpsons of Norwich	
2001	Simpsons of Norwich	
2002	A Room With A View, Norwich	Solo Exhibition
2004	Picturecraft Gallery, Holt	'A Moment In Time' Major One-Man Exhibition
2005	Picturecraft Gallery, Holt	'Fleeting Moments' Major One-Man Exhibition
2006	Picturecraft Gallery, Holt	'Sunchaser' Major One-Man Exhibition
2007	Garden Gallery, Southwold	Solo Exhibition
2007	Picturecraft Gallery, Holt	'Sunchaser (ii), New Horizons' Major One-Man Exhibition
2008	Picturecraft Gallery, Holt	'Sunchaser (iii), Atmospheric Light' Major One-Man Exhibition
2009	Picturecraft Gallery, Holt	'Sunchaser (iv), The Skies Grand Finale' Major One-Man Exhibition
2010	Picturecraft Gallery, Holt	'Sunchaser (v), Enchanted Light' Major One-Man Exhibition